The Future of Generative AI for Business

A Strategic Leadership Guide

Written by Alex Brogane

Published by Cornell-David Publishing House

Index

Chapter 1: Introduction to Generative AI
1.1. Definition and potential of generative AI
1.2. Investment trends in the AI industry
1.3. Gartner's predictions for AI's impact on industries

Chapter 2: Five Industry Use Cases for Generative AI
2.1. Drug design and discovery
2.2. Material science and inverse design
2.3. Semiconductor chip design
2.4. Synthetic data generation
2.5. Generative design of industrial parts

Chapter 3: Generative AI in Marketing and Media
3.1. Synthetically generated marketing messages
3.2. AI-generated blockbuster films
3.3. Transforming the creative process

Chapter 4: Generative AI Technologies
4.1. Classifiers and generative AI systems
4.2. Generative Pre-trained Transformer (GPT)
4.3. Digital-image generators and their applications

Chapter 5: Foundation Models in AI
5.1. Introduction to foundation models
5.2. Transformer architectures and self-supervised learning
5.3. Attention mechanisms and context learning

Chapter 6: Risks and Challenges of Generative AI
6.1. Deepfakes and malicious AI applications
6.2. Copyright issues in generative AI
6.3. Mitigating risks and responsible AI usage

Chapter 7: Embedding Generative AI in Enterprises
7.1. Selecting appropriate AI technologies
7.2. Adapting foundation models for enterprise solutions
7.3. Ensuring transparency in AI implementation

Chapter 8: Security and Risk Management for Generative AI
8.1. Identifying potential threats and vulnerabilities

8.2. Counterfeit and fraud risks in generative AI
8.3. Collaborating with security leaders
Chapter 9: Ethical and Responsible AI Use
9.1. Developing guidelines for generative AI usage
9.2. Prioritizing transparency and model usage
9.3. Open-source models and their benefits
Chapter 10: Preparing for the Future of Generative AI
10.1. Staying updated on AI trends and advancements
10.2. Integrating generative AI into enterprise strategy
10.3. Adapting to the rapidly evolving AI landscape
Chapter 11: AI's Impact on Job Markets
11.1. The changing nature of work with AI
11.2. Reskilling and upskilling the workforce
11.3. Balancing human and AI collaboration
Chapter 12: Legal and Regulatory Aspects of Generative AI
12.1. Intellectual property rights in generative AI
12.2. Data privacy and synthetic data
12.3. Regulatory frameworks for AI technologies
Chapter 13: Generative AI in Emerging Markets
13.1. The potential of generative AI in developing countries
13.2. Unique challenges and opportunities
13.3. Case studies of successful AI implementations
Chapter 14: The Democratization of Generative AI
14.1. Making AI accessible to all enterprises
14.2. Open-source initiatives and their role in AI democratization
14.3. Fostering a global AI community
Chapter 15: Introduction to Computational Creativity
15.1. Defining computational creativity
15.2. The intersection of AI and human creativity
15.3. Evolution of computational creativity in AI research
Chapter 16: Creative Problem Solving with AI
16.1. AI techniques for creative problem solving
16.2. Case studies of AI-driven creative solutions
16.3. Challenges and limitations in AI-based creativity

Chapter 17: AI in Art, Music, and Literature
17.1. AI-generated visual art and styles
17.2. Composing music with AI algorithms
17.3. AI-driven storytelling and literature generation

Chapter 18: Computational Creativity in Game Design
18.1. Procedurally generated content in games
18.2. AI-driven narrative and character development
18.3. Adaptive game design using AI techniques

Chapter 19: AI and the Creative Process
19.1. Augmenting human creativity with AI
19.2. The role of AI in the creative workflow
19.3. Human-AI collaboration in creative projects

Chapter 20: Evaluating AI-Generated Creative Outputs
20.1. Measuring creativity in AI-generated content
20.2. Criteria for assessing computational creativity
20.3. Addressing biases in AI-generated creative outputs

Chapter 21: The Ethics of AI-Driven Creativity
21.1. Ownership and intellectual property in AI-generated content
21.2. Ethical considerations in computational creativity
21.3. Balancing AI innovation with ethical guidelines

Chapter 22: The Future of Computational Creativity
22.1. Predictions for AI's impact on creative industries
22.2. Emerging trends and advancements in computational creativity
22.3. Preparing for a world with AI-driven creative solutions

Chapter 23: Embracing the Future of Generative AI
23.1. Key takeaways and lessons learned
23.2. The transformative power of generative AI and computational creativity
23.3. Envisioning a better future with AI

Chapter 1: Introduction to Generative AI

Artificial Intelligence (AI) has come a long way since it was first conceptualized in the 1950s. Initially, AI research primarily focused on symbolic manipulation and expert systems, evolving over the years into the realm of machine learning and deep learning. Today, AI has transformed our society, increasingly influencing various aspects of our daily lives. One of the most exciting developments in the field of AI is the emergence of Generative AI, which has the potential to revolutionize creative problem-solving and push the boundaries of how we think about data-driven intelligence.

1.1 What is Generative AI?

Generative AI is a subset of artificial intelligence focused on creating new data instances that are consistent with an input dataset. These instances can take many forms, such as images, texts, audio files, or even entire software systems. The ability to generate novel and realistic examples opens up a world of possibilities for applications in various fields—including art, music, literature, and scientific research.

The primary goal of generative AI is to build models that can understand and replicate the underlying structure and patterns of the input data, thus enabling the generation of new instances that reflect the same characteristics. One way to think about generative AI is as a form of guided randomness, where machine learning models steer randomness based on the patterns observed in the input data.

1.2 A Brief History of Generative AI

The history of generative AI can be traced back several decades, with early developments in Bayesian networks and hidden Markov models for statistical modeling. These models were designed to capture the probability distribution over possible data instances based on observed training data, allowing for the synthesis of new instances with similar statistical patterns.

In the 2000s, research on deep learning started to gain momentum, paving the way for significant advancements in generative AI. This was primarily driven by advances in neural networks, which enabled more complex and nuanced data representations.

In recent years, several types of generative models have gained popularity, including:

- **Generative Adversarial Networks (GANs):** Introduced by Ian Goodfellow et al. in 2014, GANs are a powerful class of generative models that consist of two neural networks competing against each other. One network, the generator, creates data instances to fool the other network, the discriminator, which attempts to distinguish between real and generated instances. Through this adversarial process, both networks improve, and the generator learns to produce more realistic outputs.
- **Variational Autoencoders (VAEs):** Created by Kingma and Welling in 2013, VAEs are another popular generative model that combines deep

learning and probabilistic modeling. They consist of an encoder network to learn a latent representation of the input data and a decoder network to map this representation back to the original data space. The addition of a variational component helps capture complex underlying distributions and generate more diverse and realistic outputs.

- **Autoregressive Models:** Autoregressive models predict a data instance based on its previous observations, with each step in the prediction process conditioned on earlier steps. Examples of this approach include the Transformer architecture and the more advanced GPT (Generative Pre-trained Transformer) series.

1.3 Applications of Generative AI

Generative AI offers a wide range of applications across industries, allowing businesses and individuals to harness the power of artificial creativity. Some examples include:

1.3.1 Art and Design

Generative art is a popular area of exploration, where artists leverage AI models to create unique and captivating illustrations, paintings, and sculptures. Moreover, generative AI can simplify the design process by offering multiple suggestions based on specified criteria, allowing designers to select and refine elements to create professional and visually appealing projects.

1.3.2 Music Composition

Generative AI models like OpenAI's MuseNet can generate new music compositions in various styles and genres, encouraging collaboration and enabling composers to explore and fine-tune their creative vision. These tools can also assist in filling gaps in existing compositions or generating original musical scores for movies and games.

1.3.3 Writing and Journalism

AI models such as OpenAI's GPT-3 can produce human-like texts based on a given prompt, making it possible to create articles, stories, or other forms of written content in a matter of seconds. While this tech opens the door to automation in certain writing tasks, it also offers significant opportunities for enhancing human creative writing and exploring new perspectives.

1.3.4 Drug Discovery

Generative AI accelerates the search for novel drug candidates by modelling chemical structures and simulating synthesis routes. This approach has the potential to drastically reduce the time and cost associated with drug development while improving the overall accuracy and efficiency of identifying effective therapeutic agents.

1.4 Ethical Considerations

While the potential benefits of generative AI are immense, it's essential to consider the ethical implications of this technology. Potential issues include:

- **Copyright and Ownership:** The use of AI-generated content in arts and media raises questions about authorship and intellectual property rights. Determining who owns the copyrights and how royalties should be distributed requires careful examination and potential revisions to existing laws.
- **Misuse of AI-generated Content:** The ease of creating realistic AI-generated content has led to concerns about the spread of disinformation, deepfakes, and other malicious uses, which can have severe societal and political consequences.
- **Job Displacement:** As generative AI continues to improve, certain jobs—particularly in writing, design, and music composition—may become increasingly automated, leading to potential job loss and a need for workforce reskilling.

Overall, understanding and addressing the ethical challenges of generative AI is crucial to ensuring its responsible development and maximizing its positive impact on society.

1.5 Conclusion

Generative AI represents a significant step forward in the field of artificial intelligence, offering new ways to harness and extend human creativity. By understanding and navigating the unique challenges that generative AI presents, we can unlock the door to a wide range of applications—enabling businesses to thrive, fostering innovation, and enhancing our collective ability to imagine and create a more vibrant future.

1.1. Definition and potential of generative AI

What is Generative AI?

Generative AI represents a class of artificial intelligence algorithms that have the potential to synthesize and produce novel content or solutions autonomously, by employing techniques drawn from diverse disciplines like machine learning, neural networks, and natural language processing. These algorithms, unlike their discriminative counterparts, don't just predict or classify given data sets but are capable of generating entirely new outputs within the defined problem space.

At the core of most generative AI models lie deep learning techniques such as Generative Adversarial Networks (GANs), Variational Autoencoders (VAEs), and Recurrent Neural Networks (RNNs). By leveraging these techniques, generative AI models can learn from the complex patterns and latent variables within the training data, which enables them to generate samples of new data that exhibit similar features to the original data set.

Potential Applications of Generative AI

Generative AI holds transformative potential across a wide range of industries and domains. This section highlights some of the key applications that demonstrate the enormous possibilities of generative AI in both business and society as a whole.

1. Content Generation and Digital Media

With generative AI, digital artists and designers can create new forms of visual, auditory, and textual content, as well as leverage AI algorithms to automate parts of their creative workflows. Applications include:

- Automatic generation of images, videos, and other media content, by learning from existing examples
- Creation of realistic 3D models and textures for virtual and augmented reality applications
- Text simplification and summarization for better information consumption
- Automatic content moderation and removal of offensive or inappropriate material

2. Drug Discovery and Healthcare

Generative AI can aid in the discovery of novel drug candidates and accelerate the drug development process by predicting the chemical properties and biological activities of molecules. Such capabilities can offer significant cost and time savings in the lengthy process of drug development. Other applications in healthcare include:

- Identification of disease biomarkers and therapeutic targets
- Personalized medicine based on individual patient data
- Predictive analysis of disease progression and treatment outcomes

3. Optimization and Manufacturing

Generative design, enabled by AI algorithms, can revolutionize the way products are designed and manufactured by exploring a vast solution space and autonomously generating optimized designs based on defined constraints. Potential applications include:

- Lightweight and efficient designs for automotive and aerospace industries
- Optimization of supply chain and logistics operations
- Energy-efficient building and urban planning designs

4. Natural Language Processing

Generative AI models are playing a key role in advancing the capabilities of natural language processing systems. Applications in this domain include:

- Natural language understanding, enabling empathic and context-aware AI agents
- Automated language translation and summarization services
- Enhanced text-based chatbots and virtual assistants
- Creative storytelling and scriptwriting

5. Simulation and Training

Generative AI can create realistic virtual environments for training and simulation, which can be valuable in fields such as military, aviation, autonomous vehicles, and disaster management. By generating scenarios that closely mimic real-world situations, these systems can offer cost-effective and safe alternatives to traditional simulation methods.

Challenges and Limitations

While the potential of generative AI is undeniable, there are still several challenges and limitations that researchers and practitioners need to address to fully leverage its capabilities. Some of these challenges include:

- Ensuring the ethical use of generative AI, especially with regards to generating biased, harmful, or misleading content
- Respecting intellectual property rights and the ownership of generated content
- Ensuring computational efficiency and energy optimization for complex deep learning models, which often require large amounts of computational resources
- Ensuring the interpretability and explainability of generated outputs
- Achieving generalization across different domains without a drastic increase in model complexity
- Ensuring robustness against adversarial attacks and manipulation attempts

A deep understanding of these challenges will be crucial for the development of truly effective generative AI systems that can be integrated into the fabric of modern enterprises and contribute to the evolution of computational creativity. In the next sections of this book, we will explore the techniques, applications, and challenges of generative AI in greater detail, while highlighting the transformative role it can play in defining the future of digital creativity and enterprise innovation.

1.2. Investment trends in the AI industry

The rapid development of artificial intelligence (AI) in recent years has caught the attention of venture capitalists, corporations, and governments worldwide. AI promises massive advancements in various areas, from autonomous vehicles and robotics to medical diagnosis and climate change mitigation, resulting in significant investments. In this section, we will explore the key investment trends shaping the AI industry.

1.2.1. Steady increase in private investments

Private investments in AI startups have steadily increased over the past decade. According to data from *CB Insights*, in 2020, startups developing AI systems received over $27.6 billion in funding from venture capital (VC) firms and other investors. The number of private investment deals increased from approximately 1,900 in 2015 to over 2,700 in 2020. The increase in private investments can be attributed to several factors, including:

- Growing awareness of the transformative potential of AI applications across various industries
- Advancements in AI technologies such as natural language processing (NLP), machine vision, and generative models like GPT-3
- Improvements in AI-enabled hardware, including GPUs, TPUs, and rapid adoption of cloud infrastructure

1.2.2. Acquisitions and partnerships

Large technology companies have fueled the AI industry's growth, incorporating AI into their own products and services, and acquiring innovative AI startups to bolster their portfolio. Notable acquisitions include:

- Google's acquisition of DeepMind for an estimated $600 million, which has resulted in groundbreaking advancements in reinforcement learning and deep learning
- Intel's acquisition of Nervana Systems, a company focused on deep learning hardware, for approximately $350 million
- Apple's acquisition of Turi, an AI startup specializing in machine learning and data science, for around $200 million

Furthermore, we are witnessing a rise in partnerships between large enterprises and AI startups. Such collaborations have the potential to integrate AI technologies into existing products and develop new ones. Partnerships can lead to improved innovative capabilities for both parties while minimizing risk and maximizing long-term value.

1.2.3. Government interventions and policy implementations

Governments around the world have recognized the importance of AI and are taking steps to facilitate AI research, development, and integration into various industries. Measures include:

- Increased funding for public research institutions, incubators, and accelerators focusing on AI technologies
- Encouraging AI education, training, and AI adoption in traditional industries through incentives and grants
- Implementing supportive regulatory frameworks, including data protection laws and ethical guidelines for AI application

China's New Generation Artificial Intelligence Development Plan, for example, is a comprehensive strategy aiming to make China the world leader in AI by 2030. The European Union has also outlined ambitious plans for AI development in the form of the Coordinated Plan on AI and the Digital Europe Programme.

1.2.4. Thematic investments in AI applications

While AI has broad applications across various industries, certain areas have witnessed higher investments due to their potential for disruptive innovation or urgent global needs. Some examples include:

- **Healthcare**: AI-powered diagnostic tools, telemedicine, drug discovery, and personalized medicine applications have received significant investments, driven by the need for efficient and accessible healthcare services in an increasingly complex healthcare landscape.
- **Autonomous vehicles**: Investments in systems for self-driving cars, trucks, drones, and robots have been on the rise due to potential improvements in safety, efficiency, and reduced environmental impact.
- **Climate change mitigation**: AI applications in renewable energy, smart grids, and resource management have gained traction due to their potential contribution to addressing climate change and fostering sustainable development.

1.2.5. Focus on building AI ecosystems

As AI investments continue to grow, there is an increasing emphasis on developing comprehensive AI ecosystems that include a range of stakeholders such as technology companies, research institutions, educational providers, and policy-makers. These ecosystems help transform AI research and development into practical applications, foster collaboration, and create enabling environments for rapid technology transfer and adoption. Examples of such ecosystems include the Montreal Institute for Learning Algorithms (MILA) in Canada and the Turing AI Accelerator in the UK.

In conclusion, the AI industry is experiencing significant growth, driven by a mix of private investments, acquisitions, and government interventions. As stakeholders continue to recognize AI's potential to transform businesses, societies, and global challenges, we can expect further growth and innovation in the sector.

1.3 Gartner's Predictions for AI's Impact on Industries

As the growing influence of AI technology continues to permeate through our world, industries and enterprises must adapt to this emerging technology to stay competitive in the market. Gartner, a leading research and advisory company, has made several predictions about the future of AI and its impact on various sectors of the economy. In this section, we will explore Gartner's insights and what they mean for enterprises, particularly focusing on the following industries: healthcare, finance, retail, manufacturing, and technology.

Healthcare

Gartner anticipates significant AI-led advancements and disruption in the healthcare sector, including:

1. **Virtual nursing assistants**: By incorporating AI technology, virtual nursing assistants will provide around-the-clock services, answer questions, monitor patients, and report medical data to healthcare professionals, all while reducing the workload on human nursing staff.
2. **AI-driven diagnostics**: Leveraging machine learning, AI systems can learn to diagnose diseases more accurately and efficiently than humans. This has the potential to revolutionize patient care and reduce

the strain on medical professionals, especially in areas where there is a shortage of doctors or specialists.
3. **Drug development**: AI will play a crucial role in accelerating the discovery and development of new drugs. By using algorithms to analyze vast amounts of data, AI will be able to identify potential treatment candidates and streamline the process, making it more efficient and cost-effective.

Finance

Gartner predicts numerous AI developments in the finance industry, such as:

1. **AI-enhanced risk management**: By using AI to assess and predict potential risks, financial institutions can mitigate losses and make better-informed decisions. This can contribute to safer investments and increased trust from investors.
2. **Fraud detection**: AI's ability to identify patterns in large amounts of data makes it an excellent tool for detecting fraudulent activity in the finance sector. This technology will transform the way banks and financial institutions identify and prevent fraud, with the potential to save billions of dollars each year.
3. **Automated trading**: The rise of AI-driven trading algorithms will change the landscape of the stock market, as these tools outperform human traders in terms of speed, precision, and data-crunching capabilities. This leads to faster and more efficient trades, potentially altering the financial landscape and transforming the roles of human traders.

Retail

Retail is another industry where Gartner expects AI to cause significant disruption, including:

1. **Personalization**: AI systems will enable retailers to deliver a more personalized shopping experience by understanding customers' preferences, needs, and habits. This will result in better-targeted marketing campaigns and improved customer engagement.
2. **Demand forecasting**: AI-driven tools will analyze customer data and behavior to provide accurate demand forecasting, improving inventory management and reducing waste.
3. **Customer support**: The incorporation of AI-powered chatbots and virtual assistants will redefine customer support, streamlining the process and reducing the response time for queries.

Manufacturing

Gartner predicts AI's transformation of the manufacturing industry in multiple ways:

1. **Predictive maintenance**: AI algorithms will detect and predict equipment failures or life cycles, resulting in reduced downtime, optimized maintenance scheduling, and increased productivity.
2. **Quality control**: AI will dramatically improve quality control in manufacturing through the use of computer vision systems and machine learning algorithms, which can identify defects and irregularities more quickly and accurately than human inspectors.
3. **Supply chain optimization**: AI-powered systems will enhance the efficiency of supply chains by analyzing large volumes of data to optimize logistics, predict demand, and minimize waste.

Technology

As the driving force behind AI, the technology industry will experience significant breakthroughs, including:

1. **AI democratization**: The widespread accessibility of easy-to-use AI tools and frameworks will enable even small businesses and individuals to harness AI capabilities, leveling the playing field for innovation and development.
2. **Human-AI collaboration**: The advancement of AI technologies that can understand human emotions and context will lead to more efficient and effective collaboration between humans and machines in various industries.
3. **AI ethics and governance**: As AI becomes more prevalent, there will be increased focus on ethical considerations and the need for regulatory frameworks to govern the use of AI technologies.

Gartner's predictions paint a picture of a rapidly evolving landscape influenced by AI-driven innovations across all sectors of the economy. It is essential for enterprises and industries to adapt to these changes and embrace AI as a key driver of growth, efficiency, and competitive advantage. The future of AI is promising, and understanding its potential impact will enable enterprises to harness its vast potential and revolutionize their industries.

Chapter 2: Five Industry Use Cases for Generative AI

In this chapter, we will explore five different industries where generative AI is making a significant impact. These industries include marketing and advertising, healthcare, automotive, finance, and entertainment. The applications of generative AI within these fields are diverse, encompassing creative aspects, behavioral modeling, predictive analyses, and optimization. By understanding how generative AI shapes these industries, we can gain insights into how enterprises can harness the power of AI to improve efficiency, foster creativity, and drive success.

2.1 Marketing and Advertising

Marketing and advertising are industries that rely heavily on creativity, attention to detail, and keeping up with trends. Generative AI can revolutionize these fields by automating and enhancing various aspects of the creative process, streamlining the creation of effective campaigns, and better understanding audience behavior.

2.1.1 Content Generation

Generative models can create new content, ranging from simple and repetitive text to rich and dynamic audiovisual pieces. Marketers can use training data sets to obtain AI-generated slogans, headlines, ad copy, and more. AI-generated content allows marketing teams to quickly develop an array of creative options and discover unique, engaging concepts that resonate with their target audience.

2.1.2 Personalization

Creating personalized content can enhance the customer experience and improve conversion rates. Generative AI enables marketers to deliver more personalized messages by crafting unique variations of content tailored to each user. In this context, generative models can automatically generate visual elements and copy that fit the preferences and needs of each segment of customers.

2.1.3 Social Media Monitoring

Pattern recognition capabilities inherent in generative AI can aid in social media monitoring, mining vast amounts of data to glean audience sentiments and reveal consumer preferences. With insights generated from these AI-driven analyses, marketing teams can quickly pivot their strategy to address newfound trends, competition, or emergent consumer desires more effectively.

2.2 Healthcare

The healthcare industry is well-positioned to benefit from the advances in generative AI. From drug discovery to patient care, generative AI is revolutionizing the field, promising to improve outcomes and increase efficiency.

2.2.1 Drug Discovery

Generative AI can accelerate the process of drug discovery by allowing researchers to quickly generate and analyze new molecular structures. Machine learning algorithms can identify promising drug candidates, estimate their potency, and suggest modifications to improve their efficacy. This approach significantly reduces the time and resources required for drug development.

2.2.2 Medical Imaging

Generative models can aid in the analysis of medical imaging data, including MRI, CT, and X-ray scans. These models can quickly highlight regions of interest, detect anomalies, and provide diagnostic insights. By automating the analysis of medical images, generative AI has the potential to improve the speed and accuracy of disease detection and treatment strategies.

2.2.3 Personalized Treatment Plans

Generative AI can develop personalized treatment plans for patients by considering factors such as patient history, genetics, lifestyle, and environmental factors. AI-driven care recommendations can lead to more effective and preventative care, ultimately resulting in better patient outcomes.

2.3 Automotive

The automotive industry is continually advancing towards more autonomous and intelligent vehicles. Generative AI is playing a crucial role in the industry's development, creating safer, more efficient, and more personalized transportation options.

2.3.1 Autonomous Driving Systems

Generative AI is integral to the development of autonomous driving systems. By providing deep neural networks with complex training data, AI models can accurately recognize traffic patterns, make informed decisions, and navigate diverse driving scenarios. This technology's benefits include increased traffic efficiency, reduced accidents, and improved overall transportation systems.

2.3.2 Vehicle Design

Generative design allows automotive engineers to create innovative vehicle designs by using AI to generate and test numerous design variations. These designs can optimize factors such as weight, aerodynamics, fuel efficiency, and durability, leading to better-performing and more efficient vehicles.

2.3.3 Personalization

Generative AI can help create unique user experiences by customizing vehicle interiors based on individual preferences. Incorporating AI-driven personalization can lead to increased customer satisfaction and foster brand loyalty.

2.4 Finance

The finance industry is one of the earliest adopters of AI-driven approaches. Generative AI is elevating the industry by allowing data-driven decision-making, improving fraud detection, and predicting market trends.

2.4.1 Algorithmic Trading

Generative AI is enabling the development of more sophisticated algorithmic trading systems. These systems benefit from AI's capacity to analyze extensive data sets, identify patterns, and make trading decisions based on useful predictive models. The growing sophistication of algorithmic trading technologies contributes to increased profitability and optimized risk management.

2.4.2 Fraud Detection

Generative AI can assist financial institutions in identifying and preventing fraudulent activities. By using machine learning algorithms to recognize patterns and create profiles of legitimate transactions, these systems can quickly detect anomalies and suspend potentially fraudulent transactions.

2.4.3 Forecasting and Risk Management

Generative AI models enable financial institutions to make more informed decisions by analyzing vast amounts of historical and real-time data. Predictive analyses provide valuable insights into market trends, allowing firms to anticipate market fluctuations, optimize investment strategies, and better manage risk.

2.5 Entertainment

The entertainment industry is always on the lookout for creative and engaging content. Generative AI provides the tools needed to unleash untapped creativity, enabling the development of innovative artistic expressions and audience experiences.

2.5.1 Music and Sound Production

Generative AI can assist in composing music and soundscapes by analyzing and generating complex and varied audio sequences. These AI-assisted compositions can lead to unique and engaging audio experiences that resonate with audiences.

2.5.2 Film and Animation

Generative AI can revolutionize film and animation by automating various aspects of the creative process, such as character and scene modeling, storyboarding, and visual effects. AI-generated elements can significantly streamline production pipelines and inspire novel approaches to storytelling.

2.5.3 Video Game Design

The video game industry can benefit from the incorporation of generative AI in aspects such as level design, character generation, and procedural content creation. Generative AI can create highly customized, immersive gameplay experiences that cater to individual players' interests and preferences.

In conclusion, generative AI is transforming a diverse set of industries by driving efficiency, fueling creativity, and providing valuable insights. Understanding the various potential applications of generative AI within these industries allows enterprises to harness its power and pave the way for success in an AI-driven world.

2.1. Drug Design and Discovery

In recent years, Artificial Intelligence has been increasingly employed in various aspects of the drug design and discovery process. The advent of deep learning and various Generative AI models has significantly changed the landscape of the pharmaceutical industry, paving the way for swifter, more efficient, and innovative drug development.

2.1.1. Current Challenges in Drug Design and Discovery

The traditional process of drug design and discovery is time-consuming, expensive, and fraught with several challenges. Some of the prominent issues faced by researchers and developers include:

1. **Complexity**: The human body is an immensely complex system, and a vast range of factors affect the behavior and interaction of potential drug candidates within it. Researchers often need to consider multiple variables, such as metabolic pathways, reactions to other molecules, and potential side-effects, to determine the efficacy of a drug.
2. **Synthesis and Testing**: Experimentally synthesizing and evaluating drug candidates requires significant investment in terms of resources, laboratory space, and time, often taking several years just to identify promising candidates.

3. **Cost**: The entire drug development process, from initial discovery to clinical trials, to obtain regulatory approval, can take over a billion dollars per drug, with a high risk of failure.
4. **Time to Market**: It can take over a decade for a drug to get from the initial discovery stage to being commercially available, which can leave patients waiting for much-needed treatments.

2.1.2. Generative AI in Drug Design and Discovery

Generative AI technologies, based on deep learning models, promise to overcome these challenges by automating and accelerating different stages of drug development. The most notable advancements made with Generative AI in drug design and discovery include:

1. **De novo drug design**: Generative AI models can aid de novo drug design by creating novel chemical structures with desired properties based on chemical space exploration. These AI-generated molecules have the potential to treat diseases more effectively than the manually designed molecules.
2. **Molecular optimization**: AI algorithms can significantly enhance the optimization of drug candidates by iteratively modifying their molecular structures to achieve the desired balance between potency, selectivity, and pharmacokinetics characteristics.
3. **Target identification and validation**: Identifying therapeutic targets in a cellular or molecular system is a critical step in drug discovery. AI models can help predict how a prospective drug will act on specific

targets, further refining the hypothesis generation and validation process.
4. **Virtual high-throughput screening**: Researchers can use Generative AI models to rapidly screen millions of molecules in silico against various targets, drastically reducing time and resources spent on experimental evaluation.
5. **Predicting drug properties**: Generative AI models can predict various properties of molecules, including their solubility, stability, and binding affinity, thereby assisting the candidate selection process.
6. **Predicting potential side-effects**: These models can also help predict potential side-effects of a drug candidate, enabling identification of possible safety concerns before moving to clinical trials.

2.1.3. Notable Generative AI Models in Drug Design and Discovery

Several pioneering Generative AI models have found their way into the drug design and discovery workflow. These include:

1. **Generative Adversarial Networks (GANs)**: A GAN consists of two neural networks - a generator and a discriminator. The generator creates novel structures, while the discriminator evaluates their quality. GANs have been successfully utilized in generating novel molecular structures with desired physicochemical properties.
2. **Variational Autoencoders (VAEs)**: VAEs consist of an encoder network that compresses the input data into a latent space, and a decoder network that generates outputs based on this space. VAEs enable

sampling from high-dimensional chemical space, generating original molecular structures.
3. **Recurrent Neural Networks (RNNs)**: RNNs process sequences of data, making them suitable for generating and predicting properties of molecules represented as strings (e.g., SMILES notation). RNNs can be used to create libraries of novel compounds for drug discovery.
4. **Reinforcement Learning (RL)**: RL models learn through a trial-and-error process to achieve desired outcomes, making them well-suited to optimize molecular properties. By incorporating RL techniques in the drug discovery pipeline, researchers can reveal more potent and effective drug candidates.

2.1.4. Practical Applications and Case Studies

Several pharmaceutical and biotechnology companies have already started implementing Generative AI models in their drug discovery pipelines. Some notable examples include:

1. **Insilico Medicine**: This company developed an AI-based drug discovery platform implementing GANs and RL to generate novel molecules, cutting down the time from target identification to lead compound optimization from years to weeks.
2. **Atomwise**: Atomwise's AI platform, AtomNet™, uses deep learning to predict the binding affinity of small molecules to proteins, enabling efficient virtual screening and lead optimization.
3. **Exscientia**: Exscientia developed an AI-driven platform called Centaur Chemist™, which combines

various AI techniques, including RL, to explore the chemical space and optimize drug candidates.
4. **BenevolentAI**: Focused on developing AI-driven drug discovery solutions, BenevolentAI uses machine learning algorithms to mine data and identify promising drug candidates with desired properties.

2.1.5. Future Outlook

The future of drug design and discovery with Generative AI is very promising. As computational power increases and more high-quality data becomes accessible, AI-driven techniques will continue to mature, leading to:

1. Improved efficiency in the drug discovery pipeline, enabling faster development of novel drugs.
2. Reduced costs and higher return on investment in R&D efforts.
3. More personalized medicine, with drugs optimized for specific patient populations.
4. Discovery of novel treatments for diseases currently deemed undruggable.

In conclusion, Generative AI has the potential to revolutionize drug design and discovery, enabling faster, more efficient, and innovative drug development. This advancement in computational creativity will ultimately benefit millions of patients worldwide, leading to better treatments and, consequently, improved overall human health.

2.2. Material Science and Inverse Design

The impact of AI on material science is profound and far-reaching. As we advance the understanding of the interaction between atoms, molecules, and nanoparticles, we continue to discover new materials with unique properties that have the potential to revolutionize industries. AI-powered predictions and algorithms have been showing their potential to drive this field to new frontiers, not only by accelerating the rate of discovery but also by enabling the generation of entirely new material structures that were once considered impossible.

Evolution of AI in Material Science

While material science once relied on experimentalists to discover materials with desirable properties, AI-based computational methods now offer a complementary yet powerful approach. These computational tools have proven to be indispensable in material science, aiding in the design, analysis, and optimization of new materials. The adoption of such accelerated methods has led to significant progress in the development and commercialization of high-performance materials.

In particular, applications of *generative AI*, alongside data mining, machine learning, and optimization, have resulted in notable advancements in the pace and scope of materials discovery. With the ability to process vast and complex libraries of datasets, AI-based material predictions have led to the discovery of groundbreaking materials and optimized structures.

Inverse Design: A Paradigm Shift

Inverse Design is an emerging approach in material science that relies on AI to support the development of a desired material or structure from the onset. Rather than iterative experimentation and optimization, Inverse Design flips the conventional design process on its head. Traditionally, a material's potential was discovered through trial and error, but Inverse Design offers a smarter and more efficient pathway.

By integrating AI algorithms with computational materials science, Inverse Design offers a more efficient route to achieving desirable properties for specific applications. This method starts with a defined target for performance and utilizes the immense computational power of AI to identify optimal material configurations that can satisfy such requirements. With vast libraries of datasets, AI can then mine these data to identify relevant patterns or relationships, ultimately guiding the design process.

This shift in the design approach allows researchers to explore more complex material structures and even structures that don't yet exist, leading to unprecedented discoveries.

Inverse Design in Material Science

The application of Inverse Design in material science is transforming the trajectory of the field. Some prominent examples include:

- **Photonic Materials**: With the ubiquity of high-performance electronic devices, the demand for more efficient light-based signal processing continues to grow. Photonic materials with engineered optical properties can help materialize this goal. Inverse

Design methods have allowed researchers to predict optimal configurations of photonic crystals to achieve desired spectral properties.
- **Metamaterials**: As materials with engineered microstructures or nanostructures, metamaterials exhibit unique, human-engineered properties not found in nature. Inverse Design, synthesizing both AI methodologies and physics-based simulations, offers vast potential in predicting metamaterial structures that can produce these bespoke properties.
- **Biomaterials**: Biomaterials are essential in fields such as healthcare, pharmaceutics, and agriculture. Inverse Design offers new approaches to engineering nanoscale biomaterials with unique properties, tailoring them to specific applications and enabling the development of more effective therapies and diagnostics.
- **Energy Storage and Generation**: Inverse Design is being used to generate new materials for energy applications, such as batteries or solar cells. AI can assist in the quest to develop materials that can provide more extended energy storage or efficient energy transfer, helping mitigate global energy challenges.

The Future of Inverse Design in Material Science

The potential applications of Inverse Design in material science are limitless. Accelerating the development of new materials through Inverse Design will lead to immense economic value and advances in fields ranging from medicine to energy production. As enterprises increasingly adopt generative AI models for a wide range of applications, the efficacy of the material design process will continue to exponentially improve. Despite some limitations due to incomplete data sets and computational constraints, with continued advancements in AI, the integration of various computational methods and the establishment of universal databases, the future of Inverse Design promises creative and intelligent solutions that are reshaping material science.

2.3 Semiconductor Chip Design

Semiconductor chip design is a complex and highly specialized field dedicated to creating highly sophisticated and optimized chips for various applications, such as computing, communication, and control systems. These chips can range from simple microcontroller devices to highly complex processors and graphics processing units. With the growing demands for efficient and powerful computing systems, semiconductor chip design has become a critical aspect in the development of innovative technology solutions for enterprises.

Artificial intelligence has made significant strides in recent years, promising disruptive advancements in many industries. Generative AI, a subset of AI focused on the creation of new and innovative outputs such as designs, code, and content, has emerged as a powerful tool in navigating the complexities of semiconductor chip design, offering a wide range of unprecedented opportunities to improve the process, reduce development costs, and increase the speed of innovation for enterprises.

Generative AI Applications in Semiconductor Chip Design

1. Generative Design

Generative design is an iterative design process that leverages the power of AI algorithms and computational power of machines to explore a vast number of possible design solutions and rapidly converge on optimal designs. This approach enables chip design teams to reduce the time dedicated to manual exploration of design trade-offs and focus on more strategic tasks.

Generative AI can optimize chip designs for various criteria, such as power consumption, performance, and space efficiency. By combining AI-powered algorithms with human insights and domain expertise, companies can significantly accelerate development cycles and create highly optimized semiconductor devices that are better suited for real-world applications.

2. Predictive Chip Modeling and Simulation

Accurate modeling and simulation of semiconductor designs are critical to identifying and resolving issues before transitioning into the fabrication stage. Generative AI can be applied to predict key design attributes and simulate various scenarios based on data input, ensuring greater accuracy and early identification of possible design issues.

This results in a faster, more informed decision-making process and smooths the transition between design, testing, and production for semiconductor devices. Additionally, it enables a proactive approach to managing risk while minimizing the likelihood of expensive redesigns and production delays.

3. Intelligent Test Case Generation

As semiconductor chips increase in complexity, effective testing becomes vital for validating the functions and performance of the final product. Currently, the process involves manually generating test cases – a tedious and time-consuming task. However, generative AI can automatically generate test cases that specifically target vulnerabilities or flaws in the design, reducing the time and resources expended on manual testing.

Through the application of AI, semiconductor chip designers can identify critical test scenarios and generate well-organized test suites in a much shorter time frame. This ensures comprehensive testing and expedited iterations, leading to faster time to market and improved product quality.

4. Manufacturing Process Optimization

Semiconductor manufacturing is a highly complex and costly process. Generative AI can be employed to optimize manufacturing process parameters, reducing production costs, and minimizing waste. By analyzing historical manufacturing data and running simulations, generative AI algorithms can optimize for yield, process variation, and fabrication constraints, thereby increasing efficiency and reducing costs for semiconductor manufacturers.

Future Outlook and Challenges

The increasing application of generative AI in semiconductor chip design is expected to deliver significant advances in the design, testing, and fabrication of semiconductors. However, there are challenges to be overcome, including:

- **Dataset Quality:** For generative AI to be effective, it requires high-quality datasets to train the models correctly. In the case of semiconductor design, obtaining such datasets often involves negotiating multiple layers of intellectual property and authority, posing roadblocks to the seamless implementation of AI solutions.
- **Computation Requirements:** The application of generative AI in semiconductor chip design requires significant computational power, which can be resource-intensive and expensive. Consequently, the challenge lies in balancing between the advantages offered by generative AI and the associated high costs of utilization.
- **Implementation Difficulties:** Seamless integration of AI-powered solutions into current industry workflows and methodologies is not without its challenges, such as cross-disciplinary cooperation, education barriers, and inertia within the industry.

Despite these challenges, the future of generative AI in the semiconductor chip design industry is encouraging. As the technology matures and becomes more accessible, the growing adoption of AI-driven solutions will empower semiconductor manufacturers to stay ahead of the competition, driving innovation at an unprecedented scale.

2.4. Synthetic Data Generation

The volume, quality, and diversity of data are essential for training efficient generative AI models. However, obtaining the required data may not always be feasible due to financial constraints, privacy concerns, or a lack of information in some domains. Consequently, synthetic data generation methods are gaining traction as they can alleviate the need for authentic samples while delivering solid performance outcomes from the AI models. In this section, we will explore the potential of synthetic data generation and how it appeals to the enterprise and computational creativity fields.

2.4.1. Understanding Synthetic Data

Synthetic data refers to artificially generated data samples that mimic the statistical properties of authentic data. These data samples are constructed using various techniques, such as computer simulations, deep learning modeling, and probabilistic modeling. The primary goal is to develop data samples that can substitute real-world data to some extent while complying with specific requirements in terms of privacy, cost, and other constraints.

2.4.2. The Significance of Synthetic Data in Generative AI

Generative AI models necessitate vast amounts of diverse and accurate data to learn correlations, patterns, and dependencies. Synthetic data provides the following benefits to enterprises in the generative AI domain:

1. **Privacy and Security:** AI-generated data can comply with data protection regulations, ensuring that sensitive information remains secure. Privacy-preserving techniques such as differential privacy can be incorporated into the data generation process to mitigate the risks of data exposure.
2. **Cost-effectiveness:** Acquiring large volumes of authentic data can be both expensive and time-consuming. By employing synthetic data,

organizations can reduce the need for data collection, annotation, and storage, leading to significant cost savings.
3. **Data Augmentation:** Synthetic data generation techniques can supplement real-world data when faced with scarcity. They can create additional samples to provide a more comprehensive dataset for training AI models, particularly in domains with limited inputs.
4. **Bias Reduction:** Generating synthetic data allows for fine-grained control over the data distribution, enabling data scientists to address potential biases by balancing and diversifying the data samples.
5. **Adaptable to Domain-specific Requirements:** Synthetic data generation can be tailored to particular domain constraints, enabling flexibility and adaptability to match the specific requirements of various industries and applications.

2.4.3. Techniques for Synthetic Data Generation

Below are some popular techniques employed for generating synthetic data:

1. **Generative Adversarial Networks (GANs):** GANs consist of two neural networks, the generator and the discriminator, which compete with one another. The generator synthesizes data samples, while the discriminator evaluates them against the real-world data. The generator iteratively refines the generated samples until they are indistinguishable from authentic data.
2. **Variational Autoencoders (VAEs):** VAEs are a type of deep learning model used for generating and reconstructing high-dimensional data samples. They encode input data into a lower-dimensional latent space before decoding it back to its original form.

VAEs balance data reconstruction accuracy and statistical properties to create new samples similar to the training data.
3. **Probabilistic Models:** Probabilistic models, such as Bayesian networks, Gaussian mixture models, and hidden Markov models, aim to describe the underlying statistical structure of data by modeling the joint probability distributions. These models allow for generating new data samples by sampling from the learned probability distributions.
4. **Data Simulation:** Computer simulations can create synthetic data with close resemblance to real-world data by implementing predefined models, rules, and algorithms. These models can account for specific complexities and behaviors of the target system or process, resulting in a more accurate representation of the real-world data.

2.4.4. Challenges and Limitations

Despite the advancements in synthetic data generation techniques, several challenges persist, which must be addressed for efficient integration within the enterprise and computational creativity space:

1. **Quality and Realism:** Ensuring that the generated samples retain the quality, diversity, and realism of the original data is crucial. Poorly constructed synthetic data can lead to suboptimal AI model performance and, in some cases, may even produce misleading or biased outcomes.
2. **Privacy Preservation:** While synthetic data generation presents the potential to address privacy concerns, there is still a risk of reverse engineering the models to extract sensitive information.

Developing robust privacy-preserving techniques to eliminate this risk remains a challenge.
3. **Domain Expertise:** It is essential to incorporate domain knowledge and expertise when designing synthetic data generation models. Failure to do so might result in unrealistic data samples that do not adequately represent the real-world phenomena or systems.

2.4.5. Future Perspectives

With improvements in generative AI techniques and the need for data privacy, synthetic data generation is set to play a vital role in the enterprise and computational creativity domains. Future developments can be expected in terms of:

1. **Interdisciplinary Efforts:** Combining knowledge across disciplines such as mathematics, computer science, and domain-specific expertise will strengthen the overall process of creating high-quality synthetic data.
2. **Advancements in models and algorithms:** As research progresses, state-of-the-art algorithms for data generation will most likely continue to improve, resulting in enhanced realism, diversity, and privacy preservation.
3. **Increased adoption and utilization:** As more organizations recognize the potential of synthetic data generation, they will adopt these techniques for various applications, including data augmentation, cost reduction, and privacy concerns.

In conclusion, synthetic data generation holds tremendous potential in driving the future of generative AI for enterprises and computational creativity. By overcoming existing challenges and limitations and facilitating interdisciplinary collaboration, it can substantially contribute to developing better-performing AI models while adhering to privacy, cost, and other constraints.

2.5 Generative Design of Industrial Parts

Generative design is a transformative approach that employs artificial intelligence (AI) and computational power to revolutionize the way industrial parts are designed, produced, and utilized. This innovative technique relies on iterative optimization processes to generate a multitude of design variations for a given component while satisfying predefined functional, performance, and manufacturing constraints. The result is the potential to optimize and create novel and highly efficient industrial parts that were previously unimaginable.

2.5.1 Evolution of Industrial Design Approach

Traditional methods of industrial design involve human intuition, creativity, and expertise in generating a restricted number of design alternatives. These methods are largely influenced by the designer's experience and knowledge, which might limit innovation and overlook hidden optimization opportunities. Over time, engineers have employed the use of computer-aided design (CAD) and manufacturing technologies, streamlining the process of modeling, analyzing, and producing complex geometries.

However, generative design transcends this approach, utilizing algorithms and AI to propose an extensive array of alternatives that cater to all conceivable design needs, operational parameters, and constraints. With the aid of AI, designers can now harness the power of computational creativity, unlocking a plethora of designs that cater to various use cases and manufacturing requirements.

2.5.2 Key Components of Generative Design

Generative design requires certain key components for its successful implementation:

1. **Objective definition**: The first step in any generative design process involves defining the objectives, or goals, of the design. Specific performance criteria, functional requirements, and manufacturing constraints must be established to focus the generative process on generating suitable solutions.
2. **Design space exploration**: Using the predefined objectives, the AI-driven generative design algorithm searches the design space, identifying possible design alternatives. Some common techniques used for generative design algorithms include topology optimization, lattice or gradient-based optimization, and bio-inspired optimization methods.
3. **Design evaluation and selection**: Each generated design must be evaluated according to its fitness, which is determined by comparing its respective attributes to the predetermined objectives. Suitable designs undergo further modifications, while the unfit ones are discarded. This iterative process continues until the required level of design optimization is achieved.

4. **Manufacturability analysis**: Once the candidate designs are refined and assessed, a manufacturability analysis is performed. This step is crucial, as it ensures the design is compatible with the chosen manufacturing process, such as additive manufacturing or traditional machining.
5. **Post-processing and validation**: Finally, the optimal design is selected for post-processing, which includes refining geometric details, performing stress tests, and validating the design's functionality. The design can then be 3D printed, fabricated, or produced through other forms of manufacturing.

2.5.3 Benefits of Generative Design for Industrial Parts

Generative design offers several advantages that can revolutionize the landscape of industrial design:

1. **Design optimization**: As the AI algorithm iteratively refines each design, the resulting parts offer optimal performance, reduced weight, and improved functionality.
2. **Reduced time-to-market**: The generative design process simplifies the design phase and eliminates the need for excessive trial-and-error iterations, drastically cutting down the time it takes to bring a product to market.
3. **Resource and cost efficiency**: By optimizing the material used in manufacturing, generative design enables a significant reduction in material waste and associated costs.
4. **Design innovation**: AI-driven generative design leads to novel and innovative solutions that may remain undiscovered through traditional design methods, potentially resulting in entirely new product categories and applications.

5. **Customization and personalization**: Generative design allows companies to create customized and bespoke components that cater to specific consumer demands or industry standards, enabling greater flexibility and adaptability to various sectors.

2.5.4 Industrial Applications

Generative design has found diverse applications across numerous industries, including:

1. **Automotive**: From lightweighting vehicle components to improving structural efficiency, generative design enables the creation of unique and innovative designs that maximize fuel efficiency and reduce emissions.
2. **Aerospace**: Aircraft manufacturers use generative design to optimize the weight and performance of critical components, enhancing overall aircraft efficiency, and reducing operating costs.
3. **Medical**: The design of medical implants and prosthetics can be optimized through generative processes, resulting in devices that are more comfortable, functional, and durable.
4. **Architecture and construction**: Landscape architecture, building design, and structural components can benefit from the optimized, organic shapes generated through AI-driven algorithms, leading to more efficient and innovative structures.

As AI-driven generative design continues to mature, its potential applications and uses will similarly expand, giving birth to a new age of computational creativity that will redefine the world of industrial design.

Chapter 3: Generative AI in Marketing and Media

In the previous chapters, we have discussed the development of artificial intelligence and its impact on various industries, introducing the concept of generative AI and its potential in transforming business processes. In this chapter, we dive deeper into the applications of generative AI in marketing and media, exploring areas like content creation, personalization, customer engagement, and other innovations that are shaping the landscape of these industries.

3.1 Overview of Generative AI in Marketing and Media

As businesses continue to grapple with an increasingly competitive landscape and ever-changing consumer preferences, marketing and media professionals must consistently adapt and innovate in order to stay ahead. Thankfully, generative AI presents a myriad of possibilities that can help these professionals drive value, improve efficiency, and create memorable experiences for their customers.

From personalized marketing campaigns to creative content generation, generative AI has the potential to transform every facet of marketing and media. Companies that recognize and adapt to this powerful technology stand to gain a significant competitive advantage in the future.

3.1.1 Key Concepts

When discussing generative AI in the context of marketing and media, it is important to have a foundational understanding of the key concepts and technologies that drive these innovations. In this section, we will briefly introduce the concepts of natural language processing (NLP), generative adversarial networks (GANs), and reinforcement learning, among others.

- **Natural Language Processing (NLP)** is a subfield of artificial intelligence that focuses on enabling computers to understand, interpret, and generate human language. NLP technologies are responsible for many of the generative AI applications in marketing and media, such as automatic content generation and chatbots.
- **Generative Adversarial Networks (GANs)** are a type of AI model consisting of two distinct networks – a generator and a discriminator. The generator creates new content (e.g., images or text) while the discriminator evaluates the quality of the generated content. GANs have been used in various marketing and media applications, including the generation of realistic images and deepfake videos.
- **Reinforcement Learning** is a type of AI technology where an agent learns to make decisions by interacting with its environment, receiving feedback, and adjusting its actions accordingly. This approach can be used to optimize marketing strategies, create adaptive recommendation systems, and improve customer engagement.

Now that we have laid the groundwork, let's delve into some specific use cases of generative AI in marketing and media.

3.2 Content Creation

One of the most significant applications of generative AI in marketing and media is its ability to revolutionize the content creation process. With the help of NLP and GANs, companies can generate high-quality written and visual content at scale.

3.2.1 Copywriting and Content Generation

Generative AI tools have significantly impacted the way marketers create written content like email copy, product descriptions, and social media posts. Using NLP and machine learning algorithms, these tools can generate coherent and engaging text in just a few seconds. Some examples include GPT-3 (Generative Pre-trained Transformer 3) by OpenAI, which is capable of generating highly convincing text on a range of topics.

One of the primary advantages of using AI for content generation is the unparalleled speed and scale it provides. This allows companies to create a larger volume of content, freeing up marketers and copywriters to focus on more strategic and creative tasks.

3.2.2 Image and Video Generation

A picture is worth a thousand words, yet generating compelling visual content has historically been a time-consuming and costly endeavor. Generative AI tools like GANs have begun to change that narrative by producing realistic images, video thumbnails, and even deepfake videos. This technology allows marketers to create highly engaging and personalized visual content for campaigns or social media without being dependent on human designers, decreasing the costs and delays inherent in the creative process.

3.3 Personalization and Targeting

One key aspect of successful marketing campaigns is the ability to personalize content to resonate with target audiences. Generative AI can help companies analyze user data and behavior to create highly relevant marketing messages, resulting in increased engagement, conversion rates, and customer loyalty.

3.3.1 Customer Segmentation

Effective marketing campaigns require businesses to understand and segment their customers according to preferences, behavior, and demographics. Generative AI can process large volumes of data to identify patterns and automatically create customer segments, allowing companies to target their messaging more accurately and effectively.

3.3.2 Personalized Recommendations

One of the most common use cases for generative AI in marketing and media is the creation of personalized recommendation systems. By analyzing customer data, preferences, and behavior, these systems can provide highly relevant content and product suggestions, improving user experience and driving customer retention.

The application of reinforcement learning in recommendations further increases the sophistication of these algorithms by enabling them to adapt and learn from user behavior, continually refining their recommendations.

3.4 Customer Engagement and Communication

Generative AI can help businesses enhance customer engagement through interactive experiences and personalized communication by using technologies like chatbots and voice assistants.

3.4.1 Chatbots and Customer Support

AI-powered chatbots have become increasingly popular as a means to provide immediate and personalized customer support. By leveraging NLP, these chatbots can understand and respond to customer queries in a human-like manner. Businesses can use them to handle a wide range of tasks, including answering frequently asked questions, booking appointments, and even handling complaints.

3.4.2 Voice Assistants and Conversational AI

As voice assistants like Amazon's Alexa or Google Assistant become more commonplace, generative AI has helped to create more natural and engaging conversational experiences by generating human-like responses. This technology can be used to build intricate, voice-based marketing strategies or even develop branded voice assistants for companies, encouraging deeper customer relationships.

3.5 Impact on Marketing and Media Professionals

Despite the numerous benefits of generative AI in marketing and media, concerns exist about potential job displacement as these technologies become more widespread. However, it is essential to consider that generative AI does not replace human creativity and intuition, but rather serves as a powerful tool to augment human skills and decision-making. By embracing generative AI and learning to work collaboratively with these technologies, marketing and media professionals can leverage AI-driven insights to optimize strategic decision-making, create unique experiences, and reinvent their industries.

In the next chapter, we will explore the impact of generative AI on industries such as retail, manufacturing, and finance, shedding light on the broad scope and potential of this technology across various sectors.

3.1 Synthetically Generated Marketing Messages

As we move further into the age of artificial intelligence, businesses are constantly looking for ways to leverage this technology to enhance their marketing strategies. One of the most promising avenues to emerge from the AI revolution is the use of generative algorithms in crafting marketing messages. This section will explore synthetically generated marketing messages, their benefits, and potential applications, as well as the limitations and ethical considerations surrounding this technology.

What are Synthetically Generated Marketing Messages?

Synthetically generated marketing messages are advertisements, promotional materials, or other forms of communication crafted by AI algorithms instead of human copywriters. By employing Generative Adversarial Networks (GANs), Machine Learning (ML), or Natural Language Processing (NLP) techniques, these AI algorithms can create persuasive, engaging, and effectively personalized marketing messages.

Benefits of Synthetically Generated Marketing Messages

There are numerous benefits to incorporating AI-generated marketing messages into your business strategy:

1. **Increased Efficiency and Scale:** AI-generated marketing messages can be created rapidly, allowing businesses to quickly iterate and test different versions of their marketing materials. This efficiency also makes it possible to scale marketing efforts more easily, reaching larger audiences or tailoring messaging to specific microsegments.
2. **Personalization:** Personalization is a key component of successful marketing campaigns. AI algorithms can analyze vast amounts of customer data and create personalized messages tailored to individual preferences, habits, and behaviors, increasing the likelihood of customer engagement.
3. **Multiformat Adaptability:** Synthetically generated content can be easily adapted to various formats and mediums, from text and images to audio and video. This flexibility enables businesses to create a cohesive brand experience across all touchpoints, streamlining the customer journey.
4. **Continuous Improvement:** AI algorithms are built on large datasets, and their performance improves as they are exposed to more data. As a result, marketing messages created by AI can be constantly refined to boost the effectiveness of campaigns.
5. **Cost Reduction:** Employing AI-driven marketing messages can reduce the cost associated with hiring copywriters and marketing agencies, freeing up resources that can be invested in other areas of the business.

Applications of Synthetically Generated Marketing Messages

AI-generated marketing messages can be applied to a variety of marketing channels and techniques, such as:

1. **Email Marketing:** Personalized AI-generated subject lines and content can drive higher open and click-through rates, boosting the overall success of email campaigns.
2. **Social Media Marketing:** AI-generated captions, hashtags, and ad copy can help businesses create consistent, engaging, and timely posts across all platforms, increasing brand visibility and audience engagement.
3. **Content Marketing:** AI algorithms can produce tailored blog posts, whitepapers, or ebooks, optimizing the content for SEO and ensuring relevance to target audiences.
4. **Pay-Per-Click Advertising:** AI-generated ad copy and keyword selection can lead to more effective, targeted ad campaigns with improved click-through rates and ROI.
5. **Product Descriptions:** AI-generated product descriptions can be both more informative and engaging, improving the online shopping experience and driving sales.

Limitations and Ethical Considerations

Despite the many advantages of synthetically generated marketing messages, there are limitations and ethical concerns that businesses must consider:

1. **Loss of Human Touch:** While AI algorithms are improving, they may not yet capture the subtlety, emotion, and cultural nuances of human-authored

content, potentially leading to impersonal or disconnected marketing messaging.
2. **Misrepresentation and Manipulation:** AI-generated messages can be designed to be highly persuasive, which raises the question of whether it is right to use technology that could potentially manipulate customers into making decisions they would not otherwise have made.
3. **Data Privacy:** The use of AI-generated marketing messages relies on vast amounts of customer data. The collection, storage, and utilization of this data for marketing purposes raise ethical concerns around data privacy and consent.
4. **Job Displacement:** The increased use of AI in marketing may lead to job losses for human copywriters and marketing professionals, causing concern around the socio-economic effects of automation.

In summary, synthetically generated marketing messages offer numerous benefits for enterprises looking to enhance their marketing strategies. Businesses should consider leveraging this technology to create efficient, personalized, and adaptive campaigns. However, it is crucial to remain mindful of the potential limitations and ethical concerns, finding ways to strike a balance between leveraging AI for marketing success and maintaining a human touch that fosters genuine connection with customers.

3.2. AI-generated blockbuster films

The creative potential of generative AI has not only found its way into the world of literature, but it has also begun to infiltrate the ever-evolving landscape of the film industry. As a tool for generating scripts, storylines, and even visuals, AI has an immense potential to revolutionize the way films are made and experienced. In this section, we will outline a future where AI-generated blockbuster films become mainstream, impacting both the creative process and the audience's engagement with this medium.

3.2.1. AI in film production

AI-generated storylines and scripts

The first breakthroughs in AI-generated films will likely come from the realm of storytelling, with AI algorithms creating intricate storylines and scripts based on various narrative patterns, character arcs, and genres. These AI-generated stories will be able to create compelling narratives that are personalized and developed at scale.

Screenwriters and filmmakers will be able to leverage this technology to explore unconventional ideas and themes, as well as crafting characters with diverse backgrounds and voices. By incorporating AI-generated elements into their stories, they will redefine the creative process and push the boundaries of what's possible in storytelling.

AI-powered previsualization and casting

In the pre-production phase of filmmaking, AI can also be utilized for tasks like previsualization and casting. Machine learning algorithms can analyze vast amounts of data from previous films to generate optimal shot compositions, camera movements, and lighting conditions. This will save time and money during pre-production and ensure that directors can communicate their vision effectively to their crews.

Casting is another area that AI has the potential to transform. By analyzing the traits of successful actors in specific roles or genres, AI systems can suggest the right fit for characters in an AI-generated story. This would not only benefit casting directors but would also open doors for previously overlooked actors by eliminating some aspects of human bias.

AI-driven visual effects and animation

The capabilities of AI in generating hyper-realistic graphics and visuals have already been demonstrated through technologies like deepfakes and adversarial neural networks. This has the potential to revolutionize the visual effects and animation industry, enabling filmmakers to create stunningly realistic worlds and characters without needing massive budgets or resources.

AI-driven visual effects tools will also streamline the post-production process, allowing filmmakers to make adjustments to scenes and characters in real-time. The flexibility offered by AI-generated visuals will enable creators to experiment with different visual styles and effects, further expanding the creative scope of their films.

3.2.2. The impact on consumption and audience engagement

Personalized movie experiences

As generative AI advances, it will enable the creation of films that are tailored to the preferences of individual viewers. AI-generated films will learn from the tastes and preferences of their audiences, delivering content that resonates on a personal level.

These personalized experiences could include dynamic storylines that adapt in real-time, changing based on the viewer's emotional response or engagement during the film. This level of interaction and customization will redefine the concept of a traditional "blockbuster," as audiences are offered unique cinematic experiences that cater specifically to them.

Expanding the horizon of genres and narrative styles

With AI-generated films making their way into mainstream cinema, we can expect not only an explosion of content but also a diversification of genres and narrative styles. The creativity and novelty offered by generative AI will introduce genres and themes that blend storytelling with cutting-edge technology.

These new hybrids will offer enriching and thought-provoking experiences for audiences, pushing the boundaries of traditional storytelling and forcing creators and viewers alike to rethink the way they engage with film.

3.2.3. Challenges and considerations

While the emergence of AI-generated blockbuster films presents an exciting future for both creators and audiences, it also raises a number of ethical and practical concerns.

The decline of human creativity

One fear is that the widespread adoption of AI-generated content could lead to a decline in human creativity, as the roles of screenwriters, directors, and other creative professionals become marginalized. However, it's worth considering that AI will always remain a tool, and the human touch will still be required to ensure a well-rounded, emotionally rich film that resonates with audiences on a deeper level.

Attribution and copyright

As AI-generated content becomes more prevalent, it raises questions about copyright and ownership. If an AI-generated screenplay is signed by a human screenwriter, can the original AI algorithm be credited as a co-writer? How should royalties be distributed? Working out the legal and ethical nuances of these questions is crucial as AI-generated films become more mainstream.

Ethical concerns

With the potential for AI-generated films to cater to individual preferences, there is a risk of encouraging echo chambers or perpetuating harmful stereotypes. As AI-generated content creators, it is important to remain vigilant in balancing personalization with responsible and ethical storytelling.

3.2.4. Conclusion

As generative AI continues to develop and infiltrate the world of film and entertainment, its impact on the industry is only set to grow. AI-generated blockbuster films have the potential to not only revolutionize the creative process but also transform the way in which we consume and engage with cinema.

Although many challenges and concerns loom on the horizon, the potential benefits of AI-generated films for both creators and audiences are immense. By embracing and adapting to this technology, the film industry can pave the way for a new era of cinema that leverages AI's capabilities to tell powerful, engaging stories that resonate with global audiences.

3.3. Transforming the creative process

As we venture deeper into the realm of generative AI and its potential impact on enterprises, it becomes crucial to understand how this technology can transform the core aspect of innovation - the creative process. From ideation to execution, many elements contribute to a breakthrough invention or solution that shifts paradigms.

In this section, we'll be investigating how generative AI intersects with the creative process, its implications on various industries, and the potential shifts in the way we perceive and approach creativity.

3.3.1. Redefining ideation with generative AI

Traditionally, the ideation phase of the creative process involves brainstorming sessions, collecting references, and experimenting with various methods to conjure novel ideas. Incorporating generative AI into this stage provides a plethora of possibilities by removing limitations imposed by the human mind and expanding the creative space.

This transformative capability can be attributed to the ability of generative AI to analyze vast amounts of data, identify patterns, and generate new concepts that human collaborators might not have envisioned. By suggesting innovative ideas based on advanced data analysis, the AI can leapfrog conventional thinking and stimulate humans to explore uncharted territories. This symbiosis enables designers, engineers, and artists to reach beyond their imagination and tap into the infinite potential of generative AI.

3.3.2. Expediting concept validation and iteration

One of the most resource-intensive stages in the creative process is validating and iterating on ideas or designs. This often involves multiple iterations and resources in terms of time, money, and human effort. Generative AI holds the potential to considerably accelerate this stage by evaluating vast possibilities within a shorter time frame and autonomously generating variations that align with the design specifications.

With the help of advanced algorithms and computational power, generative AI models, like GANs (Generative Adversarial Networks), can quickly test and refine prototypes. For instance, in generative design, computer-aided design (CAD) systems can assess structural and functional elements of a design, simulating the performance of multiple iterations and providing insights that guide engineers towards an optimal solution.

3.3.3. Personalization and customization at scale

Whether it's marketing content, product design, or user experience, catering to individual preferences has become a determinative factor for success in today's competitive market. This demand for personalization and customization can be met effectively by leveraging generative AI.

Generative models can tailor content or design according to specific requirements drawn from user data or preferences, generating personalized solutions at scale. Customizable products with unique features, personalized marketing campaigns, or tailored user experiences on digital platforms can vastly enhance customer satisfaction and engagement. This potential for mass customization can disrupt the existing dynamics of various industries and set new benchmarks for success.

3.3.4. Democratizing creative expertise

The mammoth task of comprehending and transforming vast data has traditionally been carried out by domain experts who possess specialized knowledge and experience. However, generative AI's potential to identify patterns, derive insights, and create novel outcomes has the potential to democratize access to creative expertise.

Regardless of their experience level, professionals and enthusiasts alike can leverage this technology to explore new terrains in their respective domains. Be it music production, writing, product development, or scientific discovery, access to AI-powered tools can diminish barriers that limit creative potential and facilitate a more equitable playing field for innovation.

3.3.5. Shaping ethical considerations and collaborations

The application of generative AI in the creative process necessitates a shift in the way we perceive ownership, authorship, and collaboration. As AI-generated content becomes more prevalent, questions surrounding intellectual property, creative responsibility, and originality will arise, prompting a reevaluation of ethical stances and copyright laws.

Moreover, embracing a collaborative approach between humans and AI, where the skills and expertise of both entities synergize, would prove imperative to navigating the creative landscape of the future. This collaboration might manifest as a fusion of human intuition, empathy, and contextual understanding with AI's analytical prowess and infinite creative potential.

Conclusion

In conclusion, generative AI holds the key to unlocking unprecedented possibilities in the creative process for enterprises and individuals alike. As we witness the dawn of a new era of computational creativity, it is crucial to adapt and evolve our mindset and methodologies to harness this transformative technology's true potential. The future of innovation will be characterized not just by the power of AI, but by the successful collaboration between human and artificial intelligence.

Chapter 4: Generative AI Technologies

In this chapter, we delve into the various generative AI technologies that power computational creativity and enterprise solutions. We'll explore how these technologies are shaping the future of AI and their potential impact on businesses across various sectors.

4.1 Overview of Generative AI Technologies

Generative AI technologies fall under a broader category of machine learning algorithms known as generative models. These models learn to generate new data by capturing the underlying patterns and structures present in the training data. Some of the most notable generative AI technologies include:

1. Generative Adversarial Networks (GANs)
2. Variational Autoencoders (VAEs)
3. Recurrent Neural Networks (RNNs)
4. Transformer Models
5. Reinforcement Learning (RL) based approaches

Let's discuss each of these technologies in more detail.

4.2 Generative Adversarial Networks (GANs)

Generative Adversarial Networks (GANs) were introduced in 2014 by Ian Goodfellow and have since become one of the most popular and widely used generative AI techniques. GANs consist of two neural networks, namely the generator and discriminator, that compete against each other in a zero-sum game.

The generator's primary objective is to produce realistic data samples, whereas the discriminator's goal is to distinguish between real data samples and the generated samples. By optimizing this competition, GANs gradually improve the quality of the generated data.

GANs have found numerous applications, such as image synthesis, data augmentation, and style transfer. GANs have also been used to generate realistic images, video, and audio content, and even create artwork that has been auctioned at major art galleries.

4.3 Variational Autoencoders (VAEs)

Variational Autoencoders (VAEs) are another popular generative model that combines deep learning and Bayesian inference. VAEs consist of two main components: an encoder and a decoder. The encoder learns a compressed representation of the input data and the decoder reconstructs the data from the compressed representation.

Unlike traditional autoencoders, VAEs optimize a trade-off between data reconstruction and the compression of the latent space, resulting in a smoother and more structured latent space. This makes VAEs particularly suitable for generating new samples by interpolating between points in the latent space.

VAEs have numerous applications, including data denoising, anomaly detection, data synthesis, and image editing. They have been used for generating realistic images, 3D models, and game levels.

4.4 Recurrent Neural Networks (RNNs) and Language Models

Recurrent Neural Networks (RNNs) are a class of neural networks that specialize in processing and generating sequential data. RNNs contain loops that allow information to persist between different time steps of a sequence. This enables RNNs to learn complex temporal patterns present in data such as text, audio, and video.

Among various RNN architectures, Long Short-Term Memory (LSTM) and Gated Recurrent Units (GRU) have proven to be particularly effective in capturing long-term dependencies. RNNs have been the backbone of many significant advances in natural language processing (NLP), speech recognition, and time-series analysis.

Language models, a subclass of RNNs, learn the underlying structure and statistical patterns in textual data. Transformer models, which we will discuss next, have emerged as a more powerful alternative to traditional RNNs for language modeling tasks.

4.5 Transformer Models

Transformer models, introduced in 2017 by Vaswani et al., have revolutionized the field of NLP, outperforming RNN-based approaches on a wide range of tasks, including machine translation, text summarization, and sentiment analysis.

The key innovation of the Transformer architecture is the self-attention mechanism, which allows the model to weigh the importance of different tokens in a sequence based on their contextual relevance. This enables Transformer models to efficiently capture long-range dependencies in text data and generates more accurate and coherent outputs.

OpenAI's GPT-3, a state-of-the-art generative language model, is based on the Transformer architecture and has showcased the potential for generating contextually relevant, creative text.

4.6 Reinforcement Learning (RL) based Approaches

Reinforcement Learning (RL) is a subfield of AI that revolves around training agents to perform actions in an environment to maximize a reward signal. RL has shown promising results in generating creative content in domains such as music, art, and game design.

In the context of generative AI, RL algorithms can guide the optimization of generative models to produce more diverse and appealing content. For instance, RL can be used to fine-tune GANs or guide the sampling process of language models to generate more creative and coherent text.

4.7 Future Directions

Generative AI technologies continue to evolve at a rapid pace, with advancements in unsupervised and self-supervised learning, multitask learning, and transfer learning promising more efficient and versatile models. These technologies could potentially unlock new possibilities for enhancing creativity and driving innovation in enterprises.

In the following chapters, we will explore various applications of generative AI in different industry sectors and discuss strategies for effectively leveraging generative AI in enterprises.

4.1 Classifiers and generative AI systems

In this section, we will explore the relationship between classifiers and generative AI systems, delving into their characteristics, strengths, and applications in various domains. Understanding the fundamental differences and similarities between these two categories of AI systems is paramount for enterprises seeking to harness the power of computational creativity and generative AI.

4.1.1 Introduction to Classifiers

Classifiers, also known as discriminative models, are a category of AI systems that focus on determining the boundary between different classes or categories. These models are trained to recognize patterns, features, or attributes within a given dataset and subsequently classify new, unseen data into predefined categories. A classifier's primary objective is to maximize the margin between different classes, ensuring the model can discriminate between them with high accuracy.

Some common examples of classifiers include:

1. **Logistic Regression**: A statistical method for analyzing a dataset with one or more independent variables that determine an outcome, often expressed as a binary variable.
2. **Support Vector Machines (SVM)**: A machine learning technique that constructs a hyperplane in a high-dimensional space, separating different classes.
3. **Decision Trees**: A flowchart-like structure used to classify input data into different classes by recursively splitting the dataset based on specific attributes.
4. **Neural Networks**: Multi-layered models that can learn non-linear mappings between input and output layers, used for a wide range of classification tasks.

4.1.2 Introduction to Generative AI Systems

Generative AI systems, on the other hand, focus on learning the underlying structure or distribution of the data to generate new, previously unseen samples.

These models not only learn the boundaries between different classes but also understand the probability distribution across the entire dataset. This enables generative systems to create new instances that are coherent and representative of the original dataset.

Some well-known examples of generative models include:

1. **Generative Adversarial Networks (GANs)**: A framework in which two neural networks, the generator and the discriminator, compete against each other to learn the data distribution and generate realistic new samples.
2. **Variational Autoencoders (VAEs)**: A neural network architecture that learns a latent space representation of the data, enabling efficient generation of new instances.
3. **Markov Chain Monte Carlo (MCMC)**: A class of algorithms used to sample from a probability distribution, often used in Bayesian inference for generative models.
4. **Restricted Boltzmann Machines (RBMs)**: A type of generative neural network designed to learn the probability distribution of a dataset.

4.1.3 Comparing Classifiers and Generative AI Systems

While both classifiers and generative systems aim to make sense of data, their approaches and applications differ significantly. We will explore some of these differences below:

1. **Objective**: As mentioned earlier, classifiers aim to find boundaries between classes or categories in a

dataset, while generative systems focus on learning the data distribution to generate new samples.

2. **Model Flexibility**: Generative models tend to be more flexible and expressive than classifiers, as they capture the entire data distribution, including complex interdependencies among variables. However, this can sometimes make them more challenging to train and require greater computational resources.

3. **Data Efficiency**: Classifier models can exploit small labeled datasets more effectively, as their primary focus is on learning the decision boundaries between classes. Generative systems typically require larger datasets to learn the underlying structure and distribution accurately.

4. **Supervised vs. Unsupervised Learning**: Classifiers often rely on supervised learning, which requires labeled data for training. In contrast, many generative models can be trained using unsupervised learning methods, leveraging unlabeled data for learning.

5. **Applications**: The use-cases for classifiers and generative AI systems also differ. Classifiers are used in many real-world applications such as image and speech recognition, spam filtering, and fraud detection. Generative models, on the other hand, have found success in designing novel molecules in drug discovery, generating realistic images, creating music, and enhancing data augmentation processes.

4.1.4 Convergence of Classifiers and Generative AI Systems

Despite their distinctions, recent developments have blurred the lines between classifiers and generative models as they complement and enhance each other in various ways:

1. **Transfer Learning**: Pre-trained generative models can be fine-tuned for specific classification tasks, leveraging the rich feature extraction capabilities they possess.
2. **Semi-supervised Learning**: Generative systems can be used alongside classifiers to enable semi-supervised learning, wherein generative models aid in the generation of additional labeled data for training the classifier.
3. **Adversarial Training**: In GANs, the generator and the discriminator (a classifier) work adversarially to improve each other's capabilities, ultimately leading to the generation of higher-quality and more realistic samples.
4. **Data Augmentation**: Generative models can be employed to generate new training data, enabling classifiers to learn from a more diverse and robust dataset.

As we continue to explore the future of generative AI in enterprises and computational creativity, it is crucial to understand the strengths and limitations of both classifiers and generative systems. By leveraging the best of both worlds, organizations can achieve unprecedented levels of innovation, problem-solving, optimization, and ultimately, a stronger competitive edge.

4.2. Generative Pre-trained Transformer (GPT)

Generative Pre-trained Transformer (GPT) is a cutting-edge AI technology that has shown remarkable results in natural language understanding and generation tasks. Developed by OpenAI, the GPT model has been evolved through several versions, each proving to be more effective and sophisticated than the previous. In this section, we will delve deep into the evolution of GPT models, their working principles, and how they are shaping the future of generative AI for enterprises and computational creativity.

4.2.1. The Evolution of GPT Models

GPT models have gone through steady advancements over the years, with three major iterations released by OpenAI.

GPT-1

Introduced in June 2018, GPT-1 provided a strong foundation for the future of generative AI in the field of natural language processing. With 117 million parameters, GPT-1 was trained on the BooksCorpus dataset, which contains over 7,000 unpublished books. The model's primary purpose was text generation, and it demonstrated significant competency in various tasks, such as translation, question-answering, and text summarization.

GPT-2

In February 2019, OpenAI unveiled the second iteration, GPT-2, which marked a substantial improvement over its predecessor. GPT-2 consisted of a whopping 1.5 billion parameters, granting it a deeper understanding of language patterns and greater generative capability. Trained on the WebText dataset, which encompasses approximately 45 million web pages, GPT-2 was initially deemed "too dangerous" to release entirely due to its high capacity for generating realistic, context-aware content. However, by November 2019, OpenAI fully released GPT-2, confident in the research community and AI ecosystem's ability to handle potential misuse.

GPT-3

The most recent and groundbreaking iteration, GPT-3, was released in June 2020. Encompassing a colossal 175 billion parameters, GPT-3 dwarfed its predecessor in both size and competency. Trained on a dataset called WebText2, which is an enhanced version of the dataset used for GPT-2, GPT-3 is capable of performing various NLP tasks with minimal fine-tuning. Its capability ranges from text generation and context-aware sentiment analysis to code generation and natural language interfaces for software. GPT-3 has shown promise in changing the AI landscape profoundly and becoming a pivotal force in enterprises and computational creativity.

4.2.2. GPT Architecture and Training Methodology

GPT models are built on the foundational principles of the Transformer architecture, which was introduced by Vaswani et al. in the paper "Attention is All You Need" (2017). Unlike traditional sequence-to-sequence models that rely on recurrent neural networks (RNNs) or convolutional neural networks (CNNs), Transformers use self-attention mechanisms to process input sequences. When training GPT models, OpenAI employs a two-step process consisting of unsupervised pre-training and supervised fine-tuning.

Unsupervised Pre-training

During this phase, the model is trained on a large corpus of text data (e.g., web pages or books) using a language modeling objective. This task involves predicting the next word in a sequence, enabling the model to internalize the syntactic and semantic patterns present in the input data. The resulting consequences of this pre-training phase are a highly capable general-purpose language understanding system.

Supervised Fine-tuning

In the second phase, fine-tuning with labeled data sets only requires a minimal number of task-specific examples. The model is adapted to accommodate specific supervised learning objectives, such as text classification, sentiment analysis, or summarization. Consequently, fine-tuning enables GPT models to tackle a wide range of natural language processing tasks with proficiency.

4.2.3. GPT in Enterprises and Computational Creativity

The advancements in GPT models are rapidly transforming how enterprises interact with AI and opening new avenues for computational creativity.
1. **Chatbots and Customer Support**: GPT models can be utilized to create highly competent chatbots and virtual agents. Their rich language understanding enables them to respond to complex client queries, refine the customer experience, and reduce the workload on human operators.
2. **Content Generation**: GPT models provide businesses with the ability to generate contextually relevant and coherent text. This capability can be leveraged for creating marketing materials, product descriptions, or even drafting emails.
3. **Translation and Language Modeling**: GPT models can be utilized for machine translation tasks, enabling more precise and human-like translations. This application can help businesses reach global audiences and break language barriers efficiently.
4. **Code Generation**: GPT models have demonstrated an ability to generate code based on natural language inputs. This can lead to a programming revolution, with developers obtaining assistance in composing code snippets and simplifying the software development process.
5. **Artistic Expression**: The improvements in GPT models open the door for exploring computational creativity in various domains such as poetry, storytelling, and music composition.

In conclusion, GPT models act as the embodiment of the future of generative AI for enterprises and computational creativity. By continually facilitating advancements in their understanding of language and context, these models can enrich and transform industries worldwide.

4.3. Digital-Image Generators and their Applications

Generative AI technologies and algorithms have begun playing a crucial role in various domains, from natural language processing to computer vision. As these algorithms mature, generative models have become more sophisticated, leading to a new breed of applications that leverage the power of these models to generate new and innovative content. One such application is digital-image generators, which are AI-driven tools that generate high-quality images based on input data or descriptions. This section delves into digital-image generators, covers their technology, and discusses the different applications in which these generators are being utilized.

4.3.1. Understanding Digital-Image Generators

Digital-image generators, also known as AI image synthesizers, leverage the power of generative AI models such as Generative Adversarial Networks (GANs) and Variational Autoencoders (VAEs) to generate new images. These models learn the underlying statistical distribution of a given dataset and leverage that knowledge to generate new images that are statistically similar to the training data.

GANs, introduced by Ian Goodfellow, consist of two neural networks: a generator and a discriminator. The generator creates fake images or data, while the discriminator distinguishes between real and generated samples. Through multiple iterations, the generator improves its ability to create more realistic images, and the discriminator becomes better at telling the difference between real and fake images. The result is a powerful generative model that can synthesize high-quality images.

VAEs, developed by Kingma and Welling, are generative models that use neural networks to learn to encode the data into a lower-dimensional latent space efficiently. The decoder part of the VAE then uses the points in this latent space to generate new images similar to the samples in the training dataset.

4.3.2. Application Areas of Digital-Image Generators

Digital-image generators have found applications across various industries, including, but not limited to, advertising, film, gaming, and e-commerce. Following are some examples of their applications:

4.3.2.1. Art and Design

AI-generated images can serve as a creative tool for artists and designers, helping them rapidly explore a wide range of visual styles and ideas. This technology can augment an artist's imagination and open up new dimensions of creative expression.

NVIDIA's GauGAN is an example of a digital-image generator that allows users to draw simple sketches, which are then transformed into realistic landscapes using GANs. GAN Paint Studio, developed by researchers at the MIT-IBM Watson AI Lab, is another tool that generates photorealistic images from user-drawn sketches.

4.3.2.2. Advertising and Marketing

Digital-image generators can create a myriad of new visuals, catering to the requirements of different advertisements or marketing campaigns. They can help businesses create unique content and reduce time spent on the design and production of marketing material.

For instance, creative agencies can use AI-generated images to create product mockups and generate various design assets quickly, saving time and resources.

4.3.2.3. Gaming

Digital-image generators enable game designers to produce textured content, such as terrain, characters, and objects, at a faster pace. They can also assist in procedural generation to create vast and diverse game worlds.

For example, the game No Man's Sky uses procedural generation to create an expansive universe with more than 18 quintillion planets for players to explore. AI-generated assets can help populate these worlds with unique and varied flora, fauna, and other elements to make for a more immersive gaming experience.

4.3.2.4. E-commerce

AI-generated images can help e-commerce companies generate product images without the need for physical photoshoots. These images can be used for product listings, advertisements, or other promotional material.

For example, a company called DataGrid used GANs to develop a dataset of human-like models that can be used for clothing advertising. This can help e-commerce businesses save on hiring models and organizing shoots for each clothing item.

4.3.3. Future Prospects

As digital-image generators continue to improve and generate more realistic images, they will find new applications across diverse areas. Some potential future developments include:

4.3.3.1. Visual Storytelling

Digital-image generators could assist in visualizing narrative concepts and create compelling visual stories based on text input. This would allow filmmakers, graphic novelists, and other storytellers to quickly generate visual representations of their ideas.

4.3.3.2. Virtual Reality and Simulation

AI-generated assets can significantly aid in creating hyper-realistic virtual environments for training simulations, virtual tourism, and immersive experiences.

4.3.3.3. Personalized Content Creation

Combining digital-image generators with user preferences could lead to the creation of personalized visual content, such as wallpapers, artwork, and designs tailored to individual tastes.

However, along with the development of these novel applications, addressing ethical concerns—like responsibility, accountability, and the potential for deepfake generation—will be important in shaping the progression of digital-image generators.

In conclusion, digital-image generators are transforming the way images are designed and consumed. As the technology evolves, their applications across various sectors will continue to grow, enabling new creative possibilities while also addressing relevant ethical concerns.

Chapter 5: Foundation Models in AI

This chapter will explore foundation models in AI with particular focus on their relevance for enterprises and computational creativity. In doing so, we will delve into the history of these models, their architecture, their strengths and limitations, as well as the opportunities they present for progress in future generations of AI.

5.1 A Brief History of Foundation Models in AI

In the second decade of the 21st century, significant advances were witnessed in the AI landscape as ambitious projects and new models were introduced. These models, known as foundation models, have gradually come to redefine AI approaches, especially in the areas of natural language processing (NLP), image recognition, and computational creativity. Key milestones in the development of the foundation models include:

5.1.1 Google's BERT

Introduced in 2018, Google's Bidirectional Encoder Representations from Transformers (BERT) emerged as a groundbreaking foundation model for NLP tasks. BERT transformed pre-existing models, like word2vec, by replacing them with context-aware, bidirectional language models that could better understand semantics.

5.1.2 OpenAI's GPT

In the same year, OpenAI introduced Generative Pretrained Transformers (GPT). As an autoregressive transformer, GPT could generate text of unmatched quality at the time, exhibiting a flavor of the generative capabilities of the advanced AI models that were to emerge.

5.1.3 GPT-2 and GPT-3

In 2019 and 2020, OpenAI released more advanced versions of the GPT architecture, GPT-2 and GPT-3. GPT-2 contained 1.5 billion parameters and managed even more impressive text generation. GPT-3 took it to another level altogether, boasting 175 billion parameters and revolutionizing AI-based language understanding, generation, and translation.

5.2 Unraveling the Architecture of Foundation Models

Foundation models are powered by an architecture that relies on deep learning techniques, primarily using transformers. Let's explore the architecture of these models, focusing on key components such as the attention mechanism and modules in the transformers.

5.2.1 Attention Mechanism

A key component of the transformer architecture is the attention mechanism, which allows models like GPT-3 to weigh the importance of input tokens when generating outputs. The attention mechanism helps foundation models learn and understand context by enabling them to focus on different parts of input sequences. This capability has significantly enhanced the context-awareness and quality of generative AI.

5.2.2 Encoder-Decoder Architecture

Many foundation models use an encoder-decoder architecture that consists of modules connected in separate stages. This architecture can process inputs and create outputs in parallel, enabling more efficient training for large models like those in the GPT series.

5.2.3 Large-Scale Pretraining

Foundation models undergo extensive pretraining on diverse datasets. By learning from vast repositories of text or images, they acquire a strong understanding of various tasks.

5.3 Strengths and Limitations of Foundation Models

As powerful as foundation models have proven, they come with certain strengths and limitations that need to be considered.

5.3.1 Strengths

1. **Scalability:** Foundation models have shown impressive scalability while working with increasingly larger datasets and parameters. This enables higher levels of complexity and parallelism in AI applications.
2. **Task Agnosticism:** These models excel at a wide range of tasks, from language translation to image recognition and synthesis, without needing task-specific modifications.
3. **Few-Shot Learning:** Foundation models can quickly adapt to new tasks with minimal fine-tuning, demonstrating remarkable few-shot learning capabilities.

5.3.2 Limitations

1. **Resource Requirements:** The sheer scale of foundation models such as GPT-3 makes them resource-intensive, consuming massive amounts of computational power and energy.
2. **Bias:** As learning is derived from large, predominantly biased datasets, these models are prone to reproduce or even amplify biases present in their training data.
3. **Lack of Comprehensibility:** Foundation models have complex internals that make them difficult to interpret and comprehend, leading to challenges in understanding how and why they produce certain outputs.

5.4 Opportunities in Enterprise Implementation and Computational Creativity

Foundation models present immense opportunities for enterprises as they lead to versatile AI solutions that can be applied across domains, including language understanding, computer vision, and creative applications.

5.4.1 Enterprise Implementation

Enterprises can deploy foundation models for various applications, such as:

1. Customer service automation
2. Summarization of lengthy texts
3. Sentiment analysis
4. Automated content generation

5.4.2 Computational Creativity

In addition to being game-changers in NLP tasks, foundation models have shown potential in enhancing computational creativity, transforming fields like music, film, and art by generating original content, collaborating with human creators, or morphing and modifying existing work.

5.5 The Future of Generative AI

Advancements in foundation models have paved the way for the next wave of AI evolution. Areas where future generations of AI can make a substantial impact include:

1. Achieving improved alignment of AI systems with human values

2. Enhancing safety and robustness while working with large and diverse datasets
3. Exploring the possibilities of AI creativity and collaboration with humans in various fields

Ultimately, the future of generative AI for enterprises and computational creativity is bound to be heavily influenced by the development and impact of foundation models. As a significant driving force in the AI landscape, decoding the full potential of foundation models and resolving their limitations will undoubtedly lead to groundbreaking advancements in the field.

5.1. Introduction to Foundation Models

The era of Artificial Intelligence (AI) has rapidly advanced, driven by significant breakthroughs in deep learning and data processing capabilities. In recent years, a new class of AI models has emerged, known as "Foundation Models." These models have gained substantial traction due to their ability to create a wide range of creative and computational applications while providing rapid domain adaptation with minimal fine-tuning. This section will delve into the concept of foundation models, explore their importance, and discuss their growth trajectory alongside the implications for enterprises and computational creativity.

5.1.1. What are Foundation Models?

Foundation models are large-scale, pre-trained models that serve as a base for various machine learning applications. These models are trained on diverse and extensive datasets, incorporating an extensive range of knowledge learned from the data during the pretraining phase. Using a method known as transfer learning, foundation models can be fine-tuned for specific tasks or applications, allowing them to perform well even with smaller and less diverse datasets.

Some of the well-known foundation models include OpenAI's GPT-3 (an advanced language model), BERT, and RoBERTa (used for natural language understanding and generation), and Vision Transformer models, such as ViT and DALL-E (used for image understanding and generation).

A key quality of foundation models is that they adapt to multiple domains and tasks with relatively little or no domain-specific training data. This ability has accelerated their adoption and made them essential components of cutting-edge AI systems and applications.

5.1.2. The Growing Importance of Foundation Models

With the onset of big data and advanced computational resources, AI models have drastically evolved, leading to a shift towards foundation models that can adapt to various tasks and domains effectively. These models have a significant edge over those specifically designed for a single application. The advantages of foundation models include:

- **Versatility:** Since they are pretrained on large and diverse datasets, these models possess a solid

foundation that allows them to be applied to numerous tasks or domains.
- **Efficiency:** Using transfer learning, foundation models require smaller datasets and fewer labeled data for fine-tuning and adaptation, making them efficient alternatives for organizations without access to large or expensive data resources.
- **Scalability:** Foundation models are inherently scalable, as they can learn from massive amounts of data sourced from multiple domains. This enables them to improve their performance over time by exploiting continuous advancements in data, computing power, and AI research.
- **Speed:** Fine-tuning these models for specific tasks is typically faster than training models from scratch, thereby enabling organizations to develop and deploy AI-based solutions more quickly and efficiently.

5.1.3. Foundation Models in Computational Creativity and Enterprise Applications

The versatility, efficiency, and scalability of foundation models have propelled their adoption in the context of computational creativity and enterprise application development. From natural language processing to computer vision, these models have demonstrated their potential to advance the state of the art in various domains.

For example, OpenAI's GPT-3 has exhibited impressive performance in diverse computational creativity tasks, such as text generation, language translation, code completion, artistic creations, and more. Similarly, BERT and RoBERTa have been transformative for various natural language understanding applications, such as sentiment analysis, document summarization, and information extraction.

In the enterprise context, organizations can leverage foundation models to develop AI-powered services that enhance customer experiences, automate processes, augment human decision-making, and drive innovation. Potential use cases include virtual assistants, content generation, image recognition, trend analysis, and anomaly detection, just to name a few.

5.1.4. The Challenges and Risks of Foundation Models

Despite the numerous benefits offered by foundation models, their adoption brings forth multiple challenges and risks, too. Some of these concerns include:

- **Model Bias:** Since foundation models are trained on vast, diverse datasets, they are also susceptible to inherent biases in the data, which may lead to biased outputs and harmful consequences.
- **Ethical and Societal Concerns:** The use of foundation models in AI systems raises concerns regarding privacy, fairness, accountability, and transparency. Addressing these concerns requires active cooperation among researchers, policymakers, and corporate entities.
- **Resource Requirements:** Large-scale foundation models require considerable computational power and energy for their training, which may pose financial and environmental challenges.

- **Security:** The rapid development and adoption of foundation models heighten the potential for adversarial attacks, highlighting the need for comprehensive security frameworks to ensure their safe and responsible deployment.

5.1.5. The Road Ahead for Foundation Models

As foundation models continue to evolve and shape the future of AI, understanding their potential and limitations becomes crucial for organizations seeking to benefit from these transformative models. By fostering interdisciplinary collaborations, investing in research and development, addressing ethical and societal concerns, and adopting responsible deployment practices, enterprises can harness the power of foundation models for creating groundbreaking applications and solutions that define the next era of computational creativity and AI-driven growth.

5.2 Transformer Architectures and Self-Supervised Learning

The rapid development of NLP and AI techniques witnessed a shift in neural network architectures, from simple recurrent structures to more advanced transformer-based models. To appreciate the role of self-supervised learning in the progress of generative AI, we must first understand the concept of transformer architecture.

5.2.1 What is a Transformer Architecture?

Introduced by Vaswani et al. in the 2017 paper, "Attention Is All You Need." A transformer architecture is a neural network model that effectively processes long-range dependencies in sequential data by employing parallel attention mechanisms known as self-attention. This novel attention mechanism takes advantage of the contextual relationships within the input and output sequences to learn and represent the patterns in the data. One of the main advantages of transformer architecture is its capacity for parallel computation, which allows for more efficient training and faster deployment, as opposed to traditional recurrent neural networks.

5.2.2 The Building Blocks of Transformers

Two main components form the building blocks of the transformer architecture:

1. **Self-Attention Mechanism**: A mechanism that enables the model to extract contextual relationships in the input data by weighting relevant tokens in the sequence. These weights (attention scores) are learned during training, allowing the model to focus on important parts of the input when performing a specific task.
2. **Position-wise Feed-Forward Networks (FFN)**: A fully-connected network that operates separately on each position in the sequence. This FFN helps in processing the output of self-attention mechanisms by applying position-wise non-linear transformations, further enhancing the model's expressive power.

These components, along with positional encodings to incorporate the order of the sequence, compose the core of the transformer architecture. One major distinction in transformers is between the encoder and decoder layers. The encoder deals with input sequences, and the decoder generates output sequences. These layers can be stacked to create deeper transformer models, improving their capability to learn complex patterns but increasing computational costs.

5.2.3 Self-Supervised Learning in Transformers

Self-supervised learning has shown great promise in training transformer models for a wide array of tasks, primarily due to the ability of such models to derive meaningful representations from unlabeled data. By exploiting the structure of the input data, self-supervised learning methods enable transformers to learn by predicting parts of the input or generating augmented views of the data.

A notable example of self-supervised learning in transformers is BERT (Bidirectional Encoder Representations from Transformers), introduced by Google AI in 2018. BERT revolutionized the field of NLP by pretraining an unsupervised transformer model using two novel self-supervised tasks:

1. **Masked Language Modeling (MLM)**: The model learns to predict masked words in the input sequence by taking the surrounding context into account. This bidirectional technique helps in the development of robust contextual representations for the input data.
2. **Next Sentence Prediction (NSP)**: To learn relationships between sentences, the model is trained to predict whether two sequences are adjacent in the original text or not.

By pretraining the transformer model using these self-supervised tasks, BERT obtains powerful context-aware representations that can be adapted to a wide range of downstream NLP tasks with minimal fine-tuning, such as sentiment analysis, question answering, and named entity recognition.

5.2.4 Advances in Transformer Architectures

Since the introduction of the original transformer architecture and BERT, there have been many advances in the development of larger, more sophisticated transformer models like GPT-3 (Generative Pre-trained Transformer 3) by OpenAI. These models employ deep architectures and extensive computational resources to achieve state-of-the-art performance in various language understanding tasks, surpassing even human-level understanding in some cases.

The principle of self-supervised learning has significantly contributed to these advances, providing an efficient training mechanism for these large-scale models. However, the increased complexity of these architectures poses new challenges in terms of computational resources, memory constraints, and ethical considerations, which future research will need to address.

5.2.5 Impact on Enterprise and Computational Creativity

The development of transformer architectures and the embrace of self-supervised learning have had profound implications for enterprise and computational creativity. These advancements have led to a new breed of AI systems capable of generating high-quality content, providing context-aware recommendations, and automating complex decision-making processes. Some promising applications of generative AI in the enterprise realm include automated content generation, AI-driven insights, personalized user experiences, and the automation of tasks previously deemed exclusive to human intelligence.

In conclusion, transformer architectures have pushed the boundaries of what is possible with generative AI and self-supervised learning. The continuous innovation in the field presents exciting opportunities for enterprises and computational creativity applications that were once considered beyond reach. The future of generative AI promises powerful, context-aware systems capable of learning autonomously, understanding complex patterns, and generating valuable insights for enterprises on an unprecedented level.

5.3. Attention Mechanisms and Context Learning

As advanced AI and deep learning architectures continue to revolutionize the landscape of various industries, new approaches are emerging to fine-tune models and create even more effective tools. One such approach is the attention mechanism, which allows models to selectively focus on specific aspects of input data, and aids in better context learning. In this section, we will explore how attention mechanisms enable context learning, their integration into various AI models, and the implications for businesses and computational creativity.

5.3.1. Attention Mechanisms: An Overview

Traditional neural networks process input data as a whole, without paying specific attention to individual components that affect the final outcome. An attention mechanism, inspired by the human cognitive process, alleviates this limitation by permitting models to assign importance scores to different input parts, and to adjust these scores dynamically as new information is encountered. Such a strategy allows the model to prioritize certain aspects of the data required for successful processing and prediction.

The attention mechanism has been a game-changer, significantly improving performance in a wide range of applications, including machine translation, image captioning, speech recognition, and document summarization, among others.

5.3.2. Context Learning: The Role of Attention

Context plays a critical role in understanding and interpreting information. In human communication, the intended meaning of words or sentences often depends heavily on the context in which they are used. Similarly, models that can grasp the context surrounding their input data can make more effective predictions and generate more accurate results.

Attention mechanisms have become a powerful means of bolstering context learning in AI models. By assigning varying importance to different parts of input data, attention mechanisms enable models to prioritize and emphasize elements that may provide additional context to interpret the given data. This results in a more nuanced understanding of the task at hand, leading to improved performance and enhanced context-aware output generation.

5.3.3. Integration of Attention Mechanisms in AI Models

Attention mechanisms can be incorporated into different AI architectures, depending on the specific use case and requirements. Two dominant approaches that integrate attention mechanisms include:

1. **Self-attention:** Also known as *intra-attention*, self-attention is a technique whereby a neural network calculates the importance of individual input elements relative to other elements within the same input sequence. By enabling the model to emphasize certain parts of the input data, self-attention fosters a more comprehensive understanding of the input's context. Prominent models that employ self-attention include the Transformer architecture, which has demonstrated exceptional performance in natural language processing tasks.
2. **Sequence-to-sequence attention:** In sequence-to-sequence models, attention mechanisms are used to align input and output sequences better. By selectively focusing on different portions of the input sequence while generating output, these models can create more contextually relevant results. This approach has been particularly successful in neural machine translation systems, where attention greatly aids in the accurate translation of various languages.

5.3.4. Business Applications and Computational Creativity

The integration of attention mechanisms and enhanced context learning in AI models has numerous real-world applications that can benefit organizations:

- **Machine translation:** Attention mechanisms have transformed the field of machine translation, helping organizations communicate more effectively with global audiences.
- **Sentiment analysis:** By enabling models to capture the context in which words and phrases are used, attention mechanisms have enriched sentiment analysis applications for industries such as customer service and social media monitoring.
- **Document summarization:** Advanced AI models possess the ability to generate concise summaries of long documents, alleviating the need for manual effort and saving time for businesses.
- **Conversational AI:** Attention mechanisms improve chatbot and virtual assistant capabilities by allowing them to better understand context across extended conversations, enhancing their overall performance and effectiveness.

In the realm of computational creativity, attention mechanisms and context learning enable AI models to generate more context-aware content, aiding in the creation of stronger literary works, marketing strategies, and other creative outputs. This has the potential to reshape industries that rely heavily on generating quality content, including advertising, journalism, and entertainment.

5.3.5. Conclusion

Attention mechanisms and context learning spearhead the advancement of AI models, permitting organizations to operate more efficiently and capitalize on computational creativity. As AI continues to evolve, the integration of attention mechanisms will undoubtedly lead to the development of even more sophisticated and robust algorithms, reshaping the landscape of various industries and reshaping the way businesses operate. Overall, attention mechanisms represent a key breakthrough that enhances the performance of AI models and paves the way for future innovations in deep learning and machine intelligence.

Chapter 6: Risks and Challenges of Generative AI

As the potential of generative AI becomes more apparent, and more organizations begin to see its value for innovation and creativity, it is also essential to discuss what happens when things go wrong. While this cutting-edge technology has the potential to transform the way businesses operate, it is not without its risks and challenges. In this chapter, we will delve into various concerns related to the adoption of generative AI and how organizations can navigate these obstacles to create a responsible and effective strategy around AI-powered tools.

6.1 Data Privacy and Security

A core aspect of any AI's development, including generative algorithms, is the data being used to train the models. Data privacy and security become paramount concerns, as this technology relies heavily on access to large quantities of data, often sourced from different points and some even with ethical and legal restrictions.

6.1.1 Data Misuse and Leakage

A significant concern is the potential misuse or leaking of sensitive data, which could lead to reputational, financial, and even regulatory repercussions. For instance, an AI model might inadvertently reveal personally identifiable information (PII) or confidential data points when generating content or outputs. Companies must implement robust data security and privacy measures, such as data anonymization and access controls, to mitigate this risk.

6.1.2 Regulatory Compliance

Data protection regulations, such as the General Data Protection Regulation (GDPR) and California Consumer Privacy Act (CCPA), have a significant impact on how organizations handle data. Non-compliance can result in substantial fines and other penalties. Companies adopting generative AI should ensure their solutions adhere to these regulations and be proactive in addressing any potential legal roadblocks.

6.2 Bias and Discrimination

Generative AI is not immune to the biases present in the data it is trained on. This can lead to unintended outcomes that perpetuate harmful stereotypes and discrimination.

6.2.1 Bias in Training Data

Training data is the foundation upon which generative models learn to create outputs. However, if the training data is biased, the model's results may reflect and even amplify those biases. Careful selection and curation of training data should be a priority to prevent biased outputs.

6.2.2 Discrimination in Generated Outputs

When a model generates biased outputs, it can perpetuate discrimination against specific demographics, races, or individuals. Companies must be diligent in monitoring their AI-generated content and be prepared to address any instances of discriminatory outputs proactively. This can include retraining the AI with less biased data, implementing a review process, or adopting new techniques to detect and mitigate biases in the AI system.

6.3 Ethical Concerns

The ethical implications of generative AI are far-reaching and complex. As these algorithms become more sophisticated, they raise new ethical questions about the nature of intellectual property, creative control, and consent.

6.3.1 Intellectual Property and Ownership

Generative AI challenges the traditional notions of intellectual property and ownership. As AI-generated content becomes more commonplace, it raises questions of who owns the rights to that content, the value of human creative processes, and the potential for AI-generated content to commodify creativity.

6.3.2 AI Agent Accountability

The use of generative AI in decision-making processes or creative activities may lead to situations where the AI system's actions have significant consequences. This raises the question of accountability, with current frameworks often unable to attribute the responsibility of AI-generated content or decisions solely to the system or the developers.

6.3.3 Consent and Control

Another ethical concern with generative AI is that content or decisions may be generated without the consent or knowledge of the subjects involved. For example, AI-generated images of real people or creative work based on an artist's style could create ethical dilemmas as they may infringe upon the rights and choices of the subject.

6.4 Malicious Uses and Control of Generative AI

The power of generative AI can be misused for malicious purposes or lead to unintended consequences. This technology can be exploited to produce deepfake videos, spam content, or manipulative narratives, among other harmful applications.

6.4.1 Deepfakes and Misinformation

The rise of deepfake technology, which uses generative AI to create realistic but fake images, videos, or audiorecordings, presents significant risks. These can include deception through manipulated content, erosion of trust in media, and potential threats to national security, all of which can contribute to the spread of misinformation.

6.4.2 Content Filters and Digital Rights Management

Generative AI's ability to generate content quickly and in vast quantities can lead to cases where the technology surpasses content filters, digital rights management systems, or other protective measures, potentially resulting in copyright infringement, unauthorized replication of intellectual property, or widespread production of unwanted content.

6.5 Conclusion

Generative AI, although promising, presents numerous challenges and risks that organizations must carefully navigate. By tackling data privacy and security issues, addressing biases, considering ethical implications, and preparing for potential malicious uses, businesses can responsibly harness the power of generative AI to innovate and excel. A proactive, risk-aware approach and a culture of ongoing monitoring, evaluation, and adaptation will enable organizations to thrive in the future of generative AI for enterprises and computational creativity.

6.1. Deepfakes and Malicious AI Applications

As enterprises explore the potential of generative AI and computational creativity for improvement and expansion, it is essential to acknowledge and be aware of the potential malicious applications and risks associated with this incredible technology. With great power comes great responsibility, and the rise of deepfakes and other nefarious AI instances prompts necessary discussions and considerations for enterprise stakeholders.

6.1.1. Understanding Deepfakes

Deepfakes are AI-generated videos, images, or audio recordings that replace or manipulate the original content, usually intended to deceive or mislead viewers or listeners. These false pieces of information are created using generative adversarial networks (GANs), deep learning algorithms that can synthesize new content based on the vast amount of data fed into them. Given the high fidelity of deepfakes, distinguishing them from real content has become increasingly challenging.

6.1.1.1. The Emergence of Deepfakes

Deepfakes first emerged in late 2017 on Reddit, and since then, they have become a highly disturbing trend gaining significant public attention. Initially focused on swapping celebrity faces onto pornographic videos, deepfakes evolved into a tool for political manipulation, misinformation, and targeted harassment. It is increasingly difficult to identify and combat these AI-generated falsehoods as the technology improves, creating ripple effects across various industries and society.

6.1.1.2. The Technology Behind Deepfakes

Deepfakes involve two primary AI components: autoencoders and GANs. Autoencoders work by compressing the original data (video, image, or audio) into a low-dimensional (latent) representation, then reconstructing the data from the latent representation. GANs, on the other hand, train two networks — the generator and the discriminator — against each other in a zero-sum game. The generator creates realistic synthetic data, while the discriminator tries to distinguish between the generated data and real data.

These technologies, along with improvements in computing power and accessibility of AI frameworks, have significantly reduced the barriers to creating high-quality deepfakes.

6.1.2. Malicious AI Applications

While deepfakes represent a substantial concern, other AI-based applications may also be exploited for malicious purposes. Some of these applications include:

6.1.2.1. Synthetic Text Generation

AI-powered text generation models, such as OpenAI's GPT-3, can generate human-like text. These models can be utilized for generating realistic fake news, fabricated reviews, or impersonating individuals in personalized phishing attacks.

6.1.2.2. AI-Generated Voice Cloning

Advanced voice synthesis algorithms can replicate a person's voice, potentially enabling malicious actors to produce deepfake audio for nefarious purposes, such as mimicking the voice of a CEO or government official to perpetrate fraud or disinformation.

6.1.2.3. Automated Hacking

AI can be used to augment, automate, and scale hacking activities, enabling bad actors to conduct security breaches and exploit vulnerabilities more efficiently and harder to detect.

6.1.2.4. Surveillance and Privacy Invasion

AI-based facial and voice recognition precisely identify people and monitor their activities, leading to intrusion into individual privacy or abuse by oppressive regimes.

6.1.3. Mitigation Measures

To counteract deepfakes and malicious AI applications, it is crucial to develop and implement both technical and policy-based countermeasures, such as:

6.1.3.1. Deepfake Detection Technologies

Technological advancements must be harnessed to detect and combat deepfakes, such as deep learning models trained specifically to identify manipulated or fabricated content. However, it is crucial to acknowledge that bad actors will continue refining their techniques, leading to an ongoing cat-and-mouse game between detection and deception algorithms.

6.1.3.2. Open and Transparent AI

Developing AI in an open and transparent manner allows for increased scrutiny of its systems, leading to better understanding, evaluation, and validation of the AI's actions. This step can help in identifying potential vulnerabilities and addressing them proactively.

6.1.3.3. Policy and Regulation

Governments and international organizations should play an active role in formulating and updating policies and regulations for responsible AI use, ensuring that malicious actors bear legal consequences for their actions.

6.1.3.4. Public Awareness and Education

Promoting public understanding of AI technologies, fostering digital literacy and critical thinking skills will help individuals better recognize manipulated content and protect against misinformation.

6.1.4. Conclusion

As artificial intelligence continues to transform the world, it is incumbent upon enterprises to be aware of the potential malicious applications and pitfalls associated with these powerful tools. By adopting a proactive and responsible approach towards AI development and deployment, businesses can not only mitigate the risks of harmful AI manifestations but also contribute to a safer and more equitable AI ecosystem.

6.2 Copyright issues in generative AI

In an increasingly digital world driven by artificial intelligence advancements, copyright issues have become more complex than ever. The intersection of generative AI and intellectual property law presents numerous legal questions that challenge traditional notions of idea ownership, authorship, and protection. This section delves into some of the current and future copyright issues arising from generative AI systems in enterprises and computational creativity.

6.2.1 AI as a creator and copyright infringement

Generative AI systems that generate creative works have the potential to infringe on existing copyrighted material. As these systems become more adept at creating original content, the possibility of replicates, derivative works, or works that parallel existing intellectual property may increase. For instance:

- Text generators could produce written works that inadvertently mirror already copyrighted content.

- AI-generated music, videos, or visual art could employ elements heavily influenced by copyrighted material.

In these cases, questions of liability arise. Can a business be held responsible for an AI-generated product that unintentionally infringes on copyrights – even if the business owner was unaware of the issue? This unique scenario necessitates a thorough evaluation of existing copyright laws and regulations.

6.2.2 Defining authorship for AI-generated works

Traditionally, copyright laws protect the rights of human authors and creators, allowing them to reap economic benefits while also maintaining the originality and integrity of their work. However, AI-generated content problems arise when determining an "author" in the legal sense. Some key themes to consider include:

- Can an AI system be considered an author if it creates content without human intervention?
- Are human operators or developers of AI systems the rightful authors of AI-generated works?
- If businesses own the AI systems generating content, do they bear the responsibility of authorship?

Presently, most copyright laws do not account for these complexities, and their evolution will largely depend on upcoming court rulings, legislative reforms, and international treaties.

6.2.3 Attributing moral rights to AI-generated works

Moral rights, a critical aspect of copyright law, include the author's right of attribution, right of integrity, and right to oppose false attribution. These rights protect the ethical and reputational aspects of a creator's work. However, moral rights pose queries when connected to artificial intelligence:

- Can moral rights apply to AI-generated works without acknowledging the AI system as a legal entity?
- How do moral rights function for AI-generated art when it comes to crediting the source material, algorithms, or operators?
- If user data is employed to train AI systems that generate content, do users have any moral rights over generated works?

These questions reflect a need to redefine or expand the scope of moral rights in copyright law, particularly concerning generative AI.

6.2.4 Public domain and fair use implications

The public domain and fair usage principles have a crucial role in fostering creativity and the sharing of information. For instance, AI systems can use public domain works to generate new content, raising certain inquiries:

- How do copyright laws apply to AI-generated works based on public domain materials, and is protection warranted?
- Can AI-generated works be considered transformative and fit under the notion of fair usage?
- What are the implications of generative AI on the existing equilibrium between protecting authors' rights

and promoting public access to culture and knowledge? Finding a balance between these interests is essential to maintain a robust creative ecosystem that supports both human and AI-generated works.

6.2.5 Cross-jurisdictional complexities

Intellectual property laws vary across territories, bringing a host of challenges when generative AI systems produce content spanning multiple jurisdictions. For global enterprises, considering these discrepancies is vital, including:

- The scope of copyright protection for AI-generated works depending on their country of origin or use.
- Transferring, licensing, or enforcing copyright for AI-generated works across jurisdictions with divergent legal standards.
- Reconciling issues related to moral rights, authorship, or infringement in an international context.

Cross-jurisdictional complexities emphasize the need for harmonization or cooperation between nations to address AI's impact on copyright systems uniformly.

6.2.6 Preparing for the future of copyright and generative AI

It is evident that copyright law and its practical application need to evolve to cater to generative AI advancements. A few recommendations to better prepare for this future include:

- Encouraging dialogue among regulators, businesses, and AI developers to develop

comprehensive and forward-looking copyright frameworks.
- Updating intellectual property legislation to define authorship, ownership, and moral rights concerning AI-generated works.
- Creating universally accepted standards and collaboration between nations to address transnational copyright issues.
- Establishing best practices for businesses to use generative AI ethically and minimize legal risks.

In conclusion, businesses navigating copyright issues in generative AI must stay informed about the dynamic legal landscape to protect their interests and foster creativity in emerging technologies. As this field evolves, businesses, creators, and regulators must work together to strike a balance that protects traditional authorship while embracing AI-driven innovation.

6.3. Mitigating Risks and Responsible AI Usage

As the field of generative AI continues to advance, it offers enterprises great potential for growth, efficiency, and development. Computational creativity can fuel innovation with unprecedented possibilities while simultaneously enhancing human-AI collaboration. However, with great capabilities come immense challenges and risks. Ensuring responsible AI use is crucial to reap the benefits while mitigating these risks.

Optimizing AI systems for their intended usage and embedding ethical practices and guidelines into development is paramount. In this section, we explore various ways to achieve this through accurate evaluation, collaboration, fairness, transparency, consideration of impact, and the establishment of clear regulatory frameworks.

6.3.1. Evaluation of AI Performance

Evaluating performance is critical for any technology. With generative AI, it becomes even more important due to the technology's potential impact on users and organizations.

- Supervised evaluation techniques that compare generated outputs (e.g., images, texts) to a ground-truth baseline can help assess AI quality. However, this might become challenging when dealing with AI-generated outputs with many potential ground truths.
- Unsupervised evaluation methods can be beneficial in such cases, as they measure the correlation between ground truth and predictions with no set correct answer. This can enable a more creative exploration of possible solutions.
- Human evaluation of AI-generated outputs is vital to ensure quality, relevance, and ethical considerations are addressed. Inputs from domain experts can be incorporated into AI models for ground-truth validation and optimization.
- Regularly updating and upgrading the training data with relevant and recent information can improve AI predictions and suggestions.

6.3.2. Collaborative Creation

Human-AI collaboration can become an essential part of the AI development process. By ensuring complementary roles between human creativity and

AI capabilities, we can avoid an overdependence on AI systems.

• Emphasizing a human touch: AI technologies should be designed to assist and empower human creativity rather than replace it. Encouraging human oversight and intervention promotes the more responsible use of AI systems.
• Establishing clear boundaries: By defining limits for AI involvement in the creative process, we can maintain human control and assure ethical standards are observed.

6.3.3. Fairness and Bias Consideration

Mitigating bias in generative AI is essential to ensure fairness and avoid propagating stereotypes and discrimination.

• Diverse data sets: Training data should be representative of a wide variety of perspectives and encompass different sources to minimize the risk of bias.
• Regularly auditing AI models: Regular assessment of AI models can help identify potential pitfalls and biases that might stem from training data or model parameters.
• Establishing fairness metrics: Metrics such as demographic parity, equalized odds, and calibration can be used to ensure fair and unbiased decision making across different groups.

6.3.4. Transparency through Explainable AI

Generative AI models have been criticized for their "black-box" nature, meaning their decision-making processes are often not understandable by humans.

Explainable AI (XAI) aims to make AI decisions more transparent, justifiable, and accountable.

• Offering explanations: By providing clear and comprehensible explanations to end-users, organizations can enhance user trust and ensure responsible AI use.
• Model visualization techniques: Visualizing model components can help experts analyze and interpret complex AI systems' inner workings.

6.3.5. Consideration of Societal and Economic Impact

Assessing the possible consequences of generative AI on society and economies can help avoid potential drawbacks and harms.

• Impact assessments: Regular assessments on the long-term effects of generative AI deployments can help identify potential risks and benefits for society and stakeholders.
• Stakeholder engagement: Involving different stakeholders (e.g., policymakers, employees, customers) in the AI development process can help businesses address relevant concerns and forge stronger collaborative relationships.

6.3.6. Regulatory Frameworks and Guidelines

Establishing clear regulatory frameworks and guidelines is crucial to addressing generative AI's ethical and legal implications.

• Developing policies: Governments and regulatory bodies must establish policies that enforce responsible AI usage, covering aspects such as data usage, privacy, and security.

- International cooperation: Collaborative efforts among nations and organizations can help develop shared guidelines and standards across the global AI ecosystem.
- Accountability mechanisms: Ensuring responsibility is attributed to the correct individuals and organizations when AI systems cause undesired outcomes can help create a more ethical and responsible AI landscape.

By embracing these principles and practices, companies can not only mitigate the risks and challenges posed by generative AI but also harness its full potential for innovation and synergistic human-computer collaboration.

Chapter 7: Embedding Generative AI in Enterprises

7.1 Introduction

In recent years, Generative AI has emerged as a powerful innovation tool that allows enterprises to automate and improve their creative and decision-making processes. With the potential to disrupt business models and redefine industries, the time has come to discuss how organizations can benefit from embedding Generative AI into their operations.

In this chapter, we will explore the process of integrating Generative AI into various business functions, from product design and manufacturing to customer engagement and beyond. We will also discuss the challenges and opportunities for organizations embarking on this journey to embrace generative technologies and witness their transformation.

7.2 Generative AI for Product Design and Development

Generative AI algorithms can accelerate the design process and minimize the need for trial-and-error by using historical data to generate new concepts and ideas automatically. This can help streamline the development cycle, reduce costs, and increase the likelihood of developing innovative products that resonate with customers.

7.2.1 Integration and Implementation

1. **Evaluate and Choose the Right Tools:** Leverage existing generative AI platforms such as TensorFlow or PyTorch, and assess compatibility with your existing infrastructure.
2. **Prototype and Test**: Establish a proof-of-concept to gauge the efficiency of generative AI-driven design improvements, test against real-world scenarios, and fine-tune the algorithms and models accordingly.
3. **Streamline Data Collection and Processing**: Establish a structured pipeline for data collection, preprocessing, and normalization to ensure the generative models are receiving high-quality inputs for superior performance.
4. **Apply Iterative Design**: Integrate generative AI into your existing design workflow and retrain the model iteratively with feedback from human designers to create a truly symbiotic relationship.

7.2.2 Case Studies

1. **Generative Design in Aerospace Industry**: Airbus leveraged generative AI to automate the design of their partition walls, resulting in a lighter and more durable solution, increasing fuel efficiency and reducing carbon emission.
2. **Smart Manufacturing and 3D Printing**: General Electric employed generative AI in the additive manufacturing process for developing parts for their

aircraft engines, substantially reducing production time and costs.

7.3 Generative AI for Personalized Customer Experience

Generative AI can engage customers by providing personalized recommendations, content curation, and interactive experiences.

7.3.1 Integration and Implementation

1. **Invest in Data Collection and Segmentation**: Gather comprehensive customer data (behavioral, demographic, and psychographic) to fuel the generative AI models.
2. **Create an Experience Delivery Platform**: Develop an infrastructure that leverages generative AI to personalize and deliver various customer touchpoints, including recommendations, communication campaigns, and interface design.
3. **Conduct Cohort-Based Experimental Controls**: Design experiments to optimize customer experiences and measure the impact of personalized AI features using control groups and key performance indicators.

7.3.2 Case Studies

1. **Walmart's Dynamic Pricing Algorithm**: Walmart uses generative AI models to optimize and customize pricing in real-time based on millions of data points, including customer preferences, regional preferences, and competitive pressures.

2. **Netflix's Content Recommendations**: Netflix uses generative AI algorithms to analyze user data and deliver highly personalized content recommendations, driving greater customer engagement and satisfaction.

7.4 Generative AI for Process Automation and Optimization

Generative AI can optimize internal workflows and decision-making by automating repetitive tasks and providing insights on how to enhance operational efficiency.

7.4.1 Integration and Implementation

1. **Identify Areas of Improvement**: Assess key workflows and decision-making processes to identify bottlenecks, inefficiencies, or opportunities for automation.
2. **Invest in Infrastructure and Training**: Develop the necessary technical infrastructure, data pipelines, and human expertise needed to support generative AI.
3. **Implement Continuous Improvement**: Measure the effectiveness of generative AI in optimizing processes, and iteratively refine the algorithms to drive greater efficiency.

7.4.2 Case Studies

1. **Generative AI in Supply Chain Management**: Amazon uses generative AI-based algorithms to optimize inventory management, warehouse routing,

and product delivery to enhance operational efficiency.
2. **AI-Driven Workforce Optimization**: Xerox leveraged generative AI to re-engineer its call center staffing and scheduling, generating a consistent, optimal workforce plan that decreased staffing costs and improved service levels.

7.5 Challenges and Opportunities

As organizations integrate generative AI into their operations, they will encounter a range of challenges and opportunities. Embedding AI can be resource and time-intensive; enterprises must make the necessary investments in infrastructure, talent, and data management.

Additionally, organizations may face ethical concerns over transparency, control, and legal implications. Regulators are increasingly scrutinizing AI deployments, and enterprises must be prepared to navigate the evolving regulatory landscape, ensuring compliance and building trust among customers and employees.

However, if enterprises can address these challenges, they will unlock the true potential of generative AI in transforming their operations, products, services, and customer experience, all while driving growth and competitive advantage.

7.6 Conclusion

Integrating Generative AI into an enterprise is a major step that requires forethought, investment, and commitment. However, the potential payoffs are immense, as it can drive innovation and growth by automating internal and customer-facing processes, optimizing decision-making, and sparking creative breakthroughs. Enterprises that embrace this technology now will be better positioned for success in the years to come.

7.1. Selecting Appropriate AI Technologies

Artificial Intelligence technologies have become pervasive in almost every industry, driven by rapid advancements in hardware and machine learning algorithms. AI's potential to improve the functioning of organizations, automate essential tasks, and gain insights hidden within large datasets has made it an indispensable tool for enterprises. To reap the benefits offered by AI, it is crucial that proper planning, evaluation, and selection of the appropriate technologies take place. In this section, we will discuss key factors that must be considered while selecting the right AI technology suite for your business.

Assessing the problem and desired outcomes

The first step is to clearly identify the business problems to be addressed by AI and the desired outcomes. Ensuring that the problem's scope is well-defined will help the organization focus its efforts and resources in solving the issue at hand. Identify whether the problem is to streamline operations, analyze data for decision-making, optimize resource allocation, create more personalized customer experiences or something else. Once the problem and its desired outcome are outlined, organizations can match AI technologies that best solve the specific issue.

Exploring various AI technologies

While selecting an AI solution, organizations should explore a wide range of available technologies. These technologies can be divided into the following categories based on their typical applications:

1. **Machine Learning (ML):** ML tools use historical patterns and adapt to new data to improve model predictions. There are many subfields of machine learning, and each subfield serves a specific use case or domain.
   o Supervised Learning: Classic machine learning technique that includes regression, classification, and ensemble methods.
   o Unsupervised Learning: Includes clustering, anomaly detection, and dimensionality reduction.
   o Deep Learning: Based on neural networks, handles complex problems such as image recognition, speech recognition, and natural language processing.
2. **Natural Language Processing (NLP):** NLP enables machines to read, interpret, and generate human language. This includes chatbots, sentiment analysis, and machine translation.
3. **Computer Vision:** Computer vision technologies enable machines to interpret and derive meaningful context from visual data, such as images and videos. Examples include facial recognition, object detection, and video analytics.
4. **Robotic Process Automation (RPA):** RPA automates manual, repetitive tasks that consume a significant amount of time and resources. Examples include data processing, data cleaning, and data entry.
5. **Intelligent Automation (IA):** IA combines RPA with AI/ML, making it possible to automate more

complex tasks that require human-like cognitive skills, such as understanding text or images.

6. **Expert Systems:** These AI technologies emulate decision-making processes of human experts, typically in a rule-based, deterministic manner.
7. **Reinforcement Learning:** Reinforcement learning trains algorithms through a reward-based mechanism, allowing the model to learn complex behaviors without explicit supervision.

Identifying use-case suitability and maturity

A crucial step in selecting the right AI technology is understanding which solution is best suited for a particular use case. Use-case suitability depends on the complexity, data availability, and desired performance level of the AI solution. Evaluating the maturity of AI technologies and the advancements made in each field is essential to make a well-informed choice.

Phased implementation and integration

As AI technologies mature and become widely adopted, organizations may need to incrementally adopt various AI solutions for different stages of problem-solving or decision-making. For instance, initial decision support may come from rule-based systems, followed by ML-based predictive models and eventually more advanced deep learning solutions.

Implementing AI technologies in a phased manner reduces the risk of disruption to the existing workflow and increases the likelihood of successful integration. Additionally, it allows organizations to learn from and iterate on their AI deployments, progressively improving the effectiveness of the AI solution.

Vendor evaluation

Research and evaluate potential vendors that provide AI products or services to find the best fit for your organization's needs. Consider factors such as technical expertise, product capabilities, customer support, domain-specific experience, and the ability to customize AI models for your specific requirements.

Ethical considerations and explainability

With increased use of AI technologies, it is essential to set up guidelines and practices that ensure ethical use and transparency in decision-making. Modern AI systems might produce complex and hard-to-interpret results; thus, selecting AI technologies that offer explainability can be beneficial. Transparent AI methodologies can help in understanding the reasons behind AI-generated insights and maintaining user trust.

Cost and resource constraints

Lastly, the costs and resource constraints associated with the implementation and maintenance of AI technologies must be taken into account. The long-term feasibility of the selected technologies, the personnel needed to manage the AI implementation, and any additional physical infrastructure or computing resources required should be calculated to ensure a successful AI deployment.

In conclusion, selecting the appropriate AI technology requires a comprehensive understanding of the various AI tools and algorithms available, the problem at hand, and the desired outcome. By thoroughly investigating and considering these factors, organizations can make informed decisions and drive positive ROI through the implementation of AI technologies in their processes.

7.2. Adapting foundation models for enterprise solutions

The rise of foundation models is changing the landscape of AI adoption and has the potential to drastically impact various industries, including the enterprise sector. Foundation models, such as GPT-3 and BERT, are pre-trained on vast amounts of data and can be fine-tuned for specific tasks, making them powerful tools for diverse applications in the enterprise, including natural language processing, machine translation, and summarization.

However, as powerful as these models are, they may not always be perfectly suited for every enterprise solution out of the box. As researchers and developers work on incorporating the generative capabilities of foundation models into enterprise solutions, it's essential to adapt them to fit the unique needs of each industry and use case.

In this section, we will discuss several strategies for adapting foundation models for enterprise solutions, focusing on data curation, fine-tuning, model scaling, and software integration.

7.2.1. Data curation for enterprise-specific needs

One of the key steps in adapting foundation models for enterprise solutions is data curation, which involves creating high-quality and relevant datasets that are representative of the problem you are trying to solve. This step is critical, as the performance of these models will greatly depend on the data they have been trained upon. There are three main steps in curating data for enterprise purposes:

1. **Data collection:** Collecting data relevant to the use case and broad enough to cover various possible scenarios that might be encountered in the specific domain is essential. This can include using open-source datasets when available, collecting data from internal company sources or even purchasing data sets if necessary.
2. **Data cleaning and preprocessing:** Not all data collected will be clean and useful for training. There might be errors, inconsistencies and duplicate entries, which need to be cleaned before the data can be used further. Moreover, preprocessing often involves tokenization, normalization, stemming, and more to make the data suitable for training a model.
3. **Data labeling:** Supervised fine-tuning often requires annotated datasets. In some cases, the target output needs to be manually annotated by domain experts or using crowd-sourcing platforms. It's important to ensure data labeling is consistent and

accurate to ensure the model, once fine-tuned, will produce meaningful results.

7.2.2. Fine-tuning for enterprise tasks

While foundation models are pre-trained to have general knowledge of various domains, they may lack the specific knowledge and expertise required for a certain enterprise task. Fine-tuning is an essential step in adapting these models to fulfill the unique requirements of each enterprise use case. By fine-tuning the models on domain-specific data, we can significantly improve their performance in the relevant tasks.

It's important to choose an appropriate loss function and evaluation metric that aligns with the end goals of the enterprise task. Additionally, monitoring the fine-tuning process ensures that the model does not overfit or diverge from the desired outcomes.

7.2.3. Model scaling and adaptation

Foundation models come in various sizes and configurations, with trade-offs between computational resources, training time, and performance. In order to adapt these models to fit the needs of an enterprise, it's crucial to consider the computational budget available and the latency requirements of the specific use case.

- **Model scaling:** Scaling the model size up or down, depending on the available resources and user requirements, can be done by selecting a model with a different number of layers and/or attention heads. However, it is essential to ensure that the model's size does not negatively affect the model's performance.

- **Quantization and compression:** To adapt to edge devices or other resource-limited environments, model compression techniques like quantization can help reduce the model's memory footprint and computational requirements without significant performance degradation.
- **Parallelization and distributed training:** In some cases, the available computational resources can be harnessed more effectively through the parallelization of model training or prediction tasks. This can substantially accelerate the fine-tuning and deployment processes.

7.2.4. Integration with existing software systems and infrastructure

Finally, to effectively leverage foundation models for an enterprise solution, it's vital to ensure seamless integration with the existing software systems and infrastructure of the organization. This may involve the development of connectors, APIs, or other interfaces that allow the foundation models to interact with other systems and data sources.

- **Data connectors:** Enable the movement of data between the machine learning pipeline and the rest of the organization's infrastructure, such as databases, data lakes, or other storage systems.
- **API development:** To make the models easily accessible and deployable across different platforms, wrapping them into accessible APIs can ease integration into existing workflows.

- **Monitoring and management tools:** Developing monitoring and management tools that track the model's performance, handle errors, and ensure security helps maintain a high level of reliability for enterprise solutions.

To conclude, adapting foundation models for enterprise solutions requires careful data curation, fine-tuning of the models on domain-specific data, scaling models to meet computational constraints, and integrating the models with existing software systems and infrastructure. By addressing these considerations, organizations can harness the power of generative AI for a wide range of applications, ultimately driving innovation and transformation in the enterprise sector.

7.3 Ensuring Transparency in AI Implementation

In this rapidly evolving era of AI and machine learning, organizations are adopting these advanced technologies to streamline their processes, enhance customer experiences, and unlock new market opportunities. However, these capabilities come with a range of challenges, one of which is ensuring transparency in the AI implementation process. Organizations must address this critical aspect to maintain customer trust, strengthen the robustness of these systems, and comply with regulatory norms.

Transparent AI is about understanding the factors, processes, and outcomes of an AI system's decision-making. It involves explaining how the algorithms interpret inputs, identifying the values and biases ingrained in their development, and aligning them with clearly defined ethical principles. This section presents effective strategies to ensure transparency in AI implementation across enterprises and the field of computational creativity.

7.3.1 Define Clear and Measurable Objectives

To achieve transparency, start with defining the purpose and measurable goals for the AI solution. Clearly outline the expected business outcomes and the key performance indicators (KPIs) that will be used to evaluate the system's success. This step provides a benchmark to assess the AI's alignment with organizational values, ethical principles, and legal requirements, and serves as a foundation for transparent decision-making.

7.3.2 Adopt an Interdisciplinary Approach for Model Development

Transparency requires integrating expertise from diverse fields, such as computer science, data science, ethics, social sciences, legal, and domain knowledge. Collaborating with interdisciplinary teams, therefore, becomes crucial for designing AI systems that are unbiased, interpretable, and can account for the complex and often competing objectives, constraints, and ethical trade-offs. This collaborative approach helps to ensure the AI system's values, incentives, and decision-making processes align with those of the organization and its stakeholders.

7.3.3 Establish Transparent Algorithms

Choose AI algorithms and models that are both accurate and explainable. Some algorithms, such as decision trees and linear regression, are more interpretable than others, like deep learning and neural networks. As far as reasonably possible, prioritize algorithms that provide insights into their decision-making processes. This encourages a clearer understanding of the AI's functioning and helps to identify and rectify biases or misaligned objectives.

7.3.4 Use Open Standards for Data, Models, and Explanations

Adopting and promoting open standards for data, models, and explanations can greatly enhance transparency. By making the AI's logic and reasoning open to inspection, stakeholders can scrutinize the decision-making process and evaluate consistency, fairness, and accuracy. Furthermore, open standards help to break down barriers to understanding and facilitate cross-sector coordination.

7.3.5 Rigorous Testing and Validation

Perform regular and rigorous testing, validation, and certification of AI models to ensure their reliability, accuracy, and fairness. Implement testing techniques, such as time-based cross-validation and adversarial testing, to identify potential errors or biases and make the necessary adjustments. By frequently evaluating the model's performance against the set objectives, enterprises can demonstrate their commitment to transparency and continuous improvement.

7.3.6 Clear Documentation and Auditing Processes

Comprehensive documentation throughout the AI development process is crucial for transparency. This includes recording data sources, feature selection, algorithm choice, data pre-processing, model evaluation, and explanations for predictions. Such documentation forms a crucial part of audit trails, permitting accountability in case conflicts arise regarding the AI's decision-making, potential biases, or ethical implications.

7.3.7 Engaging in Transparent Communication

Engage in open, interactive, and transparent communication with all stakeholders, including employees, customers, and regulatory authorities. Encourage input and feedback from diverse perspectives, addressing concerns, and earning trust through continuous dialogue. By communicating the goals, methods, and limitations of AI systems clearly and honestly, enterprises can facilitate responsible and informed decisions by all parties involved.

7.3.8 Preparing for Evolving Regulatory Landscape

As the regulatory landscape for AI changes and evolves, organizations must be proactive in anticipating and adapting to these shifts. Keep abreast of local and international regulations and guidelines on AI transparency and conduct an impact assessment on a regular basis.

Conclusion

Transparency in AI implementation is of paramount importance for realizing the full potential of these technologies, encompassing ethical data usage, algorithmic fairness, and increased accountability. Enterprises that prioritize transparency in their AI systems not only minimize reputational risks but also foster trust among their customers, industry peers, and regulators. By integrating the strategies outlined in this section, organizations can make responsible and informed decisions, ensuring the successful adoption of AI and computational creativity in various aspects of their business.

Chapter 8: Security and Risk Management for Generative AI

8.1 Overview

As enterprises increasingly adopt generative AI to enhance their operations, streamline decision-making, and improve customer experiences, ensuring the security and proper risk management of these AI systems becomes paramount. In this chapter, we will discuss key security risks and challenges associated with generative AI and outline strategies and best practices for mitigating them. By addressing these concerns, organizations can benefit from the transformative potential of generative AI while minimizing vulnerabilities and ensuring responsible use.

8.2 Threat Landscape

Several security risks are unique to generative AI or particularly challenging in the context of AI. These include adversarial attacks, model inversion, data poisoning, intellectual property theft, and ethical and legal challenges, which we discuss below.

8.2.1 Adversarial Attacks

An adversarial attack occurs when a nefarious actor maliciously manipulates the training, validation, or testing data used to build generative AI models to achieve a specific outcome. This modification can cause the AI system to generate incorrect predictions or classifications or modify its intended behavior. Adversarial attacks can compromise the integrity, confidentiality, and availability of AI components and systems.

Defense mechanisms:

1. Data sanitization and validation: Ensuring the accuracy and reliability of input data can help prevent adversarial attacks. Regularly auditing data pipelines and validating data sources can detect inconsistencies and remove vulnerabilities.
2. Robustness testing: Integrating adversarial examples during the training phase can help models become more resistant to such attacks by learning to identify and ignore malicious input.
3. Regular updates and monitoring: Continuously updating AI models and monitoring their behavior helps identify any abnormal activity indicating a potential adversarial attack.

8.2.2 Model Inversion

Model inversion attacks aim to extract sensitive information from generative AI models by reverse-engineering their architecture or algorithm. This can lead to privacy breaches and loss of confidential data.

Defense mechanisms:

1. Differential privacy: The use of differential privacy techniques adds noise to the model's output, making

it more challenging for attackers to extract any meaningful information.
2. Secure multi-party computation: This enables multiple parties to compute a common function while keeping their data inputs private, safeguarding sensitive information from inversion attacks.
3. Encryption: Homomorphic encryption techniques allow AI models to be trained and used on encrypted data, increasing security and privacy.

8.2.3 Data Poisoning

Data poisoning occurs when an attacker introduces malicious data points into the training set to compromise the accuracy and reliability of a generative AI model. This can lead to suboptimal performance, biased results, or unintended behavior.

Defense mechanisms:

1. Robust data collection and validation: Screening data sources for trustworthiness and adequacy helps reduce exposure to data poisoning.
2. Outlier detection algorithms: Identifying and removing outliers before training can mitigate the impact of data poisoning on AI models.
3. Regular monitoring: Continuously monitoring the model's performance can help detect any anomalies resulting from data poisoning.

8.2.4 Intellectual Property Theft

Generative AI models require significant investment, time, and talent to develop. Intellectual property theft can devalue this investment and undermine an organization's competitive advantage.

Defense mechanisms:

1. Limiting access: Implementing strict access controls and need-to-know principles can protect intellectual property from unauthorized access.
2. Watermarking: Embedding unique, trackable identifiers into AI models can help trace stolen property and deter potential thieves.
3. Legal protections: Registering AI models as intellectual property, such as through patents or trade secret protection, can provide legal recourse in case of theft.

8.2.5 Ethical and Legal Challenges

Generative AI can produce biased, discriminatory, or offensive content, raising ethical concerns and posing potential legal risks.

Defense mechanisms:

1. Unbiased data collection: Ensuring input data diversity can reduce the potential for producing biased AI outputs.
2. Fairness metrics: Assessing AI systems against relevant fairness metrics helps identify and address any discriminatory behavior.
3. Legal and regulatory compliance: Ensuring AI systems comply with applicable local and international laws and regulations can mitigate legal risks.

8.3 Best Practices for Security and Risk Management

We outline several high-level best practices for securing generative AI and managing risks effectively.

1. Develop a comprehensive risk management framework: Establishing a risk management framework that encompasses assessment, monitoring, mitigation, and remediation can help identify and address security threats proactively.
2. Promote a security-conscious culture: Encourage employees to prioritize security in all aspects, including handling sensitive data, protecting intellectual property, and adhering to ethical guidelines.
3. Adopt a multi-layered security approach: Implement layered security measures that include access controls, encryption, monitoring, detection, and response capabilities to safeguard generative AI systems.
4. Implement robust governance and accountability structures: Assign clear roles and responsibilities for security and risk management within the organization and ensure appropriate oversight.
5. Continuously enhance skills and knowledge: Stay up-to-date with the latest security developments and evolving threats to ensure that generative AI systems remain secure and reliable.

8.4 Conclusion

As the adoption of generative AI continues to grow, organizations must navigate a complex risk landscape while realizing its transformative potential. By assessing threats, adopting best practices, and developing robust risk management strategies, enterprises can benefit from generative AI's immense potential while mitigating the associated risks and maintaining security.

8.1 Identifying Potential Threats and Vulnerabilities

As the adoption of generative AI continues to grow in enterprises and creative industries, it's crucial to be aware of the potential threats and vulnerabilities that may arise. Being proactive and vigilant in identifying these issues can help organizations develop a more robust AI strategy and minimize potential risks. In this section, we will explore various threats and vulnerabilities related to generative AI.

8.1.1 Security Threats

Generative AI models can be used maliciously or inadvertently expose vulnerabilities in their design, leading to security threats. Some possible security threats include:

1. Adversarial Attacks

Generative models are susceptible to adversarial attacks, a type of cybersecurity threat in which an attacker manipulates the input data to cause the model to produce unintended and often detrimental outputs. Adversarial attacks can lead to compromised system security, compromised data, or even loss of critical infrastructure.

2. Intellectual Property Theft

Generative AI can potentially be used to steal intellectual property from enterprises or individuals by generating fake versions of protected content or mimicking the style of a specific author, artist, or brand. This can result in financial losses and damages to reputations.

3. Impersonation and Spoofing

Generative models can produce realistic forgeries of content like text, images, and videos, which can be used to impersonate individuals, corporate entities, or even governments. This can lead to fraud, identity theft, and misinformation campaigns that can undermine trust in various communication channels.

4. Data Leakage

Training data used within generative AI models can potentially contain sensitive information, such as customer data, personally identifiable information (PII), or trade secrets. If an attacker gains access to this data, it can lead to damaging data leaks and privacy violations.

8.1.2 Ethical and Social Vulnerabilities

Besides security threats, generative AI models can potentially create ethical and social vulnerabilities:

1. Bias and Discrimination

Generative AI models are trained on large datasets derived from human-generated content, which often contain biases and stereotypes. If not addressed in the training process, these biases can be perpetuated and even amplified by the AI model, leading to discriminatory behavior that can harm individuals or groups.

2. Content Moderation

As generative AI tools become more accessible, they can potentially facilitate the creation and spread of unwanted content like hate speech, propaganda, or explicit material. This can make it challenging for content moderation systems to keep pace with the volume of content being produced.

3. Disinformation and Deepfakes

Generative AI can produce convincing and manipulative content such as deepfakes, which are used to spread disinformation or bypass authentication mechanisms, potentially undermining trust in digital media and online communication.

4. Job Loss and Economic Disruption

While generative AI can lead to increased productivity and cost savings, it may also result in job displacement as certain tasks become automated. It is essential to consider the societal impact of adopting generative AI technologies.

8.1.3 Technical Vulnerabilities

Generative AI models can also exhibit technical vulnerabilities that can be exploited, leading to unintended consequences or system failures. A few examples include:

1. Overfitting

Overfitting is a common issue in AI models where the model becomes too specialized in the training data, ultimately reducing its ability to generalize to new data. This can lead to poor performance in real-world applications and can be particularly problematic for generative AI models meant to accommodate a wide range of inputs and scenarios.

2. Lack of Transparency

Many generative AI models, particularly deep learning models, are described as "black boxes" due to their complexity and lack of transparency. It can be challenging to understand how and why these models produce certain outputs, making it difficult to identify potential vulnerabilities, biases, or ethical issues.

3. Reliability and Reproducibility

Generative AI models often rely on stochastic processes during training and sampling, which can yield different outputs for the same input parameters. This can make it difficult to reproduce results, which may affect the reliability and consistency of generated content in enterprise or creative applications.

8.1.4 Mitigation Strategies

To address these threats and vulnerabilities, organizations should consider adopting the following mitigation strategies:

1. **Invest in AI security and robustness**: Develop and implement security protocols for AI systems, including threat modeling, ongoing risk assessments, and robustness testing against adversarial attacks.
2. **Monitor and address bias**: Employ systematic methods to measure and address biases in training data and AI model outputs, ensuring fairness and compliance with ethical guidelines.
3. **Implement content moderation and authentication**: Deploy sophisticated content moderation systems to detect and filter out unwanted content generated by AI tools, and supplement authentication mechanisms with additional safeguards to counter deepfakes and forgeries.
4. **Prioritize explainability and transparency**: Seek AI models and techniques that promote transparency and explainability in their decision-making processes, fostering greater accountability and trust.
5. **Invest in human-AI collaboration**: Leverage AI tools to augment human workers rather than replace them, promoting a more balanced and harmonious relationship between humans and AI technologies.

By identifying the potential threats and vulnerabilities related to generative AI, organizations can devise strategies to manage and mitigate these challenges, ensuring a more secure and responsible application of AI in enterprise and creative contexts.

8.2. Counterfeit and Fraud Risks in Generative AI

Generative AI has been instrumental in driving innovation across numerous industries. Its ability to create realistic content and streamline design processes has paved the way for faster, more efficient operations. However, as with any technological advancement, generative AI also comes with potential risks, particularly in relation to fraud and counterfeiting.

In this section, we will explore some of the key concerns and risks associated with the use of generative AI in various domains - such as the creation of forged documents, the manipulation of images or videos, and fake content generation for social engineering – and discuss how businesses can mitigate these risks.

8.2.1. Forged Documents and Identity Theft

One significant threat posed by generative AI is the potential for creating realistic forgeries of official documents, such as passports, driver's licenses, or bank statements. With convolutional neural networks (CNNs) and generative adversarial networks (GANs), it is becoming increasingly possible for malicious actors to generate fake documents indistinguishable from real ones.

This may lead to an increase in identity theft, document falsification, and financial fraud, as criminals exploit this technology for personal gain. Businesses need to be prepared for sophisticated forgeries and implement robust authentication processes to counter this threat. Some possible solutions are:

1. Strengthening digital verification systems by using multi-factor authentication, encrypted data storage, and advanced biometric identification methods.
2. Developing AI-based document verification systems capable of distinguishing between real and AI-generated forgeries.
3. Collaborating with government agencies and technology providers to establish and update safety standards and security measures.
4. Providing employee training in detecting and handling suspicious documents and communications.

8.2.2. Image and Video Manipulation

The rise of deepfakes - realistic AI-generated images or videos that portray individuals doing or saying things they have never done or said - has created a new dimension of concerns around generative AI. The potential misuse of deepfakes raises significant ethical and legal questions, particularly when it comes to political manipulation, disinformation, and reputational damage.

Businesses and individuals should be aware of the following risks:

1. Spreading misinformation campaigns: Malicious actors may create and disseminate altered images or videos of public figures, executives, or competitors to manipulate public opinion, interfere in elections, or harm business relations.
2. Blackmail and extortion: Criminals could use deepfakes to stage compromising situations and demand money, potentially causing reputational and financial damage to companies and individuals.
3. Intellectual property theft: AI-generated images, videos, and designs could be used to counterfeit products, leading to loss of revenue and harm to brand reputation.

To mitigate these threats:

1. Employ AI-based detection tools to identify and flag deepfakes and manipulated content before it goes viral and causes potential harm.
2. Establish clear guidelines and policies for employees related to the creation and distribution of deepfakes and manipulated media.
3. Educate the general public about deepfakes technology to promote awareness and critical thinking in consuming media.

8.2.3. Social Engineering and Phishing Attacks

Generative AI can also be used by cybercriminals to perpetrate social engineering attacks, such as impersonating executives through email or crafting convincing phishing attacks using AI-generated text. By leveraging AI technology, attackers can automate the creation of tailored email messages that appear legitimate and relevant to the target.

To defend against these risks:

1. Promote cybersecurity awareness and educate employees on the importance of verifying the authenticity of emails, links, and attachments before taking any action.
2. Implement AI-powered email security tools designed to detect AI-generated phishing attempts, in conjunction with traditional security measures.
3. Encourage businesses to adopt sender verification protocols and monitor employee communications for signs of compromise.

Conclusion

The potential for fraud and counterfeit activities enabled by generative AI is undoubtedly concerning. However, businesses can minimize these risks by implementing robust security measures and investing in the development of AI-driven countermeasures. As AI technologies continue to advance, it is essential for organizations to remain vigilant and proactive in safeguarding their data, assets, and reputation.

8.3. Collaborating with Security Leaders

As the adoption of generative AI and computational creativity technologies expands rapidly within enterprises, the need for effective collaboration between AI professionals and security leaders becomes critical. This chapter dives deep into the crucial role that security leaders play in ensuring robustness and security in the deployment of generative AI systems, outlines the threats faced by organizations, and provides insights to foster stronger cooperation between these two groups.

The Importance of Security in Generative AI

While the potential benefits of generative AI can be transformative, the technology also has the capability to create new security risks and enable malicious activities that can imperil the integrity of organizations. Malware, deepfakes, and targeted campaigns leveraging generative AI all pose legitimate threats to the security of data, operations, and reputations.

Security leaders must work closely with AI practitioners to address these concerns, ensuring that AI deployments adhere to established security protocols, that potential vulnerabilities are identified early, and that the appropriate mitigation strategies are in place.

Understanding the Threat Landscape

Before outlining the key considerations for AI and security collaboration, it's important to understand the different types of threats that generative AI systems can pose to an organization:

1. **Data poisoning attacks**: Adversaries can manipulate training data to introduce vulnerabilities or biases in the AI model. These can lead to compromised outputs or unintended behavior that undermines the system's reliability.

2. **Adversarial example attacks**: An attacker generates inputs deliberately designed to fool the AI system into producing incorrect or misleading output, without necessarily manipulating the underlying model.
3. **Model inversion attacks**: By probing the outputs of a trained model, attackers can infer private information about individuals used in the training data, exposing sensitive data and breaching privacy.
4. **Model stealing attacks**: An attacker creates a replica of a proprietary model by repeatedly querying the AI system, which can lead to financial losses and competitive disadvantages.
5. **Malicious AI applications**: The same generative AI techniques used to create valuable content can also be used by bad actors for nefarious purposes, like generating fake news, creating deepfakes, or crafting more convincing phishing emails.

Key Considerations for Collaboration between AI and Security

Successful collaboration between AI professionals and security leaders should consider the following key aspects:

1. **Alignment of objectives**: Establish a shared vision for the role that AI and security play in an organization, ensuring that both parties understand each other's priorities, expectations, and potential challenges.
2. **Establishing a security-focused AI development lifecycle**: Integrate security requirements from the earliest stages of AI model

design and continue throughout the entire AI development lifecycle. This includes regular security assessments and code reviews, applying security best practices for data management, and employing secure systems for model deployment.

3. **Defending against adversarial examples**: Incorporate defenses against adversarial attacks both in the development of AI models and in their deployment. These measures could include adversarial training, data augmentation, or input validation to minimize the risk of adversarial samples.

4. **Implementing privacy-preserving AI techniques**: Apply techniques like federated learning, differential privacy, and homomorphic encryption, which can help to maintain privacy while still enabling machine learning on sensitive data.

5. **Recipe for a threat model:** Create threat models to identify potential vulnerabilities in the AI system by enumerating the possible attack vectors and their potential impact. These threat models can help inform the development of mitigation strategies and guide ongoing risk assessments.

6. **Establishing clear guidelines**: Develop guidelines for employees and partners on the responsible use of AI, covering data privacy, ethical considerations, and potential legal and regulatory implications.

7. **Building a culture of security**: Encourage collaboration, communication, and knowledge sharing between the AI and security teams. Leverage AI to enhance security by using AI-powered threat detection, anomaly detection, and security automation.

8. **Monitoring and reporting**: Continuous monitoring and reporting of AI system performance and security events will help identify potential threats or performance degradation due to unforeseen events.

Regular reporting and data-driven insights can also help to demonstrate and maintain regulatory compliance.

In conclusion, the future of generative AI for enterprises and computational creativity hinges on the ability of AI professionals and security leaders to collaborate effectively, addressing threats and vulnerabilities while maximizing the potential benefits of these innovative technologies. By fostering strong communication, alignment, and best practices around security and AI, organizations can be better prepared to overcome the challenges and seize the opportunities presented by generative AI systems in the years to come.

Chapter 9: Ethical and Responsible AI Use

9.1 Introduction

The rapid advancement of Artificial Intelligence (AI) brings along numerous opportunities for growth, efficiency, and transformation across industries. However, as these technologies become more prevalent in our daily lives, it is crucial to address the ethical and responsible use of AI. This chapter will discuss the key ethical considerations that should be at the forefront of AI use, as well as provide guidelines and best practices to ensure responsible deployment and management of AI systems. The objective is to ensure that the foundations on which AI is built and utilized are in line with societal values and norms.

9.2 Key Ethical Considerations

9.2.1 Fairness and Bias

AI systems often rely on massive amounts of data to make decisions and generate insights. However, this data may contain inherent biases reflecting historical or societal inequalities. AI systems can propagate or even exacerbate these biases, leading to discriminatory outcomes for certain populations or individuals. Ensuring fairness in AI requires the identification and mitigation of biases in both the data used and the mechanisms through which AI systems are designed and deployed.

9.2.2 Transparency and Explainability

In order for individuals and organizations to trust AI systems, it is crucial that they are transparent and can be effectively explained. A lack of transparency and understanding can lead to mistrust and fear, often referred to as the "black box" problem. This can hinder the adoption and integration of AI technologies. In addition, transparency and explainability make it easier to identify when an AI system has made a mistake or been compromised, enabling more effective identification and resolution of issues.

9.2.3 Privacy and Data Security

AI systems often require substantial data collection to function effectively. This data can include sensitive information about individuals or organizations, which can be compromised in case of data breaches or unauthorized access. Ensuring proper data protection mechanisms, safeguards, and ethical data use are essential to maintaining privacy and security, fostering trust, and ensuring compliance with regulatory and legal requirements.

9.2.4 Autonomy and Human Dignity

AI systems can generate significant changes to social structures, labor relationships, and individual autonomy. Understanding the implications of these changes on human dignity and well-being is therefore a key ethical consideration. AI systems should be designed, deployed, and managed in a responsible and human-centric manner, respecting the human in the loop and ensuring that they do not infringe on individual dignity, freedom, or self-determination.

9.3 Best Practices for Ethical AI Use

9.3.1 Engage Stakeholders

In order to successfully address ethical concerns, organizations must engage with all relevant stakeholders, including employees, customers, users, regulators, and the public. This can help gather different perspectives, improve transparency and trust, and promote a shared understanding of ethical challenges and expectations. Adopting a multi-disciplinary approach that includes experts from various fields, such as AI, ethics, sociology, law, and philosophy, can also help ensure more robust and responsible AI practices.

9.3.2 Adopt Ethical AI Frameworks and Guidelines

Numerous ethical AI frameworks and guidelines have been developed by governments, industry, and academia. Organizations should consider adopting these frameworks, which can help prevent ethical pitfalls, ensure compliance with legal and regulatory standards, and improve trust and reputation. Examples of ethical AI frameworks include the EU High-Level Expert Group on AI's "AI Ethics Guidelines" and the OECD's "Principles on AI."

9.3.3 Implement Privacy by Design

Privacy by design is an approach that ensures privacy and data protection are integral components of an AI system from its initial design stages. Organizations should consider privacy by design principles, such as data minimization, user control, and purpose limitation, and implement strong and privacy-preserving cryptographic techniques. This can help to minimize the potential harm associated with data breaches or misuse, and promote trust and compliance with privacy regulations, such as the EU's General Data Protection Regulation (GDPR).

9.3.4 Develop Responsible AI Policies and Governance

Organizations should formalize their commitment to ethical AI use through the development of responsible AI policies, codes of conduct, and governance structures. These policies should clearly articulate the organization's goals, values, and expectations around AI ethics, as well as accountability and enforcement mechanisms. Regular audits of AI systems, including monitoring for fairness, bias, and compliance, can help ensure adherence to these policies and enable continuous improvement.

9.3.5 Foster Education and Training

In order to effectively address ethical challenges and ensure responsible AI use, organizations must promote a culture of AI literacy and ethics across various roles and departments. This includes implementing training programs to ensure that employees understand the ethical implications of AI, as well as providing guidance and support to help them apply ethical principles to their work. Equipping employees with the necessary knowledge and skills is essential for an organization's successful and responsible AI adoption.

9.4 Conclusion

Ethical and responsible AI use is a pressing concern for organizations and society as a whole. As AI technologies continue to advance and permeate various aspects of our lives, it is critical that we remain vigilant and purposeful in ensuring that their development and use align with our societal values and norms. By engaging stakeholders, adopting ethical AI frameworks, implementing privacy by design principles, and fostering education and training, organizations can contribute to a responsible AI future, maximizing the benefits of AI while minimizing its potential risks and harms.

9.1 Developing Guidelines for Generative AI Usage

As generative AI gains momentum and becomes increasingly more sophisticated, a wide range of enterprises and organizations are looking to leverage its power to enhance their businesses, improve decision-making capabilities, and drive innovation. However, as with any technological advancement, it is important to establish clear guidelines and best practices to ensure the ethical, responsible, and productive use of generative AI technologies.

This section will delve into several essential guidelines that organizations should consider when integrating generative AI into their operations.

Understand the Capabilities and Limitations of Generative AI

Before incorporating generative AI into any enterprise workflows or products, it is crucial to understand both the capabilities and limitations of the technology. Organizations should familiarize themselves with the latest advancements and study how these tools have been used in similar industries or projects. This knowledge will help the organization select appropriate applications for generative AI and set realistic expectations for its performance.

Establish Clear Goals and Objectives

Enterprises must set clear and measurable goals when deploying generative AI solutions. Identifying the specific problems that the organization wants to address and the desired outcomes will help ensure that the AI tools' objectives are aligned with the company's broader goals. Organizations should also determine specific metrics that can be used to measure the success and effectiveness of the generative AI solution in achieving the established goals.

Prioritize Data Quality and Transparency

Generative AI relies on large volumes of data to learn and create novel outputs. Therefore, the quality of the input data is crucial to the success of these algorithms. Organizations should prioritize data cleaning, verification, and validation to ensure that the information being fed into the AI models is accurate and representative. Providing proper labels and annotations for the training data can facilitate more accurate and precise outputs.

Moreover, documenting and communicating the processes involved in data collection, curation, and analysis can help maintain transparency and build trust with stakeholders. Transparent data practices will also allow organizations to troubleshoot and fine-tune their AI models more effectively, resulting in more reliable predictions and outcomes.

Address Ethical and Bias Considerations

Generative AI can inadvertently perpetuate and amplify existing societal biases, as the training data might inherently contain skewed and biased information. It is essential that organizations acknowledge this potential issue and actively work to mitigate the risks associated with biased AI-generated outputs. This can be achieved through the use of robust methodologies for bias identification, as well as the employment of a diverse team of domain experts and data scientists who bring varied perspectives to the development process.

Enterprises should also consider the ethical implications of using generative AI, particularly when it comes to generating content that may be misleading, offensive, or potentially harmful. Establishing a strong ethical framework and guidelines for AI-driven content generation and personalization can help prevent misuse and misappropriation of the technology.

Foster Collaboration and Communication

Generative AI technologies are still in their nascent stage and continue to evolve rapidly. Collaboration between multidisciplinary teams consisting of data scientists, engineers, designers, domain experts, and decision-makers is essential to create customized AI solutions that cater to the diverse needs and objectives of the enterprise.

Regular and transparent communication across the organization will help ensure that stakeholders are kept informed, and their feedback is utilized to iteratively refine and optimize the AI systems. This collaborative approach will also facilitate the effective integration of generative AI technologies into existing workflows and systems, minimizing disruptions and maximizing productivity gains.

Monitor and Evaluate Performance

Continuous monitoring and evaluation of generative AI systems are crucial to maintaining high performance and ensuring that the system remains aligned with its intended goals. Regularly assessing the AI-generated outputs against the predetermined metrics will help inform adjustments and improvements to the algorithms, data, and workflow. This approach enables organizations to fine-tune their AI systems to better meet their unique requirements and maximize the benefits derived from these advanced technologies.

Prepare for Legal and Regulatory Compliance

As generative AI technology advances, it is likely that new regulations and legal frameworks will emerge to address potential concerns and risks associated with their use. Enterprises should stay informed about legal developments in the AI domain, be prepared to adapt their practices accordingly, and proactively engage in shaping the regulatory landscape.

In conclusion, the deployment of generative AI technologies offers a wealth of opportunities and advantages for organizations across various industries. By adhering to the established guidelines and best practices, enterprises can maximize the benefits of generative AI while minimizing potential risks and challenges. Ultimately, responsible and ethical AI usage will contribute to sustainable growth and long-term success in the global market.

9.2. Prioritizing Transparency and Model Usage

In the era of rapid AI advancement, the corporate world has witnessed an unprecedented increase in generative AI applications for enhancing product offerings, customer experience, and internal decision-making. The powerful potential of AI has led enterprises to build transformative applications that positively impact their bottom lines. However, the powerful nature of AI also raises several concerns, particularly with respect to transparency, ethics, and model usage. It becomes critical for enterprises to commit to transparency and foster responsible AI adoption.

Understanding AI Transparency

Transparency, in the context of Artificial Intelligence, refers to the ability to trace, understand, and explain the reasoning behind AI models' decisions, predictions, and recommendations. It involves creating a clear understanding of how AI algorithms arrive at specific conclusions to ensure ethical and unbiased usage. Prioritizing transparency is crucial as it helps establish trust, enhance accountability, and improve users' understanding of AI applications.

Key reasons for Prioritizing Transparency and Model Usage

1. Explainability

Complex and opaque AI models can alienate stakeholders, making it challenging for them to trust AI-generated solutions. Explainability is a crucial component of transparency, ensuring that AI models provide clear and understandable reasons for their outputs. A transparent AI system empowers users to grasp the underlying mechanisms without needing to be experts in the field. Stakeholders must be able to comprehend and validate the system's recommendations to foster trust and confidence in AI solutions.

2. Accountability

When AI models make autonomously-based decisions, it is vital to hold human decision-makers accountable for their actions. Transparency allows for timely identification of potential errors, biases, and discrepancies within the AI system. It promotes effective communication and collaboration with stakeholders, granting enterprises the ability to adapt and improve their decision-making processes.

3. Ethical Considerations

One of the most significant challenges in AI deployment lies in ensuring ethical usage, particularly when battling against biased datasets and potential discriminatory practices. Transparent AI models permit the unbiased evaluation of algorithmic decision-making, ensuring a more ethical balance in outcomes. By prioritizing transparency, enterprises can maintain ethical standards and promote positive societal impacts.

4. Compliance with Regulations

Legal and regulatory landscapes surrounding AI are rapidly evolving. Adopting transparent AI models aligns with current and foreseeable regulatory requirements, particularly those relating to privacy and data protection. Transparent AI practices address regulatory concerns and enhance overall compliance, reducing the risk of legal consequences, financial implications, and potential reputational damage.

5. Competitive Advantage

When enterprises prioritize transparency and model usage, they are more likely to cultivate a reputation for ethical AI deployment. As a result, businesses enjoy increased customer trust, support, and loyalty, emerging as industry leaders in responsible AI technology. Transparent AI practices are essential for long-term growth and a sustainable competitive advantage.

Strategies for Promoting Transparency and Model Usage

1. Collaboration and Open Communication

AI development should be a collaborative process, involving interdisciplinary teams of experts, stakeholders, and relevant communities. Adopting open communication channels helps foster a shared understanding of AI systems, leading to the co-creation of transparent and ethical applications.

2. Data Management and Processing

Enterprises must ensure that datasets used to train AI models are representative, diverse, and unbiased. By incorporating effective data management practices, organizations can identify potential biases, improve data quality, and utilize relevant datasets for specific applications.

3. Use of Transparent Models and Algorithms

Emphasize the use of simple, interpretable, and explainable models that deliver expected results without sacrificing accuracy or performance. Transparent models allow users to understand AI system behavior better, leading to more robust applications and improved decision-making.

4. Continuous Monitoring and Evaluation

AI models must be continuously monitored and evaluated to identify and address biases, errors, and data discrepancies. Regular evaluation enables organizations to adapt their decision-making processes, refine their models, and maintain overall transparency.

5. Education and Awareness

Fostering a well-informed, skilled workforce is essential for developing and deploying transparent AI systems. Equipping employees with knowledge about AI best practices, technological advancements, and ethical considerations is critical for sustainable and responsible AI adoption within enterprises.

Conclusion

Prioritizing transparency and model usage is vital for businesses looking to leverage the power of generative AI responsibly. Transparency promotes explainability, accountability, ethical decision-making, regulatory compliance, and competitive advantage. By fostering transparent AI practices, enterprises can unlock the untapped potential of AI technology and pave the way for a revolution in computational creativity.

9.3 Open-source Models and Their Benefits

In recent years, open-source Artificial Intelligence (AI) models have become increasingly popular, with large technology companies, research institutions, and individual developers sharing their AI research and tools with the rest of the world. This has led to the democratization of AI and a rapid acceleration in the development and adoption of AI by organizations of all sizes. In this section, we will explore the benefits that open-source models bring to enterprises and the field of computational creativity and discuss noteworthy examples of open-source AI models and platforms.

9.3.1 Democratization of AI

The open-source approach to AI development has significantly expanded the access and usage of AI technologies beyond the traditional confines of large enterprises and specialized institutions. By offering well-documented, easy-to-use, and regularly updated AI models and tools, more developers and organizations can harness the power of AI without necessarily having the budget or the expert knowledge to develop their own models from scratch. This broad access to AI resources is essential for fostering a wave of innovation that spans across industries and scales, as developers can experiment with different approaches to AI and develop new, more creative applications with less initial investment.

9.3.2 Faster Innovation and Improved AI Models

The sharing of AI models and frameworks leads to a collaborative ecosystem that enables rapid advancements in AI technology. When researchers and developers are open about their work, it allows others to build upon them, identify potential improvements, and apply the technology in novel ways. This collaborative dynamic ultimately leads to a faster pace of innovation and superior AI models, as multiple teams and individuals iterate on each other's work in real-time.

For example, TensorFlow, an open-source AI library developed by Google, enables organizations and researchers to develop and deploy machine learning models with ease. As an open-source project, other members of the AI community can contribute to the library, providing a wide range of pre-trained models, tools, and resources to improve the performance and applicability of the framework.

9.3.3 Cost Efficiency

Developing AI models can be a costly and time-consuming endeavor, especially if an organization does not have the expertise or resources to conduct the research internally. Open-source AI models offer a cost-effective solution to this problem, as they are freely available for enterprises to implement and modify as needed.

Adopting open-source AI models can save organizations substantial amounts of time and money, as the initial investment in research and development has already been made by the open-source community. Furthermore, as the community continues to improve the model, organizations can also benefit from those advancements without additional investments.

9.3.4 Platform Independence and Customization

When organizations utilize open-source AI models, they gain the freedom to choose and customize their AI infrastructure as per their requirements. Open-source models are designed to work on a variety of platforms, allowing organizations to avoid vendor lock-in and retain the flexibility to change or modify their AI infrastructure as needed.

Moreover, organizations can customize the open-source AI models to better suit their specific needs, whether that means retraining the model with their own data, modifying the architecture of the model, or improving the performance of the model to meet their unique requirements.

9.3.5 Talent Attraction and Retention

Enterprises that contribute to open-source AI projects are more likely to attract top-tier AI talent, who are motivated by the opportunity to work on high-profile, cutting-edge projects. By joining the open-source AI community, an organization immediately gains access to a network of AI enthusiasts and experts, enabling them to recruit the best minds in the field more easily.

9.3.6 Notable Examples of Open-Source AI Models and Platforms

Several open-source AI models and platforms have gained considerable attention and usage in recent years. Here are some notable examples:

1. **TensorFlow**: Developed and maintained by Google Brain, TensorFlow is one of the most popular open-source AI libraries for machine learning and neural network development. TensorFlow's flexibility and extensive collection of tools, resources, and pre-trained models make it suitable for use in various fields, from computer vision to natural language processing.
2. **PyTorch**: Developed by Facebook AI Research, PyTorch is a user-friendly, open-source deep learning framework that supports a broad range of AI models and provides enhanced performance through Tensor computations and GPU acceleration.
3. **GPT (Generative Pre-trained Transformer)**: Developed by OpenAI, GPT is a series of state-of-the-art open-source models for natural language processing tasks. With GPT-3, the most recent version, developers have found staggering success in tasks like text summarization, translation, and even code generation – demonstrating the power of large-scale open-source AI models.
4. **Keras**: As a user-friendly, high-level neural network library, Keras enables rapid development and prototyping of deep learning models by offering an easy-to-understand API and modular components.

Keras is built on top of TensorFlow and other high-performance backends, making it ideal for developers who want to remain flexible in their choice of AI framework.

In conclusion, open-source AI models provide numerous benefits to enterprises and the field of computational creativity, from democratizing access to AI tools to fostering faster innovation and cost efficiency. By adopting open-source AI models or contributing to the open-source community, organizations can become an active part of the AI movement and leverage the power of AI to fuel their business success and create transformative applications.

Chapter 10: Preparing for the Future of Generative AI

As the field of generative AI continues to advance rapidly, embracing its potential for enterprises and computational creativity requires proper preparation. This chapter will discuss frameworks and recommendations for organizations to adapt to the future of generative AI. We will explore the importance of investments, workforce training, ethical considerations, and integration with existing business processes.

10.1 Identifying Opportunities for Generative AI in Your Industry

Changes in technology bring about new opportunities for innovation and growth. To capitalize on the future of generative AI, businesses must begin by identifying the most impactful applications in their industry.

To achieve this, consider the following steps:

1. **Research industry-specific AI advancements**: Be aware of the latest AI developments in your industry, and consider how generative AI fits into the picture. Understand if there are existing business cases or pioneers who have successfully integrated generative AI in your domain.

2. **Evaluate pain-points in your business**: Determine the critical areas of your business where generative AI could provide a solution or enhance existing processes. Some examples include:
   o Automating repetitive or mundane tasks
   o Enhancing creativity in design or content generation
   o Optimizing supply chain management, inventory control, or resource allocation
3. **Collaborate with stakeholders**: Forge connections and dialogue with various stakeholders—including employees, customers, and partners—to validate potential use cases and gather feedback.

10.2 Developing a Generative AI Strategy

Once generative AI opportunities are identified, it is crucial to create a comprehensive strategy for implementation. This includes technological investments, workforce development, and ethical considerations.

10.2.1 Technological Investments

Investing in the right technology plays a significant role in a successful generative AI strategy. Businesses must:

1. **Choose an AI framework**: Select an AI framework that best serves your organization's needs, considering factors such as scalability, flexibility, and performance. Popular choices include TensorFlow, PyTorch, and Keras.

2. **Build or buy AI solutions**: Determine whether building an in-house AI solution or purchasing an off-the-shelf product is more appropriate for your business needs.
3. **Ensure robust infrastructure**: Ensure your organization's infrastructure is capable of supporting high-performance computing needs, including necessary data storage and processing capabilities.
4. **Invest in collaboration tools**: Implement tools that facilitate seamless collaboration between data scientists, developers, and other business stakeholders to accelerate the development and deployment of AI solutions.

10.2.2 Workforce Development

A skilled workforce is essential to ensuring success in the adoption of AI technologies. Keep in mind the following approaches to developing your workforce:

1. **Train employees**: Invest in providing training and upskilling opportunities for your current employees in AI, machine learning, and data analysis.
2. **Hire talent**: Hire AI and data science experts who can provide valuable insights, recommendations, and skills to guide decision-making within the organization.
3. **Foster a culture of innovation**: Encourage a culture that rewards experimentation, collaboration, and learning, enabling employees to stay updated, creative, and adaptable to new technologies.

10.2.3 Ethical Considerations

It is important to consider the ethical implications of implementing generative AI in your organization. This includes:

1. **Transparency**: Be transparent about the use of generative AI, its data sources, capabilities, and limitations with stakeholders.
2. **Bias mitigation**: Use unbiased training data and engage in periodic audits to ensure that your AI systems do not propagate or perpetuate unfair bias.
3. **Data privacy**: Be mindful of data privacy and security concerns when collecting, storing, and processing personal information.
4. **Human oversight**: Maintain a degree of human oversight on critical decisions, ensuring that AI isn't making decisions that may adversely affect individuals or the organization.

10.3 Integrating Generative AI into Business Processes

Successfully integrating generative AI into existing business processes requires planning, collaboration, and continuous iteration. Consider the following steps to ensure successful integration:

1. **Align AI adoption with business objectives**: Ensure that your generative AI creations align with your organization's goals and priorities.
2. **Establish metrics**: Define measurable metrics for the success and effectiveness of your generative AI implementation.
3. **Develop a cross-functional team**: Foster collaboration between various teams, such as data science, IT, marketing, and others, to ensure seamless integration of AI technology.

4. **Monitor AI performance**: Continuously evaluate the performance and impact of your generative AI implementation with regular reviews and data-driven analyses.
5. **Iterate and improve**: Encourage an agile mindset, allowing for adjustments and improvements based on evaluation and feedback.

In conclusion, the future of generative AI holds promising potential for enterprises and computational creativity. By identifying opportunities, developing a comprehensive strategy, and integrating AI into business processes, organizations can embrace this powerful technology to drive growth, innovation, and transformation.

10.1. Staying updated on AI trends and advancements

As the field of artificial intelligence (AI) progresses at a rapid pace, staying informed about the latest trends and advancements becomes essential for enterprises, researchers, developers, and students. This chapter will discuss various available resources and strategies to follow AI trends, research breakthroughs, and industrial applications. We will also discuss how to be an active participant in the AI community and stay ahead in this constantly evolving field.

10.1.1. Following AI Research

Many prominent research institutes, universities, and organizations publish their AI-related work in the form of research papers, technical reports, or whitepapers. Below is a list of resources to monitor for staying updated on AI research:

1. **ArXiv**: ArXiv is a widely-used platform where researchers often publish their work before submission to formal conferences or journals. Subscribe to appropriate categories like Computer Science (cs)/AI, Machine Learning, or Neural and Evolutionary Computing.
2. **Research Journals**: Many research journals publish AI-related papers. Popular ones include Nature Machine Intelligence, IEEE Transactions on

Pattern Analysis and Machine Intelligence (PAMI), and Journal of Artificial Intelligence Research (JAIR).
3. **Conference Proceedings**: Keep an eye on proceedings from major AI conferences like NeurIPS, ICML, ACL, and IJCAI.
4. **AI Research Labs**: Follow updates from renowned AI research labs, such as OpenAI, Google Research, DeepMind, and Facebook AI.
5. **Preprint Sharing**: Platforms like Semantic Scholar, Google Scholar, and ResearchGate let you search for and follow the work of individual researchers or institutions.

10.1.2. Following AI News, Blogs, and Podcasts

To stay updated on AI news, blog articles, and podcasts, follow these online resources:

1. **AI News Sources**: Websites like AI in Business, AI Trends, and Synced provide regular news and updates on AI advancements and applications.
2. **Company Blogs**: AI-focused companies or organizations, like OpenAI, Google Research, DeepMind, NVIDIA Developer Blog, and Towards Data Science, publish blog posts written by researchers and developers working on the latest AI breakthroughs.
3. **AI Podcasts**: There are numerous interesting AI podcasts that discuss various topics in the AI field, such as The AI Alignment Podcast, The Ed Mylett Show, and Artificial Intelligence (AI) podcast by Lex Fridman.

10.1.3. Engaging with the AI Community

Join online communities, forums, and social media to engage with AI enthusiasts, researchers, and professionals from across the globe:

1. **AI Subreddits**: Reddit has multiple subreddits dedicated to AI-related discussions, such as r/MachineLearning, r/artificial, r/learnmachinelearning. Subscribe to and participate in these vibrant communities.
2. **LinkedIn Groups**: Join AI-related groups on LinkedIn, like Artificial Intelligence and Deep Learning, Artificial Intelligence (AI), or Machine Learning & AI for networking opportunities and to stay on top of industry trends.
3. **AI Meetups**: Participating in local AI Meetups or attending international AI conferences will provide you with opportunities to connect with like-minded individuals, academics, and industry professionals.
4. **Discussion Forums**: Engage in discussions on AI-focused forums, like the AI Stack Exchange or ML Mastery Forums.

10.1.4. Online Learning Resources and MOOCs

Stay ahead in the field by refining your AI skills with online courses and learning resources:

1. **AI Courses**: Websites like Coursera, edX, and Udacity offer AI and machine learning courses taught by leading experts and researchers.

2. **AI Tutorials and Workshops**: AI conferences usually offer free or paid workshops and tutorials. For example, NeurIPS, ICML, and ACL provide technical workshops for attendees.
3. **Online Code Repositories**: Platforms like GitHub and GitLab host open-source AI projects and libraries. Following these repositories can help learn AI techniques from real-world code implementations.

As AI continues to grow and expand across various domains, staying updated on its trends and advancements is crucial for both individuals and organizations. By consistently following research, news, blogs, and the broader AI community, and leveraging online learning resources, you can stay ahead in this fast-paced landscape and, ultimately, unleash the potential of generative AI and computational creativity in your enterprise.

10.2. Integrating Generative AI into Enterprise Strategy

Generative AI has become a significant player in shaping the future of enterprises and computational creativity. Integrating this technology into your organization's strategy will not only allow you to stay competitive, but it can also lead to increased innovation, process optimization, and cost-effectiveness. In this section, we will discuss several key aspects of embedding generative AI within your enterprise strategy.

10.2.1. Identifying Strategic Goals and Opportunities

In order to effectively integrate generative AI into your enterprise strategy, it is crucial to begin with a clear understanding of the strategic goals and opportunities that can be leveraged by adopting this technology.

1. **Innovation and Creativity**: One of the main benefits of generative AI is its potential to enable new and creative solutions to traditional problems. Thus, incorporate innovation and creativity as a strategic objective that can be achieved using generative AI.
2. **Optimization**: Generative AI systems can identify and suggest improvements in various areas of your organization. Define your objectives around process optimization, cost reduction, and efficiency.

3. **Personalization**: Generative AI can create highly personalized experiences for customers, employees, and other stakeholders. Consider how personalization can be utilized to create value and better experiences across the enterprise.
4. **Data Analysis**: Generative AI has the ability to process large amounts of data and generate insights previously unavailable to human operators. Strategically align your organization with the goal of becoming more data-driven and harnessing the insights provided by these algorithms.

10.2.2. Assessing the Current State of your Organization

Before embarking on the journey of incorporating generative AI into your enterprise strategy, it is essential to assess your organization's current state. This analysis allows you to identify areas where generative AI deployment can make the most significant impact.

1. **Data Infrastructure**: Assess whether your organization has sufficient data infrastructure, storage, and management systems to handle the large amounts of information required for generative AI.
2. **Current AI Capabilities**: Evaluate the current state of AI adoption in your organization. This will inform decisions around the need for upskilling employees, creating new teams, or hiring AI experts.
3. **Organizational Readiness**: Consider your organization's culture, existing processes and systems, and openness to change. Understanding these factors will assist in facilitating the smooth

implementation of generative AI into your enterprise strategy.

10.2.3. Building a Roadmap for Integration

Once you have a solid understanding of your organization's strategic goals and current state, the next step is to create a roadmap to guide the implementation of generative AI in your organization.

1. **Gap Analysis**: Identify the gaps between your organization's current state and the desired state you aim to reach by integrating generative AI. This will inform your priorities and help you develop a realistic plan.
2. **Setting Milestones**: Determine key milestones that mark significant progress towards integrating generative AI. This can include the implementation of a specific solution, achieving a certain level of employee proficiency, or reaching a certain percentage of AI-driven processes.
3. **Resource Allocation**: Allocate the necessary resources, including budget, time, and personnel, to support the implementation of generative AI. This requires the involvement of stakeholders from various departments, such as IT, HR, finance, and operations.
4. **Collaboration and Partnerships**: Establish partnerships with technology providers, academic institutions, and other organizations to boost your generative AI capabilities. Collaborations can help accelerate the integration process, reduce costs, and bring in external expertise.

10.2.4. Fostering an AI-driven Culture

The successful implementation of generative AI within your enterprise strategy heavily depends on the acceptance and buy-in of your employees. To achieve this, cultivate an AI-driven culture within your organization.

1. **Top-Down Leadership**: The commitment and involvement of top executives in promoting generative AI as a strategic priority are crucial. Executives must lead by example and advocate for the value and importance of AI adoption.
2. **Education and Training**: Upskilling employees and providing continuous learning opportunities are essential to ensure a smooth transition to generative AI. This can be done through training sessions, workshops, and dedicated resources like online tutorials or AI-focused newsletters.
3. **Cross-Functional Teams**: Encourage collaboration among various departments to facilitate the sharing of knowledge, skills, and insights related to generative AI. This will foster a sense of collective ownership and accelerate the pace of AI adoption.
4. **Ethics and Responsible AI**: Promote responsible AI practices by incorporating ethical considerations into your organization's decision-making processes. Develop and implement guidelines, policies, and frameworks around AI ethics and ensure employees are aware of their responsibilities when using generative AI systems.

10.2.5. Tracking Progress and Continuous Improvement

Integration of generative AI systems is an ongoing process that requires continuous monitoring, evaluation, and improvement.

1. **Performance Metrics**: Establish metrics to measure the success of your generative AI initiatives, such as cost savings, improvements in efficiency, or increased revenue. Track and analyze these metrics regularly to ensure progress towards your strategic goals.
2. **Feedback and Iteration**: Solicit feedback from employees, customers, and other stakeholders on the performance of your generative AI systems. Use this feedback to make adjustments and enhancements to ensure the systems continue to meet the intended objectives.
3. **Maintaining Agility**: As generative AI technology evolves at a rapid pace, it is essential to stay updated with the latest advancements and maintain the flexibility to adapt your strategy accordingly. Conduct periodic reviews and reassessments of your generative AI integration roadmap to ensure it remains aligned with current developments and opportunities.

By identifying strategic goals, assessing the current state, building a roadmap, fostering an AI-driven culture, and tracking progress, organizations can effectively integrate generative AI into their enterprise strategy. This process will enable continuous improvement and ensure your organization remains at the forefront of technology and market trends.

10.3. Adapting to the Rapidly Evolving AI Landscape

The advent of generative AI has unlocked unprecedented capabilities and opportunities for enterprises in their quest for innovation and optimization. As the landscape of artificial intelligence becomes more intricate and sophisticated, it is essential for businesses to stay nimble and adapt to these rapid changes or risk falling behind in this increasingly competitive ecosystem. In this section, we will delve into strategies that can help organizations adapt to the evolving AI landscape all while fostering computational creativity.

10.3.1. Dedicated Resources and Structure for AI R&D

One of the most critical steps for organizations to stay abreast of the AI landscape is to allocate resources and create a dedicated structure for AI research and development (R&D). This can be accomplished by:

1. Establishing a specialized AI team - This team should consist of data scientists, AI engineers, and domain-specific experts who possess a deep understanding of machine learning and generative AI technologies.
2. Allocating budget and resources - For AI R&D to be effective, organizations must invest time, money, and resources into acquiring the necessary hardware, software tools, and datasets required to experiment with new AI models and techniques.

3. Collaborations and partnerships - Partnering with academic institutions or third-party AI research organizations can provide access to external knowledge, expertise, and technology sharing.
4. Continuous education - Encourage and arrange for the AI team to attend conferences, workshops, and training programs to stay updated on the latest AI developments.

10.3.2. Monitoring the AI Landscape

By keeping a watchful eye on emerging trends, breakthroughs, and innovations in AI, organizations can identify new techniques and tools that can benefit their business processes. To do this effectively, leaders should follow established publications, research papers, and technical blogs that cover AI advancements. Additionally, participating in AI-focused conferences and seminars will facilitate exposure to new research and use cases as well as provide networking opportunities with other AI practitioners.

10.3.3. Agile Experimentation

An agile approach to AI R&D is crucial in adapting to the changing landscape. This hinges on the ability to develop, test, and iterate on AI models quickly and efficiently. Teams should be encouraged to take risks, explore new techniques, and learn from failures. Some practical ways to foster agile experimentation include:

1. Rapid prototyping - Develop initial drafts of AI models quickly to test their performance and identify potential improvements.

2. Incremental optimization - Adjust and refine models iteratively, incorporating feedback and improvements at each stage.
3. Cross-functional collaboration - Encourage collaboration between AI teams and other departments to facilitate knowledge transfer and promote innovation.

10.3.4. Developing a Culture of AI-Driven Innovation

Organizations should aim to create a culture that embraces and supports AI-driven innovation. This can be achieved by:

1. Encouraging a growth mindset - Promote a culture where learning from failures is valued and expected, and knowledge sharing is encouraged among team members.
2. Inclusiveness and diversity - Assemble AI teams with a diverse set of skills, experiences, and backgrounds. This diversity will enable fresh perspectives that drive creativity in problem-solving and model development.
3. Support from leadership - Top management must actively support and participate in AI initiatives to foster a sense of unity and commitment toward AI-driven innovation.

10.3.5. Ethics and Responsible AI Usage

The rapidly changing AI landscape brings not only new possibilities but also ethical challenges in areas like bias, privacy, and transparency. Enterprises must strive to develop and deploy AI models responsibly, by following best practices such as:

1. Data management - Ensure that the data used for AI model development is accurate, unbiased, and respects users' privacy.
2. Continuous assessment - Regularly evaluate AI models and systems for any biases or ethical issues, and address them proactively.
3. Transparent communication - Clearly communicate the purpose and implications of AI-driven changes with all stakeholders, including employees and users.

Conclusion

The AI landscape is continually evolving, bringing forth both immense opportunities and challenges for enterprises. To adapt successfully and maintain a competitive edge, organizations must invest in dedicated AI R&D, monitor the AI landscape actively, follow an agile approach to experimentation, foster a culture of AI-driven innovation, and imbibe ethical practices throughout AI development and deployment. By embracing these strategies, enterprises will be able to harness the potential of generative AI and computational creativity to propel their business growth and success into the future.

Enhancing Enterprise Capabilities through Generative AI and Computational Creativity

As we move towards a future where technology plays an increasingly dominant role in all aspects of society, businesses will need to adapt and evolve with it. One of the most promising advancements that have the potential to reshape how enterprises operate is generative AI, a subset of artificial intelligence that focuses on creating new content and ideas through algorithms.

This section of the book will explore the potential applications of generative AI and computational creativity for enterprises, discussing how they can enhance decision-making, foster innovation, and drive growth. We will also discuss the challenges and considerations for organizations that seek to leverage these technologies in their operations.

Applications of Generative AI in Enterprises

1. Product Development and Design

Generative AI can revolutionize the process of product development and design by generating numerous iterations of a concept or prototype, allowing businesses to select the best-suited options for their target markets. This can not only help in reducing the time and resources spent on R&D but also ensures a more comprehensive exploration of possibilities. The use of generative AI for design can lead to the creation of products that are more functional, aesthetically appealing, and tailored to individual users.

2. Content Creation and Marketing

Content is an essential aspect of any enterprise's marketing strategy, and generative AI algorithms such as natural language processing (NLP) and generative adversarial networks (GANs) can aid in the creation and curation of content at scale. This can range from generating engaging and personalized copy for ad campaigns, to creating tailored social media content and analyzing user preferences for targeted marketing efforts.

3. Supply Chain Optimization

Generative AI can be employed to optimize and streamline supply chain processes, from demand forecasting to inventory management and logistics. By leveraging AI-generated models that predict market trends and customer behavior, enterprises can better anticipate demand and make informed decisions concerning production, distribution, and procurement. This can lead to reduced waste, lower costs, and improved efficiency.

4. Financial Analysis and Decision-Making

Financial decision-making can be significantly enhanced through the use of generative AI models that can simulate potential market scenarios, analyze trends, and forecast future growth. Enterprises can use these predictions to manage risk, guide investments, and make strategic decisions based on comprehensive insights provided by the generative AI models.

Challenges and Considerations for Implementing Generative AI

As promising as the applications of generative AI in enterprises may be, there are various challenges and considerations that organizations must address before fully embracing these emerging technologies.

1. Ethical Considerations

Generative AI has the potential to create content that is indistinguishable from human-generated content, which raises several ethical concerns. Issues such as plagiarism, generating misinformation or biased content, and the potential to manipulate public opinion must be considered during the implementation of generative AI in enterprise functions.

2. Data Privacy and Security

Generative AI algorithms typically require large volumes of data for training and refining their performance. This raises concerns about the privacy and security of user data, especially with ever-evolving data protection regulations. Companies must establish robust data governance frameworks and practices to ensure compliance and protect the privacy of their users.

3. Technical Expertise and Infrastructure

The implementation of generative AI in enterprises requires a solid technical foundation, including the necessary infrastructure and skilled professionals. Companies need to invest in cultivating talent and building the necessary infrastructure to harness the full potential of generative AI and computational creativity.

4. Integration with Existing Systems

A significant challenge for enterprises is integrating generative AI technologies with existing processes and systems. Careful planning and a change management strategy are required to ensure that AI-driven processes can work harmoniously with conventional methods and human employees, delivering optimal results without causing disruption.

Conclusion

The future of generative AI and computational creativity promises a wealth of opportunities for enterprises to enhance their capabilities, streamline processes, and improve decision-making. However, companies must also navigate the challenges and considerations presented by these technologies to ensure their successful integration and long-term sustainability. Through thoughtful planning and strategic investment, enterprises can leverage generative AI to drive growth and thrive in the competitive landscape of the future.

Chapter 11: AI's Impact on Job Markets

Introduction

The evolution of five major technological shifts has altered the nature of work: mechanization, industrial revolution, computerization, automation, and now artificial intelligence. These developments have greatly impacted employment and job markets across the globe. Today, a new era of AI and machine learning is opening unprecedented possibilities to perform tasks that once required human intelligence. This revolution in AI and computational creativity has raised concerns about how it will affect job markets, employment opportunities, and human roles in the future.

In this chapter, we will delve into the impact of AI on the job market, the types of jobs that may be vulnerable to automation, and the potential for new job creation due to AI technologies. Furthermore, we will discuss how the nature of work may change and how to prepare for the challenges and opportunities that AI presents.

AI Vulnerability in Job Markets

As artificial intelligence and machine learning advance, there is a growing potential for automation in a wide range of industries. According to recent research, almost half of all current jobs could be automated within the next two decades. The most vulnerable jobs to automation include:

1. **Low-skilled jobs**: These jobs involve manual or repetitive tasks, such as cashiers, warehouse workers, and fast-food servers. AI-powered machines and robots can easily perform such tasks with higher efficiency and reduced error rates.
2. **Middle-skilled jobs**: Occupations that involve routine decision-making and data processing, such as accounting clerks, customer service agents, and administrative assistants, can be replaced by AI systems that analyze data faster and make decisions more logically.
3. **High-skilled jobs**: Even highly-skilled occupations that include diagnosing diseases, legal research, and financial analysis are susceptible to automation. AI algorithms can process massive amounts of data in a short time, which outperforms human experts in speed and accuracy.

It is essential to note that AI and automation might not completely eliminate these jobs but transform them instead. Furthermore, as the adoption of AI technology increases, new industries and job opportunities may emerge.

AI-Driven Job Creation

Despite the apparent threat to employment, AI could also generate new job opportunities. Historically, technological advancements have enhanced productivity, created new industries, and thus resulted in job creation. The emergence of AI technologies may follow a similar trend by creating new roles, such as:

1. **AI trainers and explainers**: The development of AI algorithms requires humans to train, maintain, and explain the AI systems' decision-making processes. People with interdisciplinary knowledge in AI, ethics, and domain expertise will be in high demand.
2. **Data scientists and engineers**: As organizations increasingly rely on data-driven decision-making, there will be an increasing need for professionals who can efficiently manage large data sets, create effective AI models, and apply statistical techniques.
3. **AI ethics officers**: As AI technologies become more integrated into businesses, there will be concerns regarding privacy, security, and ethical implications. Organizations will require AI ethics officers to ensure their AI systems align with ethical guidelines.
4. **Personalized service providers**: With the increased integration of AI, personalized services will become more accessible and affordable, opening up new opportunities for entrepreneurs and niche service experts.

Adapting to the AI Revolution

The ongoing AI transformation will require both individuals and organizations to adapt, innovate, and reskill to succeed in the evolving job market. Some recommendations to prepare for this change include:

1. **Lifelong learning**: Continual upskilling and reskilling will be essential to stay relevant and employable in the AI-driven job market. Individuals should proactively seek to develop new skills and

knowledge in areas such as data analytics, programming, and decision-making.
2. **Adopt a growth mindset**: Cultivating a mindset of curiosity, adaptability, and resilience will enable individuals to thrive in an evolving job market. Openness to new experiences and embracing change are crucial for personal and professional development.
3. **Pursue interdisciplinary studies**: With AI technologies becoming more pervasive, future professions will demand integration and collaboration between various fields of expertise. Pursuing interdisciplinary studies will provide a competitive edge in the AI-driven job market.
4. **Emphasize soft skills**: As AI systems and automation take on more routine tasks, the importance of uniquely human skills such as creativity, empathy, and negotiation will increase. Developing strong soft skills will be vital to excel in the jobs of the future.

Conclusion

The advent of AI technologies brings with it the potential for significant disruption in job markets worldwide. Its impact on employment opportunities is a dual-edged sword, posing threats to certain jobs while also creating new possibilities. It is critical that individuals and organizations recognize the potential shifts in the job market and take proactive measures to adapt, reskill, and embrace the evolution of work in the AI era.

The ongoing challenge for society is to strike a balance between embracing the benefits of AI while also ensuring that it does not lead to widespread displacement of human workers. Through collaboration among business leaders, policymakers, and educational institutions, we can navigate the challenges and unlock the opportunities that AI presents for the future of work.

11.1. The changing nature of work with AI

The rapid progress of artificial intelligence (AI) has been on a steady march over the past few decades, as computational power increases and machine learning algorithms grow more robust. As these developments continue to accelerate, AI's potential to disrupt and redefine industries becomes increasingly apparent. In this context, it is crucial for businesses to understand the changing nature of work as AI becomes more prevalent and to evaluate how it may affect the work structure, job requirements, and workforce management.

11.1.1. Shift from manual to cognitive tasks

One of the most prominent ways AI is set to change work is through the shift it enables from manual and repetitive tasks to more cognitive and value-adding tasks. AI systems are excellent at handling routine, rules-based jobs that can be explicitly defined and are predictable. By offloading such tasks to AI, employees can focus their higher-order cognitive skills on solving complex problems, driving innovation, and creating new business opportunities.

This transition, however, represents a significant challenge for workforce upskilling and reskilling. Companies must invest in training and development programs to prepare their employees for the new era of work characterized by a focus on human-machine collaboration and cognitive tasks. This involves not just learning new technical skills, but also honing the so-called "soft skills" like negotiation, empathy, and adaptability, as well as leadership qualities that can help them guide AI implementations.

11.1.2. Redefining job roles and the work structure

As AI takes on a more prominent role in the workplace, job roles and work structures will inevitably evolve. Entire professions might not disappear, but specific tasks within these professions could be significantly altered. This can lead to a redefinition of job roles, where employees are expected to focus on areas where they can deliver the most value and leverage AI to supplement their work.

For instance, the role of customer service agents might shift towards handling more complex and emotive issues that require a high degree of empathy and soft skills. Similarly, a physician could focus more on personalized patient care, while AI takes care of data-driven diagnostics and treatment optimizations.

As the shift toward the gig economy accelerates, AI could contribute to a more dynamic work structure, where job opportunities are modular and can evolve in response to market demands. Companies will need to consider how they can realign their organizational structures and policies to adapt to the changing requirements of their workforce and job roles.

11.1.3. AI-enhanced decision-making and collaboration

AI's ability to process vast amounts of data and provide deep insights can lead to better decision-making for businesses. AI-powered data analysis allows organizations to make better-informed decisions, thereby enhancing efficiency and competitiveness. Moreover, emerging developments in AI, such as natural language processing and machine reasoning, can enhance human-machine collaboration and enable teams to make more well-rounded, more effective decisions.

As organizations become more reliant on AI for decision-making, there will be a need for employees skilled at interpreting, understanding, and communicating outputs from AI systems. This signifies the increasing importance of data literacy and a greater reliance on workers capable of navigating the complex and data-rich environments that AI systems inhabit.

11.1.4. Remote work and digital talent

The adoption of AI, combined with the recent shift to remote work due to the COVID-19 pandemic, has the potential to reshape the way organizations manage their talent. With the democratization of AI and the increasing reliance on cloud and digital technologies, enterprises can easily access global talent pools and select the best-suited candidates – regardless of their geographic location.

Moreover, the use of AI-powered tools coupled with remote work arrangements can lower the barrier to entry for individuals with varying skill levels and backgrounds, promoting diversity and inclusion in the workplace. The growing access to advanced AI tools can also empower smaller organizations to scale up rapidly by tapping into a wider pool of digitally-savvy talent.

In closing, the changing nature of work with AI represents both opportunities and challenges for enterprises. As AI continues to evolve, businesses should be proactive in assessing potential disruptions and preparing their workforce to navigate this transformative era. This necessitates a focus on promoting lifelong learning, embracing new ways of collaboration, and leveraging the right technologies to tap into the immense potential that AI promises to unleash.

11.2. Reskilling and Upskilling the Workforce

As the development of Generative AI accelerates and its applications spread across various industries, it is essential to understand the potential impacts on the workforce. It is important for organizations to prepare their employees with the appropriate skills that complement AI technologies while mitigating the potential risks and challenges.

In this section, we will discuss what reskilling and upskilling mean and their importance in the age of AI, the significant role that organizations and governments play in this process, and the strategies required for successful implementation of these initiatives.

Understanding Reskilling and Upskilling

Reskilling refers to the process of learning new skills or retraining employees to adapt to new job roles or tasks. Reskilling enables workers to transition from one job sector to another, helping them adapt to the ever-changing market demands influenced by technological advances.

Upskilling, on the other hand, is about improving the existing skills and knowledge set of employees to enhance their performance in their current roles. Upskilling initiatives may involve offering additional training programs, workshops, or learning opportunities which can be accessed online or on-site.

The Importance of Reskilling and Upskilling in the AI Age

As Generative AI technologies continue to evolve, organizations must develop strategies for maintaining a skilled workforce that can adapt and excel in this rapidly changing environment. Here are some key reasons why reskilling and upskilling initiatives are crucial:

1. **Employment Sustainability**: As the demand for AI-driven solutions increases, some job roles may be rendered obsolete or see a sharp decline in demand.

However, the same technological advances also create new job opportunities. Reskilling can help affected employees transition into these new roles.
2. **Increased Productivity**: Organizations can benefit from upskilling their workers by investing in their professional development, leading to higher productivity and an overall more competitive workforce.
3. **Innovation and Collaboration**: A workforce with upgraded skills is likely to be more innovative and better equipped to work with AI technologies, which directly benefits organizations and their overall growth.
4. **Employee Engagement**: Investing in employee development can lead to improved satisfaction and retention rates, as workers feel more valued and engaged.

The Role of Organizations and Governments

Both organizations and governments play a vital role in facilitating the reskilling and upskilling of the workforce at various levels:

1. **Workforce Assessments**: Companies should regularly assess their employees to identify skill gaps and areas requiring improvement. Governments play a role in setting standards, regulations, and providing resources to facilitate these assessments.
2. **Training Programs**: Organizations should develop and offer training programs that help their employees sharpen their skills or acquire new ones. Governments can provide support through incentives and funding for such programs.

3. **Educational Institutes and Partnerships**: Collaboration between organizations, educational institutions, and governments can lead to powerful upskilling initiatives. For instance, universities can work with enterprises to develop custom curricula and certificate programs in AI and relevant fields.
4. **Inclusive Policies**: Governments should formulate policies that ensure underrepresented demographics are included in reskilling and upskilling programs, thereby promoting equal opportunities and minimizing the potential for social inequalities.

Strategies for Successful Reskilling and Upskilling Initiatives

Organizations need a strategic approach to create an efficient and future-proof workforce. Here are some strategies worth considering:

1. **Mobilizing Management**: Organizations should communicate the importance of reskilling and upskilling at all levels, including top management. This helps develop a culture of continuous learning and adaptability.
2. **Identification of High-Priority Skill Gaps**: Companies must identify critical skills needed for their long-term business goals, analyzing the existing skills of their workforce and address any gaps through reskilling or upskilling initiatives.
3. **Implementation of Flexible Learning Paths**: Provide employees with diverse learning opportunities, such as online courses, on-site workshops, or partnering with educational institutions, which can easily be adjusted and updated depending on changing industry needs.

4. **Monitoring Progress and Adapting**: Regularly evaluate the progress of reskilling and upskilling initiatives to ensure that they are meeting their objectives. Customize the programs based on feedback and any changing requirements.

In conclusion, the growth of Generative AI presents novel opportunities and challenges for enterprises. Reskilling and upskilling are imperative in the preparation and adaptation of the workforce to meet these challenges head-on. Invest in your employees' development, collaborate with governments and educational institutions, and embrace a dynamic work culture to stay ahead in the AI-driven world.

11.3. Balancing Human and AI Collaboration

As we explore the potential for generative AI in the business world, a key challenge faced is to strike the right balance between the contributions of humans and artificial intelligence. Achieving this delicate equilibrium will require a deep understanding of the strengths and limitations of both entities, as well as strategies for designing systems that can capitalize on their respective capabilities. In this section, we will discuss various aspects of this balancing act, including augmentation, division of tasks, collaboration, trust, and ethics.

11.3.1. Augmentation

When discussing the relationship between human and AI collaboration, it is essential to highlight the concept of augmentation, which refers to the enhancement of human capabilities and efficiencies by leveraging artificial intelligence. The goal is not to replace humans entirely, but rather to enable them to perform tasks more effectively and creatively by providing appropriate AI-generated inputs and suggestions.

One way to achieve this is by designing AI systems that assist with decision-making processes. For example, generative AI can generate numerous possible solutions to a given problem in a short amount of time, allowing human team members to review and refine them with their unique domain expertise. By doing so, this partnership combines the computational prowess of AI with the nuanced understanding and intuitive thinking of humans.

11.3.2. Task Division

Determining the optimal division of labor between human and AI collaborators is another critical aspect of effective collaboration. Organizations must find suitable ways to distribute tasks among human team members and AI agents based on their relative strengths.

Typically, generative AI excels in data-driven, repetitive, and time-consuming tasks that require processing large volumes of information. With its ability to generate novel content, AI can rapidly produce multiple options or ideas, surpassing traditional human capabilities. By delegating these types of tasks to AI, human workers can focus on higher-level thought processes and strategy, such as refining AI-generated ideas or managing the overall project.

As a practical example, in the marketing domain, the AI could be responsible for generating several promotional design options, while human designers oversee and choose the final design. This pairing of human expertise with AI-generated suggestions allows for efficient and effective decision-making.

11.3.3. Collaboration

Developing effective communication mechanisms and collaborative tools that facilitate seamless interaction between human workers and AI systems is crucial in fostering successful collaboration. These tools should enable AI to understand human inputs and context, and vice versa.

Augmented reality (AR), virtual reality (VR), and mixed reality (MR) technologies can serve as platforms to achieve this interaction. These technologies provide immersive environments wherein humans and AI can work simultaneously on projects, allowing for real-time feedback and adjustment. For instance, AI-generated content can be visualized in three dimensions, potentially alongside work done by human collaborators, facilitating adjustments and refinements from both parties.

11.3.4. Trust

Establishing trust between human and AI collaborators is essential in any effective partnership, and achieving this may require overcoming some inherent challenges. Transparency plays a fundamental role in trust-building: having clarity around how AI systems function and make decisions, the rationale behind the outputs, and any associated limitations will help humans understand and confidently engage with AI-generated content.

Continuous involvement of human workers in the development, training, and refining of AI systems is a suitable way to establish familiarity and understanding, thereby fostering trust. Moreover, organizations should strive to create a culture of learning and experimentation that allows team members to familiarize themselves with AI capabilities and limitations without the fear of making mistakes or reprisals.

11.3.5. Ethics

Ethical considerations should be integrated into the design and implementation of AI systems, ensuring that both human and AI collaborators operate within acceptable moral and ethical boundaries. This is especially significant when AI-generated content has the potential to affect large audiences or lead to considerable decisions that impact people's lives.

A responsible approach to AI development involves creating guidelines and principles that focus on fairness, accountability, transparency, and the avoidance of unintentional biases. Regularly monitoring and auditing AI-generated content for compliance with ethical guidelines will further instill confidence in human collaborators and minimize the risk of causing harm.

Conclusion

In conclusion, achieving a balance in human-AI collaboration is crucial for the successful adoption of generative AI in enterprise settings. By leveraging the strengths of both parties and carefully attending to factors such as augmentation, task division, collaboration, trust, and ethics, organizations can create an environment in which human workers and AI agents work synergistically to achieve optimal results in computational creativity and business innovation. Ultimately, the future of generative AI will thrive in a collaborative landscape that capitalizes on the unique capabilities and strengths of both humans and AI systems.

Chapter 12: Legal and Regulatory Aspects of Generative AI

Introduction

As generative AI technologies develop and mature, their potential applications and implications for enterprises, governments, and individuals will also transform how we define the boundaries of ownership, accountability, and privacy. As such, there is an urgent need for devising legal and regulatory frameworks that can strike a balance between encouraging innovation, protecting stakeholders, and ensuring the responsible use of AI technologies.

In this chapter, we will explore an assortment of legal and regulatory issues that arise from the utilization of generative AI in various sectors. We will also discuss the roles and responsibilities of different stakeholders in mitigating potential risks and establishing best practices.

Ownership and Intellectual Property

Generative AI's ability to create novel content or analyze large datasets poses several questions around intellectual property rights, ownership, and attribution. It is essential to consider the following:

1. **AI-generated works:** Who is the rightful owner of AI-generated content, and is it entitled to copyright protection? One argument is that the creator of the AI system should be considered as the owner. However, the counterargument is that AI-generated works lack human authorship and should thus, not be granted copyright protection. Establishing a framework that clarifies ownership and copyright issues will be critical in ensuring that the rights of creators and users, both human and AI, are safeguarded.
2. **AI-assisted works:** Many AI tools, such as generative adversarial networks (GANs) and natural language processors (NLP), can be used for aiding human creators in generating new content, helping to reveal novel insights or predicting future trends. In these cases, how can we distinguish between the roles and contributions of AI systems and their human collaborators? There is a need for agreements that outline data and model ownership, licensing rights, and profit-sharing arrangements between stakeholders.
3. **Infringements:** AI systems might inadvertently infringe upon existing intellectual property rights by generating similar or derivative works. How can we mitigate the risks associated with such infringements and hold the liable party accountable? Organizations may need to implement robust monitoring and review processes to avoid inadvertent infringements and integrate attribution mechanisms that give credit to the original content creators.

Data Privacy and Security

Generative AI technologies often rely on vast amounts of data to train and generate novel output. As a result, concerns about data privacy and security become essential considerations for enterprises and regulators alike:

1. **Data protection:** Adhering to data protection rules, such as the General Data Protection Regulation (GDPR) in the EU, and the California Consumer Privacy Act (CCPA) in the United States, can be challenging when deploying AI technologies that require access to sensitive or personally identifiable information (PII). To mitigate the risks associated with data breaches and privacy infringements, organizations should strive to implement privacy-preserving mechanisms, such as secure multi-party computation (SMPC) or differential privacy.
2. **Bias and fairness:** Generative AI systems can often inherit and perpetuate biases present in the training data. Enterprises need to pay close attention to addressing issues of discrimination and fairness to comply with anti-discrimination legislation and maintain public trust. Ensuring transparency and releasing guidelines on AI system behavior and handling bias can help alleviate these concerns.
3. **Data breaches and hacks:** Generative AI technologies can be susceptible to adversarial attacks, whereby malicious actors feed the model erroneous or manipulated data to compromise its integrity or steal valuable information. Regulatory measures should be in place for ensuring the implementation of robust security protocols and incident reporting mechanisms.

Liability and Accountability

As generative AI systems become widely used, determining liability and accountability will become increasingly challenging:

1. **AI malfunctions and errors:** In and event where an AI system causes damages or harm, identifying who is liable for the consequences can be a complex process. A possible solution may involve establishing an AI-specific liability framework that addresses the roles and responsibilities of the AI developers, deployers, and users. This framework can also strike a balance between the need for innovation and protection of consumers from potential risks.
2. **Social and ethical implications:** Generative AI has the potential to negatively impact society, such as the spread of fake news, deepfakes, or promoting harmful biases. Companies and regulators must address these concerns by considering the social and ethical aspects of AI use and establishing guidelines or codes of conduct for responsible AI deployment.

Conclusion

Generative AI is undoubtedly transforming industries and has far-reaching implications for legal and regulatory landscapes. To ensure the responsible use and development of these technologies, governments, organizations, and technologists must collaborate to create comprehensive frameworks that address intellectual property, data privacy, security, and liability issues. Such frameworks will enable enterprises to maximize the potential of generative AI while balancing risks and protecting stakeholders' interests.

12.1. Intellectual Property Rights in Generative AI

One of the most important concerns when dealing with generative AI technology is the issue of intellectual property rights. As AI systems become increasingly proficient at generating creative work, questions surrounding ownership, originality, and the role of human intervention will become more pressing. This section will explore the intellectual property rights implications of generative AI and the need for legal and regulatory frameworks to evolve in response.

AI-generated Content and Ownership

Generative AI systems can be utilized to create various types of content, such as images, music, and text. This raises questions about who owns the rights to the generated content. Different parties may have various claims to ownership, including:

- The AI system itself: Some argue that the AI should be considered the creator and thus hold the rights to its creations.
- The AI programmer or developer: The programmer who developed the AI may claim to be the owner based on their role in creating the system that generated the content.
- The user of the AI system: In cases where the AI is used as a tool to create content, the user might

have a claim as the person guiding the AI towards the final output.
- The owner of the data used to train the AI: The AI system may be trained using copyrighted data, and the data owner may claim ownership rights to the content generated by the AI.

The Current Legal Landscape

In most jurisdictions, AI-generated content doesn't qualify for copyright protection since it is not created by a human. In the United States, for example, the U.S. Copyright Office has stated that works produced by non-humans are not copyrightable. Similarly, the European Union Intellectual Property Office (EUIPO) also requires that works be "original in the sense that they are the author's own intellectual creation" to be protected by copyright.

This means that under the current legal framework, AI-generated content may be considered in the public domain or not protected by copyright. However, in practice, some companies or copyright owners have attempted to claim rights over AI-generated content based on their input – for example, the owner of the AI system, the person who fed it data or the person who designed or commissioned the system.

Challenges and Opportunities

As AI-generated content becomes more prevalent, there is a growing need to develop a clear framework addressing the intellectual property rights associated with AI creations. This will involve tackling several challenges, including:

1. **Defining originality and creativity**: How should the law account for the unique attributes of AI-generated content, which may not be easily attributable to a human creator? Should originality and creativity be redefined, or should new categories of protectable works be created to accommodate AI-generated content?
2. **Incentivizing AI development**: Intellectual property rights often serve to incentivize innovation and creativity by granting exclusive rights to inventors or creators. Legal frameworks for AI-generated content should strike a careful balance to encourage investment and development in AI systems, while also protecting the interests of stakeholders like users and the public.
3. **Attribution and moral rights**: How should the law deal with the attribution of AI-generated content? In cases where there is no clear "human author," should there be a provision to acknowledge the AI system itself? And how should the various parties involved in AI development and use – such as programmers, data providers, and end-users – be recognized in terms of ownership or rights?
4. **Fairness and transparency**: Any legal framework addressing AI-generated content should ensure fairness, transparency, and non-discriminatory treatment for all stakeholders. This could be achieved through clear guidelines and regulations, as well as enforcement mechanisms that safeguard against misuse or abuse.

The Road Ahead

As AI systems become more entrenched in our daily lives, the question of ownership and rights in the content they generate will become increasingly important. The current intellectual property rights framework may not be adequate to account for the unique features of AI-generated content, necessitating the development of new laws and interpretations.

One potential approach could involve a mixed model, where AI-generated content is eligible for a different category of intellectual property rights – perhaps with a lower threshold of protection than traditional copyright. This could strike a balance between protection, originality, and the interests of various stakeholders.

Ultimately, the future of intellectual property rights in the context of generative AI will depend on the ability of legal systems to adapt and evolve in response to this rapidly developing technology. As lawmakers grapple with these challenges, it is clear that generative AI will continue to spur important debates about creativity, ownership, and the future of intellectual property rights.

12.2. Data Privacy and Synthetic Data

1. Introduction

As we delve deeper into the world of generative AI applications for enterprises, it is imperative to address the critical issues of data privacy and synthetic data. The increasing volume and variety of data have raised concerns about the protection of sensitive information and individuals' privacy. At the same time, synthetic data is emerging as a potential solution to mitigate these concerns. This section will discuss the importance of data privacy, the General Data Protection Regulation (GDPR), and synthetic data's role in addressing privacy-related issues.

2. The Importance of Data Privacy

Data privacy plays a crucial role in establishing trust between enterprises and consumers while ensuring regulatory compliance. The chances of data breaches have increased due to the rapidly growing volume of personal and sensitive data stored by organizations. These breaches can lead to severe consequences, including reputational damage, financial penalties, and loss of consumer trust.

Moreover, advancements in artificial intelligence have made it easier to identify and re-identify individuals using AI and ML algorithms, even in anonymized data sets. Techniques such as federated learning and differential privacy aim to address this issue by minimizing the amount of data shared and protecting sensitive information. However, these are often not sufficient to ensure total privacy.

3. The General Data Protection Regulation (GDPR)

The GDPR, a European Union-wide data protection legislation, is a crucial legal framework that governs how personal data is collected, processed, and stored. It imposes strict limitations on data processing activities, both in terms of collecting information about individuals and how it is used for various purposes, including AI training.

One of the key provisions in the GDPR is providing users with control over their data, such as the right to access, modify, or delete it. Organizations must ensure transparency in their data processing operations and make it possible for users to exercise these rights.

GDPR also requires organizations to implement appropriate technical and organizational measures to protect personal data, which poses a significant challenge for enterprises relying on large-scale AI systems that require vast amounts of data for training.

Compliance with GDPR regulations can be difficult and expensive for organizations, especially those dealing with disparate data sources, intricate data pipelines, and complex AI models. Non-compliance can result in significant fines, legal actions, and irreparable damage to an organization's reputation.

4. Synthetic Data: A Potential Solution

Synthetic data offers immense potential to address the challenges posed by data privacy requirements while still enabling enterprises to harness the power of AI. It refers to the artificial creation of data points that closely resemble the characteristics of the original data set without containing any sensitive information or revealing the identity of individuals.

4.1. Benefits of Synthetic Data

In the context of data privacy, synthetic data offers several advantages:

1. **Privacy compliance:** Since synthetic data does not contain personally identifiable information, it can circumvent privacy regulations and help enterprises

remain compliant with GDPR and other data protection laws.

2. **Reduced risk of data breaches:** As synthetic data does not contain any sensitive information, the risk of data breaches significantly decreases.

3. **Data accessibility and sharing:** Synthetic data can be openly shared between departments, organizations, and researchers without violating privacy laws, making it easier for enterprises to collaborate and innovate.

4. **Reducing bias and improving data quality:** By creating synthetic data that accurately represents various demographics, organizations can ensure unbiased AI models and improve the quality of their predictions.

4.2. Challenges and Limitations

Despite its benefits, synthetic data has its limitations:

1. **Maintaining data utility:** Ensuring that synthetic data maintains the same statistical properties and usability of the original data can be challenging. If the synthetic data does not accurately represent the original data, the resultant AI models may not perform as expected.

2. **Computational complexity:** Generating high-quality synthetic data requires sophisticated algorithms and computational resources, which may be expensive for organizations with resource constraints.

3. **Algorithmic transparency:** While synthetic data can be designed to be more transparent than original data, the underlying algorithms used to generate the synthetic data must be disclosed and explained to regulatory bodies to ensure compliance with data privacy laws.

5. Conclusion

The future of generative AI for enterprises hinges on striking a balance between harnessing the power of data-driven insights and ensuring data privacy. Synthetic data has emerged as a potential solution to overcome privacy-related challenges while maintaining data utility. As the landscape evolves, organizations must stay up-to-date with the latest developments in privacy-preserving techniques, synthetic data generation, and regulatory changes to exploit the full potential of generative AI, foster innovation, and maintain consumer trust.

12.3. Regulatory frameworks for AI technologies

As AI technologies rapidly evolve and permeate various aspects of modern society, establishing a robust regulatory framework becomes increasingly vital. This is particularly true for generative AI, which possesses tremendous potential to revolutionize how we leverage data and create new solutions. In this section, we aim to delve deeper into the importance of regulatory frameworks, explore the challenges in their formulation, and discuss several key components necessary for their success.

12.3.1. The importance of regulatory frameworks for AI

Generative AI and other AI technologies hold the promise of significant advancements across diverse fields such as healthcare, finance, and creative industries. However, they also pose numerous ethical, social, and legal challenges that need to be addressed responsibly. Regulatory frameworks are crucial for several reasons:

1. **Safety and Security**: As AI-powered systems become more autonomously capable, it is crucial to ensure their safe and secure deployment. Regulatory frameworks can help establish standards and protocols to mitigate risks and vulnerabilities, particularly in critical systems like autonomous vehicles and industrial automation.
2. **Privacy and Data Protection**: AI algorithms typically require vast amounts of data for training and optimization. A regulatory framework is necessary to safeguard personal and sensitive information, while ensuring that organizations adhere to best practices for data management and privacy protection.
3. **Accountability and Transparency**: Determining responsibility in cases of AI-generated harm can be extremely complex, given the diverse stakeholders and potential intermediaries involved. Regulatory frameworks can help create clear guidelines for attributing liability, and mandate levels of explainability and interpretability in AI systems.
4. **Ethics and fairness**: AI systems may inadvertently amplify social biases, prejudice, and discrimination. Thus, it is important to establish a set of ethical principles that can guide their design and deployment, ensuring they respect human values and maintain fairness.
5. **Innovation and Competition**: Broad accessibility to AI technologies drives widespread innovation and economic growth. Regulations can encourage healthy competition by preventing monopolies or the weaponization of AI technologies, while also providing incentives for research and development.

12.3.2. Challenges in establishing regulatory frameworks for AI

Creating an effective regulatory framework for AI technologies involves several notable challenges:

1. **Rapid Technological Advancements**: AI technologies are advancing at an unprecedented pace, which makes it difficult for regulatory bodies to keep up with the latest developments and emerging risks.
2. **Global Coordination**: AI applications and their consequences are not constrained by geographical borders. International collaboration is necessary to develop globally applicable guidelines, with harmonized approaches to privacy, data sharing, and accountability.
3. **Striking the Right Balance**: Overly restrictive regulations could hinder innovation and stifle economic growth, whereas excessively lax regulation could facilitate misuse and manipulation. Striking the right balance is crucial to maximize the benefits of AI while minimizing potential harm.
4. **Technical Expertise**: Developing and implementing AI regulatory frameworks requires a deep understanding of the technology, its potential impacts, and accompanying risks. Leveraging expert knowledge from various fields is essential to ensure well-informed and effective regulations.

12.3.3. Key components of a robust regulatory framework for AI

An effective regulatory framework for AI should encompass the following key components:

1. **Clear Definitions and Scope**: The regulatory framework should establish a clear set of definitions for AI technologies and their applications, setting the boundaries within which regulations apply.
2. **Inclusive Stakeholder Engagement**: A wide range of stakeholders, including governments, private organizations, research institutions, civil society, and the general public should be involved in the development of regulatory frameworks. This ensures representation of diverse perspectives and needs.
3. **Ethical Principles**: Regulations for AI should be guided by a common set of ethical principles, such as fairness, transparency, privacy, human augmentation, and accountability. These principles can help establish a strong value system for AI development and deployment.
4. **Standards and Best Practices**: Regulatory frameworks should be aligned with established technical standards and best practices. This includes creating benchmarks for AI system performance, testing, data management, and cybersecurity.
5. **Legal Liability and Redress Mechanisms**: The regulatory framework should establish legal liability for AI-generated harm and provide efficient mechanisms for dispute resolution and redress.
6. **Ongoing Monitoring and Evaluation**: Given the rapid pace of AI development, it is crucial to monitor the effectiveness of implemented regulations continuously, and update or modify them as needed.

In conclusion, establishing effective regulatory frameworks for AI technologies is essential to unlocking their tremendous potential while addressing the associated risks and challenges. Regulatory frameworks should be developed through a collaborative, multi-stakeholder effort that balances innovation with protecting the rights, values, and well-being of individuals and society as a whole.

Chapter 13: Generative AI in Emerging Markets

13.1 Introduction

In the constantly evolving technological landscape, the concept of artificial intelligence (AI) has become ubiquitous, and its capabilities continue to widen. One area where AI has shown immense potential is that of emerging markets. In this chapter, we explore the role of Generative AI in emerging markets, examining how these technologies can transform industries, create new opportunities, and foster innovation in the developing world. These markets offer companies untapped growth potential, and these same companies are recognizing the value of using AI-driven solutions to unleash that potential.

Generative AI refers to the subset of AI technologies that can create something new, from a piece of music to an entire business model. By combining data analysis, pattern recognition, and deep learning algorithms, Generative AI can help organizations find creative and innovative solutions to existing problems, as well as identify new opportunities.

13.2 Generative AI Applications in Emerging Markets

13.2.1 Agriculture

In many emerging markets, agriculture forms a significant part of the economy, and AI technologies are playing a massive role in reshaping the industry. Generative AI can help farmers make better decisions, optimize processes, and enhance productivity through predictive models, risk assessment, and generating innovative agricultural practices.

For example, AI-powered drones can analyze large tracts of farmland to identify patterns in soil and environmental conditions, and recommend optimized planting and fertilization strategies. Generative AI has also shown promise in predicting crop yields and detecting diseases in crops using pattern recognition, allowing farmers to take necessary action and minimize losses.

13.2.2 Finance

Financial services in emerging markets often struggle with the challenge of reaching large populations that have historically remained unbanked or underbanked. Generative AI models can serve as valuable tools in analyzing and predicting customer behaviors, offering targeted recommendations, and improving overall financial inclusion.

For instance, AI-powered chatbots can assist customers in opening bank accounts, obtaining loans, or learning about financial products without the need for physical bank branches. Generative AI can also help financial institutions devise personalized banking services and loan products tailored to the unique needs of customers in these markets, thus expanding their coverage and enabling financial growth.

13.2.3 Healthcare

Lack of quality healthcare facilities and trained professionals is a major concern in many emerging markets. Generative AI has the potential to play a transformative role in the healthcare sector, considerably improving patient outcomes and optimizing resource allocation.

AI-driven systems can help in identifying potential health risks, generating preventive strategies, and improving disease diagnosis. For example, AI algorithms can quickly analyze medical images, such as X-rays or MRIs, to identify abnormalities and early signs of diseases. Additionally, generative AI can optimize treatment and drug development processes, leading to more effective patient care and disease management.

13.2.4 Education

Education systems in emerging markets often suffer from inadequate infrastructure, teacher shortages, and outdated curricula. Generative AI presents an opportunity to bridge this gap and enhance the quality of education in these countries.

By utilizing AI-driven platforms and tools, educators can create personalized learning experiences for students, identify their strengths and weaknesses, and offer customized feedback. Generative AI can also assist in developing innovative teaching methods or creating engaging educational content to help students excel.

13.3 Challenges and Ethical Considerations

While the benefits of Generative AI in emerging markets are immense, there are potential challenges and ethical considerations that must be addressed.

13.3.1 Data Privacy

The implementation of AI systems often involves collecting and processing massive amounts of data, which raises concerns about data privacy and security. Strict protocols and regulations must be established and enforced, particularly regarding sensitive information and GDPR in emerging markets.

13.3.2 Bias and Fairness

There is a risk that AI models could perpetuate or exacerbate societal biases if the training data used reflects existing discrimination or prejudice. Efforts must ensure that the AI systems deployed in emerging markets promote fairness and inclusivity by using diverse datasets and minimizing biases in model training.

13.3.3 Job Displacement

The automation of various tasks and processes by generative AI technologies may lead to concerns about job displacement, particularly in developing countries with limited opportunities for job diversification or reskilling. It is vital to strike a balance between embracing AI-driven innovation and protecting the workforce.

13.3.4 Digital Divide

Although AI technologies have the potential to improve life in emerging markets, they could also exacerbate the prevalent digital divide. As rural and underdeveloped areas lack the necessary infrastructure or access to technology, AI-driven services could remain out of reach for many. Investment in digital infrastructure and the promotion of digital inclusivity are necessary to counter this issue.

13.4 Conclusion

In conclusion, Generative AI presents vast opportunities for innovation and growth across various sectors in emerging markets. As governments and organizations invest in digital infrastructure and allocate necessary resources, they have the potential to significantly impact the lives of millions, bringing about tangible socio-economic benefits.

However, efforts must be made to address the inherent challenges and ethical considerations to ensure a just and inclusive growth trajectory. Collaborative efforts between governments, businesses, and local communities play a vital role in leveraging Generative AI technologies, maximizing their potential while mitigating risks, and working towards a brighter future for emerging markets globally.

13.1. The potential of generative AI in developing countries

Developing countries, despite facing numerous socio-economic challenges, hold immense potential for the application of generative AI. The unique combination of exploding population growth, increased access to technology, and a rapidly evolving workforce can pave the way for generative AI to make a significant impact, providing new opportunities and driving innovation.

13.1.1. Enhancing Quality Education

Generative AI can play an essential role in improving education in developing countries. The long-standing struggle of teacher shortages, inadequate learning materials, and poor infrastructure, can be mitigated through AI-powered tools, such as intelligent tutoring systems and adaptive learning platforms. These platforms can offer personalized learning experiences, understanding each student's strengths and weaknesses, tailoring their education accordingly. Furthermore, AI's language capabilities can be utilized for efficient translation of educational materials, making them accessible to diverse groups of students.

13.1.2. Accelerating Agriculture and Food Production

Agriculture remains a predominant source of livelihood and sustenance in developing countries. Generative AI can revolutionize local agricultural industries by generating custom crop-related insights, such as predicting weather patterns, soil quality, and potential pest risks. As a result, farmers can make data-driven decisions to optimize crop selection, planting times, and fertilization practices. Additionally, AI-powered smart irrigation and monitoring systems can help reduce water wastage and detect early signs of plant diseases, addressing global challenges like food security and limited resources.

13.1.3. Enabling Affordable Healthcare

Healthcare systems in developing countries are often overburdened, underfunded, and unable to meet the demands of rapidly growing populations. Generative AI can bridge these gaps by generating virtual healthcare assistants, enabling remote diagnostics, and facilitating knowledge-sharing between medical professionals globally. It can also be employed for detecting patterns in patient data for improved diagnosis and predicting patient outcomes. Furthermore, AI-driven drug discovery can speed up the process of developing affordable medicines, essential for addressing healthcare challenges in low-income regions.

13.1.4. Driving Innovation and Supporting Local Industries

Generative AI has the potential not only to nurture nascent startups but also to create an entrepreneurial ecosystem by deploying localized AI-driven solutions. Developing countries can harness AI-powered tools for local product design, business strategy optimization, and supply chain management, paving the way for new ventures and accelerating the growth of existing ones. Besides, generative AI technologies can encourage skill development programs, guiding the workforce to meet the requirements of emerging industries.

13.1.5. Strengthening Infrastructure and Sustainable Development

Developing countries often lack well-built infrastructure and can suffer from outdated urban planning methodologies. Generative AI can foster sustainable urban development by generating smart city solutions, optimizing transport systems, improving waste management, and enabling data-driven policy decisions. By monitoring and analyzing real-time data, AI-powered tools can optimize energy distribution and consumption, contributing to greener communities and better environmental health.

13.1.6. Enhancing Crisis Response and Management

Developing countries generally face a higher vulnerability to natural disasters, pandemics, and socioeconomic crises. Generative AI can augment their crisis response systems by providing real-time data analysis, predictive modeling, and resource optimization. Integrating AI-driven information systems across different sectors can streamline disaster management, making it more proactive and accurate, improving preparedness, response, and recovery processes.

13.1.7. Closing the Digital Divide

While decreased costs and increased accessibility have improved internet penetration in developing countries, a significant digital divide still exists. Generative AI can help bridge the gap by creating customized digital solutions, fostering local language support, and promoting digital literacy. Moreover, AI-driven solutions can ensure that disadvantaged communities receive inclusive access to essential services, like education, healthcare, and financial services.

In conclusion, generative AI holds enormous promise for revolutionizing various sectors in developing countries. To realize this potential, it is imperative to collaborate with governments, research organizations, and businesses, fostering a comprehensive approach. These endeavors can create a ripple effect, driving social, economic, and environmental changes, ultimately improving the quality of life for millions.

13.2. Unique Challenges and Opportunities

Generative AI is a rapidly growing field, offering a plethora of opportunities for enterprises and their creative processes. As with any emerging technology, generative AI brings with it several unique challenges and opportunities that businesses must navigate. In this section, we will explore some of these issues, including the barriers to entry, the ethical implications, and the potential for transformative change across industries.

13.2.1. Barriers to Entry

For many organizations, the prospect of incorporating generative AI into their workflow might be hindered by several factors:

13.2.1.1. Data Access and Quality

Quality data is the lifeblood of AI development, and this is particularly true for generative AI models. Developing a reliable and efficient generative AI system requires vast volumes of quality data to train and fine-tune the algorithms. Many small to medium-sized enterprises (SMEs) might lack access to such data, limiting their ability to leverage the power of generative AI.

13.2.1.2. Technical Expertise

The deployment and maintenance of generative AI models can be a technically challenging endeavor. It requires a deep understanding of the underlying algorithms and proficiency in programming languages such as Python, TensorFlow, or PyTorch. Many SMEs might not have the in-house expertise needed to navigate these complexities.

13.2.1.3. Computational Resources

Training generative AI models can be a computationally intensive process, especially for large-scale projects. This can lead to high costs associated with acquiring the necessary hardware or cloud computing resources. Enterprises without the required capital may find it challenging to invest in high-performance computing infrastructure.

13.2.1.4. Regulatory Compliance and Security

The rapid adoption of AI technology has given rise to new regulatory requirements to ensure the ethical and responsible use of data. Enterprises venturing into generative AI will need to comply with these regulations, which may not always be straightforward. Additionally, implementing generative AI systems may require rigorous data security measures to protect sensitive information from malicious attacks.

13.2.2. Ethical Considerations

Generative AI has the potential to revolutionize numerous industries positively. However, it also presents several ethical challenges that organizations should carefully consider:

13.2.2.1. Responsible AI Creation

Generative AI models can unwittingly generate harmful or biased content if not designed with care. Developers must ensure that their AI systems are not perpetuating biases or promoting inappropriate content. Responsible AI creation will involve actively monitoring and mitigating these risks, as well as engaging in an open discourse with stakeholders to address any concerns that may arise.

13.2.2.2. Intellectual Property and Ownership

The question of ownership and intellectual property rights for AI-generated content is yet to be resolved fully. As generated content becomes more prevalent and sophisticated, organizations will need to navigate this complex landscape and establish appropriate guidelines and practices to safeguard their interests while also being mindful of others' rights.

13.2.2.3. Impact on Employment and Creativity

Generative AI can augment and enhance human creativity, but it also raises concerns about its potential impact on employment and the role of humans in creative processes. Organizations must consider these implications and strive to balance the benefits of automation with the value of human creativity and judgment.

13.2.3. Transformative Potential

Despite the challenges outlined above, generative AI presents several opportunities to transform the creative and strategic processes across industries:

13.2.3.1. Enhanced Productivity

Generative AI systems can help automate repetitive tasks, freeing up human resources for higher-value activities. By streamlining workflows and reducing bottlenecks, organizations can significantly improve their overall productivity and competitiveness.

13.2.3.2. Novel Solutions and Ideas

Generative AI's ability to process high volumes of data and generate new content makes it uniquely positioned to help organizations discover innovative solutions to complex problems. By uncovering previously unexplored design patterns, generative AI can act as a catalyst for breakthroughs and industry advancements.

13.2.3.3. Personalization and Customer Engagement

Generative AI can analyze customer preferences, behavior, and demographics to generate customized content, products, and experiences. This level of personalization can lead to deeper customer engagement and loyalty, making it a valuable tool for organizations seeking to strengthen their customer relationships.

13.2.3.4. Collaboration and Cross-Industry Synergy

Generative AI can facilitate collaboration between human experts and machines, enabling organizations to tap into a vast pool of knowledge and expertise.

This collaborative approach can lead to new insights and breakthroughs, fostering cross-industry synergy and innovation.

13.2.4. Conclusion

The future of generative AI promises both challenges and opportunities for enterprises seeking to leverage this transformative technology. Organizations must work together—across teams, departments, and sectors—to navigate the complexities of generative AI adoption while capitalizing on its tremendous potential. By fostering responsible AI practices, addressing ethical concerns, and investing in human-AI collaboration, businesses can propel themselves to the forefront of computational creativity and generate unprecedented benefits for their customers, employees, and stakeholders.

13.3. Case Studies of Successful AI Implementations

As generative AI continues to evolve and push the boundaries of what machines can create, influential brands and innovative startups around the world have started to take notice. In this section, we explore some of the most successful AI implementations to learn from their technique and strategy. We examine a variety of industries, from fashion and art to business operations and marketing. These case studies will provide tangible examples and insights into the transformative potential of generative AI for enterprises.

13.3.1. Fashion and Design: Stitch Fix

Stitch Fix, an online personal styling service, employs generative AI algorithms to power its recommendation engine. The algorithm creates a personalized selection of clothes for each customer by combining historical data on their preferences, product characteristics, and user interactions.

Used by many customers to obtain clothing recommendations for their personalized "Fixes," the generative AI system incorporates a broad range of data points. It first learns from customer feedback on style, color, fit, and other attributes, as well as explicit customer preferences, to create a unique set of styling parameters. Next, the generative AI system blends these parameters with the company's expertise in trends and fashion industry standards, resulting in curated clothing selections that balance both customer preferences and broader apparel trends.

By leveraging generative AI in this capacity, Stitch Fix has optimized its stylist support system, enhanced customer experiences, and improved its retention rates and revenue streams.

13.3.2. Art and Creativity: Christie's Auction House

Christie's, a leading international auction house, made history in 2018 when it became the first auction house to sell an AI-generated artwork. The piece, titled "Portrait of Edmond de Belamy," was created by the

Paris-based art collective Obvious using a Generative Adversarial Network (GAN).

GANs are a type of deep learning framework, consisting of two neural networks – the generator and the discriminator. These networks can "learn" from a dataset of existing artworks to generate new and unique pieces of art. The generator creates new images while the discriminator evaluates the authenticity of the generated images based on the training data.

The auction of "Portrait of Edmond de Belamy" marked a watershed moment for the merging of art and technology, as well as the growing influence of generative AI in shaping the art world. The sale not only sparked debate about AI's role in creativity but also demonstrated the potential for AI-generated artworks to achieve substantial market value.

13.3.3. Business Operations: Google DeepMind

Google DeepMind, an innovative AI company, has successfully applied generative AI to the optimization of data center cooling. By deploying DeepMind's AI technology, Google reduced its data center cooling energy consumption by 40%.

DeepMind's AI system employs a series of neural networks to devise more efficient strategies for controlling the cooling infrastructure in data centers. These strategies include determining optimal temperatures, coordinating cooling equipment, and managing air flows. The neural networks are trained through simulations, allowing them to analyze extensive data on past performance and arrive at optimal control strategies.

This implementation exemplifies not just the power of generative AI to optimize complex systems, but also its potential to reduce energy consumption and lower greenhouse gas emissions.

13.3.4. Advertising and Marketing: Lexus

Lexus, the luxury vehicle division of Toyota, partnered with IBM Watson and creative agency The & Partnership to develop the world's first AI-scripted car commercial. The ad, titled "Driven by Intuition," features a Lexus ES executive sedan and combines visually striking sequences with a compelling narrative to appeal to viewers' emotions.

To create the script, IBM Watson analyzed a broad range of data points, including 15 years' worth of award-winning luxury advertisements, insight reports on human intuition, and relevant articles and interviews. The AI analyzed emotional and narrative elements from this information and then produced a rough script that retained human inputs for refinement.

The result was a unique and engaging car commercial that pushed the boundaries of creative advertising, highlighting the transformative potential of generative AI in the world of marketing and brand storytelling.

Conclusion

These case studies demonstrate the diverse applications of generative AI across various industries and underscore its potential to reshape enterprises. AI-powered systems are capable of significant optimization and customization, improving user experiences, and informing creative processes in ways previously thought beyond machines' reach. As generative AI continues to evolve, businesses must adapt and invest in this technology to maintain competitiveness and foster innovation in the future.

Chapter 14: The Democratization of Generative AI

14.1 Introduction

The democratization of generative AI refers to the widespread availability and accessibility of AI technology and tools to people from various backgrounds and skill levels. As generative AI continues to evolve, developers, designers, artists, and business professionals all have increased access to technology and the resources necessary to create innovative applications and solutions.

Integrating AI into business operations and decision-making is becoming increasingly popular as organizations recognize the potential benefits, which include improving customer experiences, streamlining workflows, and enhancing creative processes. As such, the democratization of generative AI plays a vital role in making these technologies accessible to a broader audience and enabling them to leverage the potential benefits of AI applications.

In this chapter, we will discuss the implications of the democratization of generative AI on various industries, as well as its potential to create a new wave of innovative and creative applications.

14.2 Key Factors Driving the Democratization of Generative AI

14.2.1 Advancements in AI Tools and Platforms

One of the primary drivers of the democratization of generative AI lies in the growing capabilities and user-friendly nature of AI tools and platforms. Through the development and introduction of robust and accessible AI frameworks, like TensorFlow and PyTorch, individuals without extensive AI backgrounds can explore and develop AI applications.

These platforms often include pre-built algorithms and libraries that allow users to experiment with AI without having extensive technical knowledge. Open source communities also add to this accessibility by contributing new developments, ensuring that AI technology remains available to everyone.

14.2.2 The Rise of AI-as-a-Service (AIaaS)

The AI-as-a-Service (AIaaS) model provides organizations with on-demand access to AI resources, tools, and infrastructure without the need for in-house development or implementation. This model has proven successful for businesses hoping to utilize AI without the knowledge, time, or resources necessary for dedicated AI projects.

With cloud-based AI platforms like Google Cloud AI, Amazon Web Services (AWS) AI, and Microsoft Azure Machine Learning, it's easier than ever for startups and small businesses to access powerful AI capabilities, lowering the barriers to entry for incorporating AI into various applications.

14.2.3 Evolving Educational Resources

Alongside advancements in AI tools and platforms, increasing educational resources provide another driver of generative AI democratization. The availability of online courses, tutorials, and workshops on AI-related topics has expanded significantly in recent years.

Platforms like Coursera, edX, Udemy, and many others offer courses in data science, machine learning, and AI development, making it easier for individuals from various backgrounds to gain essential knowledge and skills.

Such educational resources help bridge the gap between individuals who lack formal training in AI-related fields and professionals who are well-versed in the nuances of AI technology.

14.3 Potential Impact on Industries

14.3.1 Media and Entertainment

The media and entertainment industry have much to gain from the democratization of generative AI. This technology can enhance creative processes, allowing for the development of more engaging, immersive, and personalized experiences.

For example, generative AI can be used for scriptwriting, video editing, and music composition, enabling content creators to explore new ideas and styles through machine-generated suggestions. Additionally, AI-driven personalization can optimize content recommendations, ensuring that users find content that resonates with them.

14.3.2 Art and Design

Generative AI also has profound implications for the art and design world. With the accessibility of AI-driven design tools, artists can explore novel styles, techniques, and ideas.

These tools can generate new patterns, textures, and shapes, which aid designers in finding unique and aesthetically pleasing components for their work. Moreover, artists can employ generative AI in the creation of entirely AI-driven artwork, further pushing the boundaries of creativity.

14.3.3 Business and Decision-making

As AI becomes increasingly democratized, it will also play a growing role in business decisions and strategies. AI-powered analytics and automated decision-making can offer valuable insights into customer behavior, preferences, and market trends.

Combined with generative AI's potential to brainstorm innovative ideas and solutions, organizations can utilize these technologies to devise more effective strategies, taking into account a wealth of data that would be difficult or time-consuming for humans to analyze.

14.4 Future Prospects

The democratization of generative AI promises a more innovative, creative, and efficient future across industries. As AI becomes more accessible, it will drive increased experimentation, allowing more organizations to recognize the potential benefits of AI technology.

Moreover, key stakeholders should invest in education, training programs, and increased collaboration across different fields to support the democratization process. By engaging a diverse range of talent, the potential for transformative innovation in generative AI will only continue to grow.

14.1 Making AI Accessible to All Enterprises

Generative AI has the potential to revolutionize businesses by automating tedious processes, optimizing workflows, and sparking innovations. However, its true potential can only be realized when it becomes accessible and convenient for all enterprises, regardless of size or industry. In this section, we will discuss the steps necessary for making generative AI accessible to all enterprises and the likely benefits that will follow.

1. Democratizing AI technologies

To make generative AI available for various enterprises, there is a need to democratize AI technologies. This means that powerful tools and platforms that were previously reserved for large corporations or research institutions must become accessible, affordable, and user-friendly.

Efforts towards this goal are already in progress in the form of open-source libraries (TensorFlow, PyTorch) and platforms (Hugging Face, OpenAI) that aim to make it easier for developers to build AI-powered applications. Furthermore, cloud providers like AWS, Google, and Microsoft offer pre-built AI services that enable enterprises to implement machine learning models with no prior knowledge.

Moving forward, there must be more emphasis on developing low-cost, user-friendly tools and platforms that cater specifically to small and medium enterprises. These tools should enable companies to easily train, customize, and deploy AI models without requiring a deep understanding of AI or the need to hire AI specialists.

2. Collaboration and knowledge sharing

For generative AI to become widely available, collaboration between different stakeholders in the AI ecosystem is necessary. This includes academic researchers, industry leaders, and AI service providers, all of whom should join forces towards a common goal. By sharing knowledge and resources, we can accelerate AI adoption and reduce barriers to entry for smaller enterprises.

Moreover, fostering cross-industry collaboration can help identify novel use cases for generative AI in various sectors. Industry associations and consortiums should sponsor research initiatives and set up shared AI research labs that pool resources and tap into the collective intelligence of their members. Public-private partnerships could also catalyze AI adoption by small and medium-sized enterprises and help them overcome financial and knowledge constraints.

3. Education and upskilling

Another crucial factor in making generative AI available to a wider range of enterprises is the development of a workforce skilled in AI technology.

There must be an emphasis on providing education and upskilling opportunities not only for technical professionals but also for existing employees so that they can leverage AI in their day-to-day activities.

This can be achieved through the creation of dedicated AI training programs at universities and vocational schools, as well as by offering workshops, boot camps, and online courses for working professionals. Additionally, enterprises should invest in continuous upskilling programs for their employees, fostering a culture of lifelong learning and curiosity.

Moreover, investment in AI education initiatives should be inclusive, targeting underrepresented groups and ensuring equal access to opportunities that can create a diverse talent pool.

4. Establishing ethical guidelines and robust regulatory frameworks

To ensure that AI is deployed responsibly and to mitigate potential risks, companies should develop and adhere to ethical guidelines and best practices. These guidelines should focus on data privacy, algorithmic fairness, and transparency to build trust among users and stakeholders.

A robust regulatory framework is also necessary to address potential negative consequences, such as job displacement or biased decision-making. Regulators should work with industry leaders to establish clear and enforceable AI policies that protect individuals and ensure an equitable distribution of AI's benefits across enterprises.

5. Developing AI-powered applications tailored to specific industries

Generative AI solutions must be relevant to the unique challenges and opportunities of various industries to be widely adopted. By developing industry-specific AI applications, smaller enterprises can gain access to powerful tools that can improve operations and spur innovation.

These applications could range from AI-powered drug discovery platforms in the pharmaceutical industry to generative design tools for architecture and construction. The more refined and targeted these applications are towards real-world challenges, the more likely they are to be adopted by a wider range of businesses.

Conclusion

Making generative AI accessible to all enterprises is critical to unlocking its full potential for value creation and innovation. By democratizing AI tools, fostering collaboration, and investing in education and ethical guidelines, we can accelerate the adoption of generative AI across various industries and improve the overall competitiveness and efficiency of businesses worldwide.

14.2. Open-source Initiatives and their Role in AI Democratization

The past decade has witnessed a wave of rapid advancements in artificial intelligence (AI), driving enterprises towards adopting these technologies for solving challenging problems and achieving competitive advantages. However, the complexity and high entry barriers in AI also make it rather exclusive to big corporations and well-funded research organizations. In response, the development of several open-source initiatives has begun to play a critical role in democratizing access to AI capabilities.

Open-source Software Libraries and Frameworks

Various open-source software libraries and frameworks have propelled AI democratization by providing developers and researchers with easy access to tools and resources to create AI applications without needing to start from scratch. Key examples include:

1. **TensorFlow** by Google: An open-source software library for high-performance numerical computation. It is widely used in machine learning and deep learning applications, and offers flexibility to express a wide variety of algorithms on multiple platforms.
2. **PyTorch** by Facebook: Another popular machine learning library, PyTorch offers efficient tensor operations, automatic differentiation, and deep learning capabilities. Its dynamic computation graph enhances its flexibility and efficiency, making it a top choice for researchers.
3. **Scikit-learn**: A Python library for machine learning, scikit-learn offers a variety of algorithms for tasks like classification, regression, clustering, and dimensionality reduction. Its simple and efficient tools

make it accessible to both beginners and advanced users.
4. **Keras**: A high-level, user-friendly API for building and training deep learning models. Integrated with TensorFlow, Keras is designed for rapid experimentation and development, reducing the entry barrier for newcomers to the field.

These libraries and frameworks enable individuals and small organizations to access cutting-edge AI technologies, thereby fostering a more inclusive and innovative AI ecosystem.

Open Data Initiatives

AI democratization also greatly depends on the accessibility of data. High-quality, diverse datasets are integral for training and validating AI models. Open data initiatives have emerged to accommodate this need.

1. **ImageNet**: A large, publicly available dataset containing over 14 million annotated images. ImageNet has been instrumental in advancing computer vision research by offering training data for object recognition and detection algorithms.
2. **Common Crawl**: An open repository of web-crawled data from billions of pages, Common Crawl provides an extensive corpus of text for natural language processing and machine learning applications.
3. **Open Government Datasets**: Many countries, such as the United States and the United Kingdom, have released vast troves of public data for various applications, including economic analysis, weather forecasting, and healthcare. These datasets offer

substantial opportunities for AI-driven analysis and decision-making.

Pre-trained Models and Transfer Learning

Another essential development contributing to AI democratization is the rise of pre-trained models and transfer learning. Pre-trained models have been trained on large datasets and can be fine-tuned to perform specific tasks with relatively smaller datasets. Some noteworthy examples include:

1. **BERT** (Bidirectional Encoder Representations from Transformers): Developed by Google, BERT is a pre-trained language model that can be fine-tuned for tasks like sentiment analysis, named entity recognition, and machine translation.
2. **GPT-3** (Generative Pre-trained Transformer 3): Created by OpenAI, GPT-3 is a state-of-the-art language model that can perform tasks like text generation, translation, and summarization without specialized training.
3. **VGG** and **ResNet**: Popular pre-trained models for image recognition, these can be fine-tuned to recognize specific objects in new datasets, significantly reducing time and resource requirements for custom development.

Pre-trained models reduce the barrier to entry for developing AI applications by enabling smaller organizations and individuals to leverage state-of-the-art models without extensive resources.

OpenAI's Collaborative Approach

OpenAI is a notable organization committed to democratizing AI. Initially focused on research and development, the organization transitioned to a more cooperative approach to AI advancements. Collaborations with AI research communities and open sourcing the results empowers individuals and small organizations to build upon cutting-edge AI technologies.

Conclusion

Open-source initiatives play a vital role in AI democratization by lowering entry barriers, encouraging collaboration, and promoting transparency. The availability of open-source software libraries, data initiatives, and pre-trained models fosters a more inclusive AI ecosystem that not only benefits enterprises but empowers individuals to participate in shaping the future of AI development. In a world where AI continues to pervade every industry and aspect of daily life, democratizing AI access and capabilities is crucial for promoting equitable growth and driving global innovation.

14.3 Fostering a Global AI Community

Introduction: The Need for a Global AI Community

The rapid advances in artificial intelligence (AI) are reshaping industries, economies, and societies around the world. The future of AI is poised to transform business and enable breakthroughs in various fields such as science, technology, and medicine. However, the full potential of AI will be realized only if we build a strong, collaborative, and inclusive global AI community that allows different stakeholders to come together and drive innovation.

A robust global AI community is essential to support knowledge sharing, facilitate dialogue and cooperation, promote ethical guidelines, and address challenges that are inherent in the development and deployment of AI technologies. In this chapter, we will explore the key elements for fostering a global AI community, examine successful initiatives, and provide recommendations for its sustainable growth.

Elements of a Strong Global AI Community

Diversity and Inclusion

A diverse and inclusive AI community ensures representation of different perspectives, skills, and expertise. Promoting diversity and inclusivity in AI research and development can lead to better decision-making, enhanced creativity, and ethical alignment with the values of the global population. Efforts should be made to remove biases, increase access to resources, and create opportunities for underrepresented groups such as women, minorities, and socioeconomically disadvantaged individuals.

Collaboration and Knowledge Sharing

Enabling collaboration and knowledge sharing is vital in fostering an AI community that can learn from one another, combine resources, and leverage best practices. Cooperative research initiatives, partnerships among academic institutions, industry, and governments, as well as open platforms for sharing AI algorithms and datasets, can facilitate collaborative innovation.

Education and Capacity Building

Strengthening AI education, training, and workforce development is a crucial component of building the global AI community. Initiatives, such as online courses or training programs targeting professionals, researchers, and students can help in disseminating AI knowledge and creating a skilled workforce. Additionally, AI education should be integrated into primary and secondary curricula, nurturing the next generation of AI practitioners.

Ethical Considerations

Addressing ethical concerns, including bias, transparency, and accountability is fundamental for the responsible development and deployment of AI. The global AI community should work towards setting ethical standards and guidelines, and implementing best practices to ensure that AI technologies are aligned with human values and do not perpetuate inequalities, perpetrate harm, or undermine privacy.

Policy and Regulatory Frameworks

Collaborative efforts to establish international policy and regulatory frameworks ensure that AI technologies are deployed in a manner that protects the rights, safety, and interests of individuals and society at large, fostering public trust in AI. These policies and frameworks should also provide regulatory clarity and support innovation by reducing barriers to entry for AI developers and startups.

Successful Initiatives and Models

There are several organizations and initiatives that have successfully contributed to building the global AI community. Some noteworthy examples include:

1. **OpenAI**: OpenAI is a research organization that promotes and develops friendly AI for the benefit of humanity as a whole. It is committed to advancing AI through research, sharing public goods like AI research, and providing safety and ethical guidelines.
2. **Partnership on AI (PAI)**: Founded by major tech companies, including Google, IBM, and Facebook, the PAI aims to foster collaboration on AI projects, establish best practices, and promote AI research and technology while addressing the global impact of AI on society.
3. **AI for Good Global Summit**: Organized by the International Telecommunication Union (ITU) and the United Nations (UN), this annual event brings together stakeholders from governments, industry, academia, and civil society to discuss the practical implementation of AI to address global challenges and sustainable development.

Recommendations for Sustainable Growth

To foster a global AI community that thrives in the long term, we offer the following recommendations:

1. Promote dialogue and cooperation among stakeholders from diverse sectors, such as industry, academia, government, and civil society organizations.
2. Encourage partnerships to address conventional barriers that exist at the economic, technological, and geopolitical levels.
3. Support open platforms for sharing AI resources, tools, algorithms, and datasets.
4. Develop programs and initiatives to increase access to AI education and resources for underrepresented and disadvantaged groups.
5. Work towards establishing a global ethical framework for AI, embracing principles such as fairness, accountability, transparency, and security.

By creating a strong, diverse, and inclusive AI community, we can ensure that the benefits of AI are harnessed equitably and sustainably while addressing the challenges that lie ahead. Fostering a global AI community will help unlock the transformative potential of AI for enterprises and computational creativity, and ultimately shape a promising future driven by artificial intelligence.

Chapter 15: Introduction to Computational Creativity

15.1 Defining Computational Creativity

Computational creativity, often considered as the core subfield of generative AI, is a rapidly developing area of research that explores the potential of artificial intelligence and machine learning to engage in activities that are traditionally associated with human creative processes—writing, painting, music composition, etc.

The objective of computational creativity research is not only to create autonomous AI systems capable of generating new content or solutions independently but also to develop algorithms that collaborate with human minds to enhance and inspire creativity within individuals and groups, creating a synergistic creative process.

In the context of enterprises, computational creativity has shown promising potential as a powerful tool for generating novel and innovative solutions, enhancing product design, and automating processes. This chapter delves into the core concepts, methodologies, and applications of computational creativity, focusing on its potential to transform the way enterprises approach problem-solving, product development, and creative tasks in general.

15.2 Core Concepts and Methodologies

15.2.1 Divergent Thinking and Convergent Thinking

Computational creativity involves two types of thinking:

1. **Divergent thinking** – The process of generating numerous possible solutions to a single problem. This type of thinking is characterized by free and spontaneous ideation, typically aimed at discovering unconventional possibilities.
2. **Convergent thinking** – The process of critically evaluating the generated ideas and selecting the most suitable solution, considering the constraints and objectives of the problem.

Computational creativity seeks to strike a balance between divergent and convergent thinking, combining the strengths of AI-powered ideation with human expertise.

15.2.2 Generative Methods and Search-guided Algorithms

There are two primary approaches in computational creativity: generative methods and search-guided algorithms.

1. **Generative methods** – These methods involve defining rule-based systems or utilizing statistical models (e.g., neural networks) to generate new content. Examples of generative methods include procedural content generation, neural style transfer, and natural language generation algorithms.
2. **Search-guided algorithms** – These algorithms involve conducting an automated search within a predefined solution space, guided by heuristics, objective functions, or utility measures. Examples of search-guided algorithms include genetic algorithms and swarm intelligence algorithms.

15.3 Key Challenges in Computational Creativity

Computational creativity faces a myriad of challenges, some of the most prominent ones include:

1. **Evaluation** – Assessing the quality of AI-generated content is a complex task, as human evaluators might favor known and familiar solutions over novel and unconventional ones. Developing objective evaluation metrics for creativity is an ongoing challenge.
2. **Variability vs. Coherence** – Achieving a balance between variability (i.e., generating diverse solutions) and coherence (i.e., generated solutions remain applicable to the problem) is crucial for computational creativity. This challenge involves walking a fine line between novelty and usability.

3. **Domain Transferability** – Computational creativity often requires AI models to understand and integrate knowledge from various domains. Designing AI systems capable of generating content that holds relevance and meaning across diverse fields remains an ongoing challenge.

15.4 Applications of Computational Creativity

Computational creativity has found applications in various domains, including:

1. **Marketing and Advertising** – AI has been used to generate ad campaigns, slogans, and creative briefs, as well as for content curation, video editing, and graphic design.
2. **Product Design and Development** – Computational creativity has been leveraged to aid in the design of new products or services, from generating aesthetics and form factors to optimizing functionality.
3. **Entertainment and Media** – AI-generated music, movies, and video games are gaining popularity, as well as AI-assisted story generation and virtual reality experiences.
4. **Scientific Research and Inventions** – Computational creativity contributes to the generation of new scientific hypotheses, chemical structures, and patentable innovations.

15.5 The Future of Computational Creativity in Enterprises

The advancement of computational creativity will significantly reshape enterprise innovation capabilities, with potential applications for small startups to large multinational corporations. Enterprises can benefit from computational creativity by:

1. **Enhancing product development** – Integrating AI-generated solutions into the product development process can lead to more innovative designs and increased efficiency.
2. **Optimizing resource allocation** – Computational creativity can help enterprises identify opportunities for resource optimization and focus on tasks that require human expertise.
3. **Collaborative creativity** – Combining human-AI collaborative processes can lead to the generation of novel and innovative ideas, fostering a culture of creative problem-solving within enterprises.
4. **Democratizing creativity** – As computational creativity becomes more accessible, smaller organizations and individual entrepreneurs will be empowered to compete with larger enterprises, encouraging a more diverse and competitive market landscape.

In conclusion, computational creativity holds the potential to revolutionize how enterprises approach problem-solving, product development, and creative tasks. By understanding its underlying concepts, techniques, and applications, businesses can harness the power of computational creativity to drive innovation and enhance their competitive edge in the marketplace.

15.1 Defining Computational Creativity

As we delve further into the realm of generative AI and its future in enterprises, it is crucial to understand and appreciate the concept of computational creativity. To properly grasp the potential and limitations of this powerful technology, we must first define what computational creativity entails, explore its components, and examine how it ties into the larger picture of artificial intelligence.

15.1.1 A Working Definition

Computational creativity, at its core, is a subfield of artificial intelligence that deals with the development of algorithms and systems that possess creative or artistic abilities. These systems have the capacity to generate new and valuable ideas, artifacts or solutions, frequently with little to no human input. The goal of computational creativity research is to design AI systems capable of imitating, augmenting, and even surpassing human creativity across various domains, such as art, music, literature, scientific discovery, and problem-solving.

15.1.2 Key Components

While the definition provides a general overview, computational creativity comprises several key components that further elucidate the concept. Below are some critical aspects of computational creativity.

15.1.2.1 Autonomy

Autonomy refers to the system's ability to operate without direct input or guidance from humans. A computationally creative system should rely primarily on its programming, existing knowledge, and learning abilities to carry out tasks and create novel products. This autonomy distinguishes creative AI from tools that simply automate or assist in the creative process.

15.1.2.2 Novelty

True creativity implies originality, whether it pertains to ideas, design, or the development of complex artifacts. Computational creativity should, therefore, emphasize the generation of novel outcomes that are not copied or derived from prior creations. Originality is crucial; it is not enough for AI to replicate excellence—it must contribute to the creative landscape and bring forth fresh, innovative ideas and solutions.

15.1.2.3 Value

An essential aspect of computational creativity is its capacity to generate valuable outcomes, which bear artistic, functional, or intellectual significance. To deem a product truly creative, it must carry not only novelty but also value—the ability to evoke an emotional response, serve a utilitarian purpose, or contribute to human knowledge. This value-driven framework establishes criteria against which computational creativity can be assessed.

15.1.2.4 Intent

A meaningful way to separate computational creativity from mere randomness or coincidental associations is by examining the system's intent. Does the AI exhibit some form of a goal, objective, or purpose that guides its creative process? Identifying intent implies that the system demonstrates an understanding of the creative constructs, rationale, or constraints that govern the domain it operates in.

15.1.3 Relationship with Artificial Intelligence

To appreciate the broader implications of computational creativity, one must situate it within the context of artificial intelligence. Computationally creative systems draw upon a wide array of AI techniques and methodologies, such as machine learning, natural language processing, pattern recognition, and neural networks.

A symbiotic relationship exists between computational creativity and AI. As we develop advanced creative AI systems that can mimic or even surpass human creativity, we also encounter opportunities to advance our understanding of AI and its applications across diverse domains. The creative capacities of AI have the potential to transcend human limitations, opening up new opportunities for innovation and growth in various fields.

15.1.4 Possible Concerns and Ethical Considerations

The advancement of computational creativity raises a unique set of ethical and cultural concerns. For instance, as creative AI systems proliferate, it will be crucial to address issues such as attribution, copyright, and ownership rights. Determining the ethics of utilizing AI-generated content, especially when it might replicate or closely mimic human works, requires in-depth evaluation and regulation.

Furthermore, humans possess cultural, historical, and emotional narratives that influence creativity across domains. The integration of AI-based creative systems must take into account these intricacies, ensuring that they complement and supplement human expression rather than supplant it.

In conclusion, understanding computational creativity from a multifaceted perspective provides deeper insight into its potential and the unique ethical and cultural concerns it raises. As generative AI continues to unfold, anticipating the transformative implications of computational creativity on enterprises, society, and the human experience becomes ever more crucial.

15.2. The Intersection of AI and Human Creativity

The rapidly evolving field of artificial intelligence (AI) has yielded impressive innovations in areas like natural language processing, image recognition, and decision-making. As these advances continue to revolutionize our ways of living and working, new and profound intersections between AI and human creativity have emerged. In this section, we will delve into the fascinating overlap between these seemingly disparate concepts and explore the future implications for enterprises, artists, designers, inventors, and researchers alike.

15.2.1. The Creative Grounds Artificial Intelligence Can Explore

Generative AI has enabled an entirely new frontier of computational creativity. The abilities to autonomously generate music, images, text, and even ideas have broken down the boundaries between the realms of human and machine outputs. Here, we discuss the nooks and crevices of artistic and inventive endeavors that AI is already exploring.

15.2.1.1. Visual Arts

AI has increasingly found its way into the realm of visual arts, such as painting, drawing, and graphic design. Through techniques like neural style transfer and deep learning models, AI systems have been able to autonomously create digital paintings that resemble the artistic styles of various renowned painters, like Van Gogh or Picasso. Designers are leveraging AI algorithms to create logos or design elements that are visually harmonious and unique.

15.2.1.2. Music

The applications of AI in music composition, production, and performance have been on the rise for some time. AI-generated music has seen an increased acceptance amongst composers, musicians, and producers for various practical purposes – from creating soundtracks for video games and movies to composing jingles for commercials. There are popular AI-based tools such as AIVA, OpenAI's MuseNet, and Amper Music, that have the capability to compose novel pieces of music in various genres and styles.

15.2.1.3. Writing and Text Generation

As natural language processing advances, AI systems have become adept at generating written text that is contextually relevant, coherent, and engaging. AI-generated text has practical applications in content creation, journalism, marketing, and more. Examples include the GPT series models developed by OpenAI, which have displayed impressive capabilities in generating human-like text across diverse styles, themes, and languages.

15.2.1.4. Idea Generation and Exploration

Through the amalgamation of different generative AI techniques, these systems have been successful in engaging in idea generation and exploration beyond just artistic applications. AI is helping users come up with innovative ideas for new products, business strategies, research concepts, and more. Some of these systems successfully analyze and synthesize vast amounts of data, detecting patterns and connections that are not readily apparent, which can spark creative thinking.

15.2.2. Benefits of the Confluence of AI and Creativity

15.2.2.1. Enhancing Human Creativity

AI does not strive to replace human creativity; rather, it can act as a powerful tool to augment human capabilities. Combining human intuition and imagination with AI's data analysis, pattern recognition, and generative abilities can lead to unique and powerful creative outputs.

15.2.2.2. Streamlining Creative Processes

AI's ability to quickly generate, refine, and iterate on ideas means that artists, designers, and inventors can spend less time in the conceptual phase and more time refining and enhancing their final products or ideas. This accelerated process can lead to reduced time-to-market for new products and services in various industries.

15.2.2.3. Unlocking New Artistic Possibilities

The innovative techniques AI introduces to the artistic process can enable entirely new possibilities of expression. The ability for AI algorithms to synthesize highly complex datasets, analyze patterns and trends, and create generative content means that the limits of human imagination can be expanded.

15.2.3. Challenges and Ethical Considerations

15.2.3.1. Authorship and Ownership

As the lines blur between human-made and AI-generated content, questions of authorship and ownership arise. Defining legal and ethical frameworks for AI-generated art, music, and other intellectual property will be of paramount importance as the field continues to progress.

15.2.3.2. Potential for Diminished Creativity

The widespread adoption of AI technology in creative processes may generate concerns about potential complacency among artists and creative professionals. Over-reliance on AI-generated results could lead to stagnation, as individuals may be less motivated to innovate, grow, and evolve in their creative abilities.

15.2.3.3. Bias in AI Systems

The presence of bias in generative AI systems can limit the perspectives and the diversity of expressions offered in their outputs. Ensuring equity and inclusivity in AI-generated creative works will require vigilant development, training, and testing methodologies that prevent the reinforcement of existing stereotypes and biases.

15.2.4. The Future of AI and Human Creativity

As the symbiotic relationship between AI and human creativity continues to evolve, it is crucial for enterprises, artists, and researchers to remain aware of the transformative potential and challenges presented by this intersection. The collaboration and continued exploration of AI and human creative abilities will undoubtedly impact the way we create, consume, and perceive creative works in the future.

15.3. Evolution of Computational Creativity in AI Research

Through the history of Artificial Intelligence research, computational creativity has gained significant attention as AI models have evolved, improved, and diversified. This development journey has remarkably transformed the industry, pushing AI systems to be more capable of independently creating content, solving new problems, and adapting to diverse scenarios. The evolution of computational creativity can be traced back through various key milestones:

15.3.1. Early Beginnings – Simulating Creativity in Machines

Alan Turing, in 1950, first proposed the idea of simulating human intelligence in machines. It did not take long for researchers to speculate whether it is possible to simulate human creativity. Turing's work paved the way for artificial intelligence research, putting forward the question: "Can machines think?"

This challenging question was the starting point for pursuing research in computational creativity. Although this area of research was not named during its early days, researchers believed that it was only natural for AI to simulate every aspect of human intelligence, including creativity.

15.3.2. Knowledge-Based Systems – Creative Problem Solving

The 1960s and 1970s marked the advent of knowledge-based systems to solve complex problems using algorithms and heuristics. Researchers began experimenting with computational creativity by developing systems like automated theorem provers, which could solve mathematical problems creatively.

Another significant milestone during this period was the creation of the General Problem Solver (GPS) by Allen Newell and Herbert A. Simon in 1959. The GPS aimed to imitate human thought processes by using a problem's objective as a starting point and finding means to reach the goal in logical steps. The intention was to make the machine think and solve problems creatively and independently.

15.3.3. Rule-Based Systems and Emergence of Creativity

During the 1980s and 1990s, rule-based systems (like expert systems) began to emerge, adopting creative techniques in their algorithms. These systems were still primarily focused on solving problems, but they started considering creativity as a critical component to improve their capabilities.

One example of such a system is the Automatic Programming System (APS) developed by Douglas Lenat in 1983. APS was designed to create new software by generating code from existing inputs or modifying programs to suit specific requirements autonomously. The system was not only innovative but also demonstrated the potential for computational creativity in various domains.

15.3.4. Generative Systems and Artistic Creativity

In the mid-to-late 1990s, researchers started exploring computational creativity in artistic domains like music, visual arts, and storytelling. These experiments gave rise to generative systems designed to produce creative outputs.

One notable project is the AARON system by Harold Cohen, which produced paintings autonomously. The system involved deep learning techniques to generate artistic aspects and style by analyzing human artwork. Another example is David Cope's program Experiments in Musical Intelligence (EMI), which could compose music in the style of various classical composers.

These early artistic endeavors demonstrated that AI systems could create creative content and imitate human-like creativity successfully.

15.3.5. Machine Learning and Neural Networks

The 2000s saw the rise of machine learning, taking computational creativity to new heights. AI systems became more intelligent, adapting through learning and making complex decisions without explicit human interference.

The development of Deep Learning and Convolutional Neural Networks (CNNs) significantly improved the creative capabilities of AI systems, allowing them to surpass human performance levels in some tasks. Examples include AlphaGo by DeepMind, which defeated the Go world champion, and OpenAI's GPT series, capable of generating human-like text in various contexts.

15.3.6. The Future of Computational Creativity

Looking forward, the field of computational creativity is set to evolve and grow in several directions. Some key trends shaping the future of the field include:

- **Seamless blending of human and machine creativity:** AI systems will better understand human artistic intentions and collaborate seamlessly with humans, leading to more expressive and diverse creative outputs.
- **Expanding AI's creative abilities:** AI systems will improve their capabilities to create music, visuals, and narratives across different domains and genres.
- **Integrating creativity in decision-making:** AI algorithms will consider creativity as an essential factor in various decision-making scenarios, including problem-solving, planning, and design, leading to more innovative solutions.
- **Ethical considerations in AI-generated content:** With the growing capabilities of AI in generating creative content, the ethical implications should be

addressed to ensure responsible growth in the industry.

As AI research continues to advance, computational creativity will play a vital role in shaping the future of technology, pushing the boundaries of what AI systems can achieve independently and in collaboration with humans.

Chapter 16: Creative Problem Solving with AI

In this chapter, we will explore how artificial intelligence (AI) techniques can be used to enhance creative problem solving, particularly within enterprise settings. We will delve into the importance of computational creativity and discuss various aspects surrounding AI-driven solutions, such as ideation, problem formulation, and evaluation.

16.1 The Age of Computational Creativity

Traditionally, creativity has been associated with the uniquely human capacity to generate novel and valuable ideas, works of art, and innovations. However, in the era of rapidly evolving AI technology, we are witnessing a new breed of creativity—computational creativity—that enables machines to recreate many of the complex facets of human creativity. Computational creativity empowers AI systems to facilitate problem-solving, idea generation, and innovation, as well as to contribute new and original ideas, designs, and artifacts.

This emergent domain of artificial intelligence combines elements of cognitive sciences, computer science, philosophy, and the arts, to create an interdisciplinary field that seeks to understand, model, and reproduce creative behaviors. Computational creativity has the potential to revolutionize the way we approach innovation and problem-solving in enterprises and to work alongside human expertise in generating novel solutions.

16.2 AI-driven Ideation and Creative Problem Formulation

One of the major challenges in problem-solving is being able to identify the problem accurately and to question assumptions. Redefining a problem, reframing it, or changing its perspective can lead to the discovery of novel solutions. AI-driven creativity techniques enable the generation of new ideas and approaches that may not be initially obvious during human brainstorming sessions.

16.2.1 Generative AI Models for Ideation

Recent advancements in AI, particularly the development of generative models, provide new opportunities for creative problem-solving. Generative AI models, such as GANs (Generative Adversarial Networks) and VAEs (Variational Autoencoders), have demonstrated remarkable proficiency in producing novel content in the form of images, text, and even music.

By tapping into these generative models, enterprises can feed domain-specific data to generate a plethora of possible solutions or ideas, which can then be screened, selected, and refined through human expertise. This AI-enhanced ideation can dramatically expand the horizon of an organization's creative capacity by rapidly generating diverse, yet high-quality ideas.

16.2.2 Dynamic Problem Formulation

Another powerful mechanism employed by AI in problem-solving is dynamic problem formulation. Rather than relying on a predefined problem statement, AI systems can adapt their problem-solving approach based on the data they encounter. They can effectively recognize patterns, create new problem statements, or adapt to new constraints, thereby discovering alternative paths to achieving a goal.

By employing AI techniques like reinforcement learning in tackling complex problems, organizations can break down larger issues into smaller, manageable components that can iteratively generate unique solutions.

16.3 Evaluation and Selection of Ideas

Choosing the best ideas from a pool of potential solutions is a critical element of creative problem-solving. AI can aid in this process by analyzing and evaluating generated solutions based on predefined criteria or objectives. AI-driven evaluation provides a systematic approach to comparing and calculating the value of different solutions, enabling organizations to make informed decisions.

Neural networks, for instance, can be trained to recognize and score a range of solutions based on their novelty, feasibility, or other specific criteria. Pairing AI with human expertise during the evaluation process will allow for a balanced consideration of both quantitative and qualitative aspects and ensure a comprehensive approach to problem-solving.

16.4 Applications of AI-driven Creative Problem Solving in Enterprises

AI-driven creative problem-solving is applicable across various industries and domains. Some examples include:

1. **Design and Engineering**: Generative design algorithms can produce multiple design solutions for complex engineering problems. Enterprises can explore various possibilities, optimizing designs based on performance, cost, and manufacturability.
2. **Marketing and Advertising**: AI can offer personalized and tailored content recommendations, optimize campaigns, and foster creativity in copywriting and visuals.
3. **Research and Development**: Utilizing AI-driven creativity techniques for drug discovery or materials science could significantly reduce time and costs associated with traditional R&D processes.
4. **Business Strategy**: Enterprises can employ AI for scenario planning and strategy development, helping organizations to navigate dynamic and uncertain business environments.

16.5 Ethical Considerations and the Future of AI-driven Creative Problem Solving

While the advancement of AI in creative problem-solving presents significant opportunities for enterprises, it also raises ethical and practical considerations.

1. **Ownership and Intellectual Property**: As AI-generated solutions become more commonplace, questions surrounding the ownership and rights to these innovations will need to be addressed, ensuring fair distribution of benefits and protection of intellectual property.
2. **Bias and Discrimination**: AI models are only as good as the data they are trained on. To prevent the perpetuation of historical biases and discrimination, organizations must carefully review and curate their training data and develop diverse data sets.
3. **Human-AI Collaboration**: Encouraging successful collaboration between humans and creative AI systems necessitates the development of transparent, understandable, and explainable AI, so users can trust and adopt these technologies effectively.

In conclusion, embracing AI-driven creative problem-solving has the potential to revolutionize the way enterprises tackle emerging challenges and innovate. The integration of computational creativity can augment human decision-making capabilities, streamline processes, and support the ideation, development, and commercialization of novel products and services. As AI continues to advance, its influence on the creative landscape within enterprises will become increasingly significant, giving rise to new creative synergies, approaches, and opportunities.

16.1. AI Techniques for Creative Problem Solving

In this section, we will explore various AI techniques that can be integrated into enterprise applications to facilitate creative problem solving. These techniques can enhance decision-making processes, product design, and even customer experiences by harnessing the power of machine-learning and AI-driven algorithms. The following AI techniques are some of the most promising for unleashing the creative potential of enterprises:

16.1.1. Generative Adversarial Networks (GANs)

Generative Adversarial Networks (GANs) consist of two neural networks: a generator and a discriminator. The generator creates new data instances, whereas the discriminator evaluates the generated data's authenticity. During the training process, the generator improves its ability to create realistic data by attempting to deceive the discriminator, while the discriminator becomes better at detecting fake data by learning the differences between real and generated data.

GANs have already demonstrated their ability to generate innovative designs, artwork, and layouts by learning from large datasets. Businesses can use GANs to generate new product ideas, optimize product and packaging designs, and create unique visual content for marketing campaigns in industries ranging from fashion and retail to automotive and manufacturing.

16.1.2. Reinforcement Learning

Reinforcement Learning (RL) enables AI agents to learn optimal decision-making strategies through trial and error. The AI is provided with a defined goal and learns by interacting with its environment, receiving feedback in the form of rewards or penalties based on its actions.

Reinforcement Learning can help enterprises explore alternative solutions for complex problems that are difficult to tackle using traditional optimization methods. Some practical applications of RL in creative problem-solving include optimizing manufacturing processes, managing supply chain and logistics, developing intelligent recommendation systems, and creating personalized user experiences in digital applications.

16.1.3. Natural Language Processing (NLP)

Natural Language Processing (NLP) empowers AI systems to understand, analyze, and generate human language effectively. Through NLP, businesses can gain insights from unstructured textual data, such as customer reviews, social media posts, and internal documents, to identify opportunities for innovation, improvements, and problem-solving.

Applications of NLP in creative problem-solving include sentiment analysis to monitor brand perception, topic modeling to identify emerging trends, information extraction to automate knowledge management, and conversational AI for enhancing customer support.

16.1.4. Neural Style Transfer

Neural Style Transfer is an AI technique that applies the artistic style of one image to the content of another using convolutional neural networks (CNNs). This technique enables the creation of highly customizable and visually engaging content without the need for extensive artistic expertise.

Enterprises can leverage neural style transfer to inject a creative touch into their marketing materials, product designs, and packaging, or even to create immersive user experiences in virtual and augmented reality environments.

16.1.5. Autoencoders

Autoencoders are a type of unsupervised learning algorithm used for data compression and noise reduction. They consist of two neural network components: an encoder that reduces the input data's dimensionality and a decoder that reconstructs the input data from the compressed form. By capturing the most important features of the data, autoencoders can reveal patterns and relationships that might be challenging to uncover with manual analysis.

Autoencoders can be used in creative problem-solving by helping businesses identify hidden patterns and features in large datasets, such as customer behavior data, operational logs, or financial reports, leading to more effective decision-making and new opportunities.

16.1.6. Swarm Intelligence

Swarm Intelligence is inspired by the collective behavior of decentralized, self-organized systems found in nature, such as ant colonies, bird flocking, and fish schooling. By modeling and simulating these systems, AI algorithms can optimize complex problems in a distributed and efficient manner.

Industries like transportation, logistics, and telecommunications can benefit from Swarm Intelligence models to optimize their processes, such as vehicle routing, scheduling, and load balancing. Additionally, Swarm Intelligence can help devise innovative strategies for collaboration, resource allocation, and process optimization across various enterprise applications.

In summary, AI techniques offer a wealth of opportunities for embracing creative problem-solving in enterprises. By leveraging these techniques, businesses can unlock new insights, enhance decision-making processes, and ultimately drive more innovation and value for their customers. As advancements continue in these technologies, the potential for creative solutions supported by AI will only continue to grow.

16.2. Case studies of AI-driven creative solutions

AI has demonstrated its potential for both augmenting human thinking and producing original and creative outputs. These case studies showcase the range and diversity of AI-driven creative solutions successfully applied across multiple domains, from advertising and music to cooking and fashion.

16.2.1. Advertising and Marketing

- **JWT Amsterdam and ELAN Language's "The Next Rembrandt"**

In 2016, JWT Amsterdam and ELAN Language partnered to create "The Next Rembrandt," an AI-powered project that generated an entirely new painting in the style of the Dutch master, Rembrandt van Rijn. The team trained a deep learning algorithm on a dataset of Rembrandt's work, and the AI created a 3D-printed portrait with the same colors, brushstrokes, and stylistic features. The project won several awards and demonstrated how AI could be used as a creative tool to produce culturally relevant and innovative outputs.

- **Persado's AI-generated marketing language**

Persado is an AI-driven content marketing platform that uses natural language processing (NLP) and machine learning to generate persuasive marketing messages. Its algorithms can analyze and optimize a wide range of marketing content, including ads, emails, and website copy, selecting the most effective phrasing and emotional triggers to increase engagement and conversions. Clients such as Expedia, Vodafone, and eBay have seen marked improvements in their marketing metrics as a result of Persado's AI-generated language.

16.2.2. Music and Audio

- **OpenAI's MuseNet**

MuseNet, developed by OpenAI, is a deep neural network that can generate music in a wide variety of genres and styles. Drawing from a dataset of classical, jazz, rock, and pop music, the AI system can create everything from original compositions to genre-blending hybrids. Musicians and composers have embraced this technology, using MuseNet-generated tracks as inspiration or starting points for their own creations.

- **Jukedeck's AI-generated music for videos and advertising**

Jukedeck is an AI-driven music company that produces royalty-free, customizable soundtracks for videos and advertising campaigns. Its proprietary technology, based on deep learning algorithms, can analyze and imitate a diverse range of musical styles, and it can adapt specific features such as tempo, mood, and instrumentation to suit clients' needs. Notable clients include Coca-Cola, Google, and the UK's National Health Service.

16.2.3. Cooking and Food Science

- **IBM's Chef Watson**

IBM's Chef Watson is a culinary AI system that generates creative recipes using an extensive database of ingredients and cooking techniques. By applying machine learning algorithms, Chef Watson can create unusual and unexpected flavor combinations, pushing the boundaries of human culinary creativity. Numerous professional chefs, including James Briscione and Michael Laiskonis, have collaborated with Chef Watson to develop innovative dishes for their restaurants.

- **IntelligentX's AI-driven beer recipes**

IntelligentX is a British startup that utilizes AI to generate beer recipes based on consumer feedback. They have developed a range of four beers, with their AI system analyzing the consumer preferences and brewing data to optimize and improve the recipes. The result is continuously evolving, customer-tailored beer offerings that showcase the potential of AI-driven creativity in the food and drink industry.

16.2.4. Art and Design

- **Google Deep Dream AI-generated art**

Google's Deep Dream project uses AI algorithms to generate hallucinogenic and visually rich imagery based on input pictures. By feeding images through deep neural networks, Deep Dream creates surreal, dreamlike interpretations that have been used in projects ranging from album covers to fashion design.

Artists have embraced this technology, and galleries have even hosted dedicated Deep Dream exhibitions, demonstrating AI's potential in the creative art world.

- **Theano Fashion's AI-generated fashion designs**

Theano Fashion is a startup that applies AI to fashion design, using big data and machine learning to generate original clothing items based on fashion trends and user preferences. The company's AI system ingests large amounts of fashion data, analyzes patterns and trends, and generates new designs that reflect current styles while remaining unique and innovative. The results highlight the capacity for AI-driven creative solutions in the industry.

These case studies represent just a small sample of the expansive and growing possibilities for AI-driven creativity. As AI technologies continue to advance, the creative capabilities and applications across diverse domains are expected to grow exponentially, transforming how innovative solutions are generated and delivered throughout the global economy.

16.3 Challenges and Limitations in AI-based Creativity

As fascinating as AI-based creativity may seem, it is imperative to acknowledge the various challenges and limitations it faces. In this section, we will delve into the obstacles that AI and generative models encounter in different aspects of the creative process, and explore their implications for enterprises and practitioners.

16.3.1 Understanding Context and Semantics

One of the most significant challenges that AI models face is understanding context and semantics. Language models like GPT-3 can generate coherent and contextually relevant text. However, they still struggle to maintain semantic consistency over more extended conversations or passages of text. Additionally, since these models primarily rely on pattern matching, they are susceptible to adversarial attacks or generating nonsensical outputs.

Understanding the context is also crucial when generating images or other creative content. Generative models may produce visually appealing content but may lack the deeper meaning or connection to the idea they were sought to represent in the first place. This issue may lead to inappropriate or irrelevant content being created by AI, resulting in wasted resources or potential harm to a brand's integrity.

16.3.2 Emotion and Empathy

Human creativity is often driven by emotions and empathy, allowing us to produce original and expressive creations. AI models, though sophisticated, lack genuine emotional intelligence, which may hinder their ability to craft emotionally resonant or evocative content. This limitation can be particularly problematic in industries such as marketing, where personal connections and emotions play a significant role in influencing consumer behavior.

16.3.3 Unintended Bias and Ethical Considerations

AI systems are trained on large datasets, which may contain biases or controversial content. When AI models, such as generative models, learn from these datasets, they may inadvertently perpetuate the biases or create content that could be deemed offensive, politically incorrect, or morally wrong. These ethical considerations are paramount when utilizing AI to create content for public consumption or when targeting diverse demographic groups. Enterprises must be cautious about taking measures to reduce bias and avoid potential negative consequences.

16.3.4 Novelty and Originality

AI, specifically generative models, rely on existing data to generate creative outputs. As a result, the creations may not be entirely original, since they are largely dependent on the seen patterns and references. The inherent drawback is that AI may simply reinforce and regurgitate the status quo – an antithesis to the very notion of creativity, which relies on novelty, exploration, and breaking new ground.

Moreover, AI-generated content may lack the conceptual depth and thematic interconnectivity that human creators bring to the table. AI systems may struggle to match the thematic and conceptual consistency that is sometimes required, especially in complex creative endeavors such as storytelling, campaigns, or product innovation.

16.3.5 Human Collaboration and Interpretation

Creativity is an inherently human trait, and while AI can be an indispensable tool, it cannot replace human input entirely. Collaborative Human-AI systems, where humans and AI work in tandem, can yield the best results in creative tasks. However, human intervention also brings its own set of challenges, such as determining the right balance between human and AI contributions, overcoming resistance to AI-generated content, and fostering the trust and collaboration needed for successful AI adoption within organizations.

16.3.6 Legal and Intellectual Property Issues

With AI-generated content becoming increasingly prevalent, questions concerning intellectual property rights, copyrights, and legal provisions for AI-created works arise. Legal systems must adapt to address these concerns, providing clarity on how to attribute ownership and enforce rights to protect both AI-generated content and traditional human-created works.

Overall, AI-based creativity holds significant promise for enhancing and transforming the landscape of creative industries. However, by understanding and addressing the challenges and limitations discussed in this section, enterprises can develop better practices for incorporating AI safely and effectively into their creative processes, while leaving ample room for human ingenuity and innovation.

Chapter 17: AI in Art, Music, and Literature

In this chapter, we will dive deep into the world of AI-powered creativity and explore the various facets of AI in art, music, and literature. As we enter a new era of computational creativity, it is crucial for businesses to stay ahead of the curve and embrace the possibilities offered by AI technology. From the creation of unique artwork and music to the development of engaging narratives, AI is gradually reshaping the creative landscape.

AI in Art

In recent years, AI has begun to play an increasingly significant role in the world of fine arts. Thanks to advancements in deep learning and generative algorithms, AI-powered systems can now create unique and compelling pieces of art that challenge our traditional notions of creativity.

Style Transfer

One of the most commonly discussed aspects of AI in art is style transfer, which is a technique that involves using deep learning to apply the artistic style of one image to another image. This technique was popularized by the work of Gatys et al., who used deep neural networks to combine the content of one image with the style of a famous painting.

This technique has since been improved upon and utilized by various artists and businesses alike. For instance, style transfer has been used in innovative ways such as generating new product designs, customizing clothing, creating unique advertisements, game development, and more.

Generative Adversarial Networks (GANs)

Another powerful AI innovation in the world of art is the Generative Adversarial Network (GAN). GANs consist of two neural networks -- the generator and the discriminator -- that work together. The generator creates new images, while the discriminator evaluates them based on their similarity to a given dataset of images.

As a result, GANs can generate striking and convincing artworks that mimic different artistic styles or even create entirely new ones. A notable example is the artwork "Portrait of Edmond Belamy," which was created by the French art collective Obvious using GANs. This piece of AI-generated art was sold at Christie's auction house in 2018 for a staggering $432,500.

Caption: Portrait of Edmond Belamy, by Obvious

AI-Generated Sculpture

In addition to visual artwork, AI is also making its impact felt in the world of sculpture. An example is the work of Manuel Ruckstuhl, an artist who uses AI to create unique, procedurally generated sculptures. By using algorithms to design intricate three-dimensional shapes, Ruckstuhl can create intricate and unique art pieces that defy traditional sculpting methods.

AI in Music

From classical compositions to modern pop, AI is gradually weaving its way into the world of music. As AI algorithms become more advanced, they are becoming capable of generating unique music compositions by learning from existing pieces and even collaborating with human musicians.

Algorithmic Composition

One of the primary uses of AI in music is through algorithmic composition. This involves using AI algorithms to analyze existing musical pieces and generate new compositions that share similar characteristics. There are several tools based on AI, like AIVA (Artificial Intelligence Virtual Assistant), Amper, Jukedeck, and OpenAI's MuseNet, which can create music across a wide range of genres, from classical to electronic.

Neural Style Transfer for Music

Similar to the style transfer techniques used in visual art, AI researchers have also applied these ideas to music. Neural style transfer for music involves extracting the stylistic elements, such as melody, harmony, and rhythm from one piece and applying these characteristics to another composition. This opens up exciting possibilities for remixing different musical styles or creating entirely new compositions that blur the lines between genres.

AI-Assisted Music Production

AI is not only revolutionizing the creation of music, but it is also impacting the production and post-production aspects of music-making. Tools like LANDR, an AI-powered mastering service, can analyze and process recorded music to create a professionally mastered version in a matter of minutes, saving musicians time and money on traditional studio sessions.

AI in Literature

The literary world is no stranger to experimentation and innovation, and AI-generated literature is no exception.

AI-Generated Poetry

By using natural language processing and deep learning, AI models can generate text in specific styles, such as poetry. Based on the given input and a dataset of existing poetry, AI algorithms can create unique verses that emulate the style and tone of specific poets or eras. As a result, AI-generated poetry has the potential to both inspire and challenge human poets, exploring new poetic themes and styles.

AI-Generated Fiction

AI-generated fiction is another emerging and fascinating field. Researchers and writers are using AI algorithms to create short stories, novels, or even entire sagas. Motivated by challenges like the NaNoGenMo (short for National Novel Generation Month), creative coders design AI-powered tools that craft stylistically accurate and coherent narratives.

One striking example is the GPT-3 model developed by OpenAI, which can generate human-like text based on input prompts. GPT-3 can be used to help authors develop new story ideas or create engaging dialogues, demonstrating the potential AI has for enhancing the fiction-writing process.

AI-Assisted Storytelling in Games

AI-generated literature is also making its mark in the gaming industry. Games like "Her Story" and "Firewatch" implement storytelling and dialogue systems driven by AI. This allows for more dynamic and immersive story experiences that are shaped by player actions and decisions. By integrating AI technology, these games can offer players a genuinely unique experience each time they play, significantly enhancing replay value and engagement.

Conclusion

As AI continues to become an integral part of art, music, and literature, enterprises must be prepared to adapt and capitalize on this emerging technology. AI-powered creativity is not only revolutionizing traditional artistic fields but also creating entirely new possibilities for expression and innovation.

Understanding the implications and potential applications of AI in art, music, and literature is essential for businesses seeking to remain competitive in an increasingly automated world. By embracing AI-driven creativity, enterprises can unlock a wealth of untapped potential and transform the creative process in ways that were once unimaginable.

17.1. AI-generated visual art and styles

Introduction

One of the most exciting frontiers of AI technology is its application to the realm of visual art. AI-generated art has been radically transforming the art sector, creating new opportunities for artists, collectors, and curators alike. This section will discuss how generative AI models have given birth to innovative visual art styles, and how these art pieces are shaping the future of the creative enterprises.

AI-generated art: a brief history

The concept of AI-generated art can be traced back to the early 1960s, when AARON, one of the first AI art programs, was developed by Harold Cohen. AARON used symbolic AI techniques to produce drawings and paintings based on a set of rules defined by Cohen. The program achieved considerable recognition, and its artistic output was exhibited in galleries worldwide.

Fast forward to the 21st century, and AI-generated art began to gain traction due to advancements in machine learning, particularly with the invention of Generative Adversarial Networks (GANs). Proposed by Ian Goodfellow and his colleagues in 2014, GANs have become the go-to model for generating novel and realistic visual content. These models have paved the way for a new era of AI-generated art, in terms of quality and diversity.

AI-generated visual styles

As computational creativity continues to evolve, a range of AI-generated visual styles have emerged. Some of the most popular styles include:

1. Deep-dream-inspired art

Google's DeepDream is an AI-based art technique using convolutional neural networks (CNNs) to interpret and enhance images iteratively. The outcome is a mesmerizing blend of patterns and surreal visual artifacts. Artists using AI-generated DeepDream art often combine these visuals with traditional techniques, creating hybrid art pieces that defy categorization.

2. Neural style transfer

Neural style transfer is an algorithmic technique that applies the visual style of one image to another. This method combines two images—a content image and a style image (often a famous painting)—to generate a new image that retains the content of the original while reflecting the style of the other. This enables artists to create unique, AI-generated visual styles based on celebrated works of art.

3. GAN-generated portraits

Using GAN models, artists can generate lifelike yet non-existent portraits that blur the line between reality and imagination. One notable example is the "Portrait of Edmond Belamy," a piece created by the French collective Obvious in 2018. This AI-generated portrait made headlines when it sold for $432,500 at Christie's auction house, proving the potential of AI-generated art in the market.

4. AI-augmented design

AI-generated visual styles are also making waves in the design industry. AI-powered tools like RunwayML and DALL-E enable designers to prototype and iterate ideas rapidly, combining human creativity with AI-generated elements for innovative results. These emerging technologies have the potential to redefine the design process and reshape the creative landscape.

The role of AI-generated art in enterprises

AI-generated visual styles have opened up a world of possibilities for creative enterprises. Here are some potential applications:

1. **Product development**: AI-generated visuals can help designers create innovative product designs that cater to diverse consumer tastes and aesthetics.
2. **Marketing and advertising**: Unique AI-generated art can differentiate promotional campaigns, drawing attention and engagement. AI-produced visuals aid in the rapid ideation and prototyping of marketing materials.
3. **Interior and exterior design**: Architects and interior designers can use AI-generated styles to develop original design concepts, leveraging the power of neural networks to create works tailored to specific tastes and themes.
4. **Entertainment**: AI-generated art can enhance the storytelling and visual experience of movies, TV shows, and video games, introducing new visual styles and narratives that captivate audiences.

Ethics and art ownership

As AI-generated art gains prominence, questions of ethics and ownership are unavoidable. Who owns the copyright to AI-generated works: the artist who programmed the AI, the AI itself, or a combination of both? And what are the implications for creators who borrow elements from other artists to create AI-generated styles?

As of now, legal frameworks and industry standards for AI-generated art remain in their infancy. To ensure that the benefits of AI-generated art outweigh any potential pitfalls, stakeholders in the creative industry must engage in meaningful conversations about regulation, intellectual property, and best practices.

Conclusion

AI-generated visual art and styles have the power to revolutionize creative enterprises across multiple industries. As generative AI technology continues to advance, we can anticipate a future rich in captivating and imaginative visual content that reshapes not only the art world but also how we consume and appreciate creative works in our everyday lives.

17.2. Composing Music with AI Algorithms

In the past, creating music was exclusively the domain of human composers, who dedicated years to honing their craft and understanding the intricacies of music theory. However, in recent years, cutting-edge AI algorithms have increasingly been used to compose music, creating pieces that are hard to distinguish from those created by human composers. AI-generated music is not only a fascinating area of research, but it also has practical applications, such as producing background music for films, video games, and advertisements. In this section, we will delve into how AI algorithms can compose music, exploring various methods and the future of this exciting field.

AI in Music Composition: The Basics

The process of composing music can be broken down into two main components: generating the melody and constructing the harmony. Melodies are the memorable and recognizable parts of a piece, often consisting of the main theme or motif. Harmonies are the accompanying chords to the melody, providing depth and resonance to the piece.

To generate melodies, most AI algorithms employ a type of machine learning called deep learning. Deep learning models, such as recurrent neural networks (RNNs), can be trained on a dataset of existing melodies, learning the patterns and structures that make human music enjoyable. Once trained, these models can generate new melodies by predicting the next sequence of notes based on the input data.

Similarly, harmonization can also be achieved using deep learning. By training algorithms on existing chord progressions, they can learn the relationships between chords that sound pleasing to the human ear. This enables them to generate harmonizations that pair well with the generated melodies.

AI Music Composition Techniques

There are several techniques for composing music using AI algorithms. Some of these include:

1. MIDI-based Generative Models

MIDI (Musical Instrument Digital Interface) is a common protocol used for electronically encoded music data. A MIDI file contains information about each note's pitch, duration, and position in time. Researchers often use MIDI files as input data to train their models, as it allows the models to learn patterns and relationships found in the provided music.

Once trained, these models can generate new MIDI files, which can then be synthesized using various instruments to create original pieces of music. This approach is popular, as it allows for a straightforward representation of musical information that can be easily manipulated by AI algorithms.

2. Audio Waveform-based Models

While MIDI-based generative models work with abstract musical information, audio waveform-based models work directly with the raw audio data. This approach involves training deep learning models on full audio waveforms to generate new audio samples. This can result in highly realistic sounds and timbres, making the generated music more difficult to distinguish from human-made pieces.

However, this method is computationally intensive, as it requires the models to learn and process vast amounts of audio data. Recent advances in generative adversarial networks (GANs) and variational autoencoders (VAEs) have helped to tackle this challenge, making it a more viable option for AI-generated music.

3. Rule-based Systems

Rule-based systems use a set of predetermined rules or constraints to generate music. These rules can be based on music theory principles or specific styles of composition. For example, a rule-based system could generate a piece of Baroque music by following the specific harmonic and rhythmic patterns characteristic of that era.

Although rule-based systems can produce high-quality and coherent music, they can be limited in their creativity, as the output is strictly confined to the rules set by the programmer. However, they can be useful for generating music tailored to specific requirements, such as composing in a specific style or adhering to a defined structure.

Applications of AI in Music Composition

AI-generated music has numerous applications across various industries:

1. **Film and television scores**: AI can generate original music to accompany visuals or create unique themes for characters and scenes.
2. **Advertisements**: Companies can use AI-generated music for marketing campaigns, creating custom jingles or background music that aligns with their brand identity.
3. **Video game soundtracks**: AI-generated music can adapt to the gameplay, creating dynamic soundscapes that evolve with the player's actions.
4. **Personalized music**: AI can create custom playlists or compositions tailored to an individual's unique preferences or moods.
5. **Music education**: AI-generated music can be used as a tool for teaching music theory and composition, offering students access to an infinite amount of unique material to study and analyze.

The Future of AI Music Composition

As AI algorithms continue to improve and evolve, the quality and variety of generated music will also expand. With an increasing number of companies and researchers investing in this field, we can expect more advanced AI-generated music tools and applications in the future. Although some fear that AI-generated music will replace human musicians, it's more likely that it will serve as a tool for enhancing creativity and inspiring new, innovative ideas.

In conclusion, AI algorithms have demonstrated immense potential in the field of music composition, with their ability to generate unique and engaging pieces. As these models continue to advance and mature, the possibilities for AI-generated music are vast and exciting, offering tremendous opportunities for both creative expression and practical applications.

17.3. AI-driven storytelling and literature generation

Artificial Intelligence has come a long way, transforming different sectors of human life, including the way we view and create art. With the rise of Generative AI, a paradigm shift in storytelling and literature generation can be witnessed. AI-driven storytelling offers innovative narratives, transforming traditional literature paradigms, and reimagining the creative process. In this section, we'll delve deep into the applications of Generative AI for storytelling and literature and discuss its impact on the future of the literary world.

17.3.1. The concept of AI-driven storytelling and literature generation

AI-driven storytelling and literature generation involve the use of advanced generative models that can learn from massive datasets of text and create entirely new and coherent pieces of literature, such as novels, poems, scripts, and stories, while maintaining originality and creativity.

The underlying technology that powers the majority of these AI-driven systems is natural language processing (NLP). NLP algorithms can analyze text, extract patterns, draw inferences, and generate content based on the given context or inputs. The most commonly used NLP algorithms are Recurrent Neural Networks (RNNs), Long Short-Term Memory (LSTM) units, and the Transformer architecture.

In the context of generative literature, systems like OpenAI's GPT-3 have garnered massive attention for their ability to generate creative, sophisticated, and high-quality narratives.

17.3.2. Techniques in AI-driven storytelling and literature generation

Several techniques enable AI-driven systems to generate literature tailored to various contexts, themes, and styles. Some of these tactics include:

1. **Transfer learning**: Training AI models on vast datasets of popular and critically-acclaimed literature to help the model grasp general style, grammar, and structure in different languages and genres. Later, these models can be fine-tuned for specific tasks,

enabling them to generate text in the required context or style.

2. **Reinforcement learning**: It can be used to optimize AI-generated narratives for specific goals, like maximizing reader engagement, increasing emotional intensity, or achieving the desired pacing.
3. **Abstractive summarization**: The ability to condense long pieces of text into shorter versions while retaining the essence and core information can be incredibly helpful for literature generation. AI can use this capability to generate summaries, outlines, or abstracts of longer works.
4. **Style transfer**: By learning the unique textual attributes of individual authors, AI models can generate new literature that mimics the style of specific creatives, enabling users to experience narratives in the 'voice' of their favorite writers.

17.3.3. Applications of AI-driven storytelling and literature generation

The implementation of AI-driven storytelling and literature generation spans various domains, including:

1. **Book writing**: AI-generated novels, novellas, and short stories that may cater to specific genres or target audiences.
2. **Poetry generation**: AI can create poems in various styles, meters, and themes, allowing for fascinating new combinations and explorations in the world of poetry.
3. **Screenwriting**: The use of AI in script generation for films, series, plays, and other performance arts results in innovative plotlines and character development that challenge conventional storytelling.

4. **Journalism**: AI-generated news articles and reports enable faster dissemination of information and provide multiple angles in the reporting of events.
5. **Content creation**: With AI-driven storytelling, marketers and content creators can generate tailored content for specific audiences and demographics, enhancing engagement and user experience.
6. **Education**: AI-generated stories and learning materials can provide engaging and interactive modes of learning for students, promoting better comprehension and retention.

17.3.4. Challenges and ethical considerations

As with any technological innovation, AI-driven storytelling and literature generation do come with certain challenges and ethical concerns:

1. **Plagiarism and copyright issues**: Ensuring that the generated text is entirely original and does not violate any copyrights is essential. Creating strict guidelines and legislation to address AI-generated content is a pressing concern.
2. **Loss of authorship**: The question of originality and ownership of AI-generated literature poses problems related to creative control and author-identity.
3. **Loss of human touch**: The risk of losing the human element in literature raises concerns, as narratives devoid of human experiences may lack emotional resonance or connection.
4. **Job displacement**: As AI becomes more advanced and prevalent, the displacement of authors, screenwriters, and other creative professionals may become a concern.

17.3.5. The future of AI-driven storytelling and literature generation

Despite the challenges mentioned above, the prospect of AI-driven storytelling holds great potential to revolutionize literature and the creative process. As AI models continue to learn and evolve, we can expect to see more advanced and sophisticated narratives emerging. Many experts believe that collaboration between AI and human authors will define the future of literature, with AI playing a supportive role — aiding in idea generation, editing, and overall refinement of human-created narratives.

With continued advancements in AI, the future of AI-driven storytelling and literature generation looks bright, offering unparalleled creative opportunities and unprecedented artistic expression possibilities. AI's role in literature will continue to evolve as we move towards a future where human creative genius and the power of AI work in synergy to create inspiring and groundbreaking works of art.

Chapter 18: Computational Creativity in Game Design

In this chapter, we explore the applications and potential impact of generative AI and computational creativity in game design. As game designers leverage AI to develop richer, more dynamic, and intuitive gaming experiences, new opportunities and challenges arise.

1. Introduction to Generative AI in Game Design

The integration of artificial intelligence in game design is not a new concept; AI has always played a pivotal role in the development of games. Its applications primarily lay in non-player characters (NPCs), decision-making, dialogue systems, and pathfinding algorithms. However, the scope of AI in gaming is expanding exponentially with the introduction of generative AI techniques that push the boundaries of what games can offer.

Generative AI, encompassing techniques like deep learning or genetic algorithms, enables machines to generate, assess, and optimize original content that satisfies certain requirements. This has wide-ranging implications for game design, including automating content generation, enhancing procedural storytelling, and creating more adaptive and dynamic gaming experiences.

In the following sections, we delve into the various aspects of computational creativity in game design and explore its potential impact on the gaming industry.

2. Content Generation in Game Design

2.1 Procedural Content Generation

Procedural Content Generation (PCG) is an increasingly popular approach in game design, where game content (e.g., levels, maps, textures, stories, or items) is automatically generated using algorithms instead of being manually created by designers. This enables game developers to efficiently create large and complex game worlds while reducing development cost and time.

Generative AI takes PCG one step further, incorporating more advanced algorithms and computational creativity techniques to generate content that is both novel and engaging. For instance, AI-driven PCG systems can learn and adapt to a player's preferences and gameplay style, optimizing the design elements accordingly to enhance player satisfaction.

2.2 Automating Game Design

`Ganbreeder`, an online tool built on `BigGAN`, exemplifies how generative AI can facilitate content creation outside the gaming domain. BigGAN is a type of generative adversarial network (GAN) that has shown remarkable capabilities in generating highly realistic images. By leveraging similar techniques, game developers can generate assets like textures, models, and animations, significantly accelerating and simplifying the design process.

3. Computational Storytelling in Game Design

3.1 Procedural Narrative Generation

In narrative-driven games, the story is a fundamental gameplay element. Procedural Narrative Generation (PNG), a subdomain of PCG, focuses on creating dynamic and adaptive stories that change depending on player choices, actions, or preferences. This generates more interactive and immersive gaming experiences.

Computational creativity techniques can advance PNG by allowing the automatic generation of complex, elaborate, and engaging stories that cater to individual players. The machine-generated narratives are likely to be unique every time, thus enriching the player experience and increasing game replayability.

3.2 NPC Behavior and Dialogue Generation

In addition to the backbone narrative, generative AI can enhance NPC behavior and dialogue, making them more realistic and adaptive. By training AI models on sets of existing game dialogues, developers can create dialogue generators that maintain the style and tone of the game while crafting unique dialogue options based on the player's choices and interactions.

Moreover, advanced AI systems can model an NPC's "personality" and "motivation," allowing them to react to evolving situations more believably. This can immerse players deeper into the game world and foster emotional connections between players and NPCs.

4. Adaptive Gameplay and Personalization

Generative AI can elevate gameplay by adapting the game's challenges and mechanics in real-time, based on player performance, preferences, or learning curves. For example, AI-driven adaptive difficulty algorithms can assess a player's skill level, while machine learning can identify and reinforce certain player behaviors to create tailored gaming experiences.

By combining personalization with computational creativity, AI can fashion unique, adaptive, and satisfying gameplay for every player, increasing the appeal of a game, especially among audiences with varying levels of expertise and interest.

5. Challenges and Ethical Considerations

5.1 Unpredictability

Generative AI systems can be unpredictable, producing unexpected or undesirable outcomes. This unpredictability poses challenges to game developers who must ensure a consistent and polished gaming experience. Hence, integrating AI into game design may necessitate close monitoring and testing before deployment to detect and rectify anomalies, mitigating potential risks to player satisfaction.

5.2 Intellectual Property and Authorship

As generative AI becomes more prevalent in game design, new questions concerning intellectual property and authorship will arise. How do copyright laws apply to machine-generated content? Who should be credited as the creator of AI-generated game elements (e.g., character models, storylines, or level designs)? These questions remain largely unanswered, and developers must navigate these issues carefully as generative AI revolutionizes the gaming industry.

6. Conclusion

Generative AI and computational creativity have significant potential to revolutionize game design, from procedural content generation to narrative development to personalized gameplay experiences. This burgeoning field presents a wealth of opportunities for game developers, while also raising novel challenges and ethical dilemmas.

Ultimately, the sustainable and ethical adoption of generative AI in game design should focus on creating more immersive, dynamic, and engaging games that push the limits of human creativity.

18.1. Procedurally Generated Content in Games

Procedurally generated content (PGC) has revolutionized the gaming industry by dynamically creating content using algorithms and rules, rather than conventional handcrafted methods. This technique enables developers to produce vast amounts of game content such as levels, terrain, maps, objects, characters, and narratives, while greatly reducing development time and resources. In turn, this dramatically enhances the user experience—providing players with unique content and increasing replayability.

How Procedurally Generated Content Works

In procedural generation, algorithms define and govern the creation process, which automatically produces content based on pre-established rules and templates set by the developer. This is in contrast to traditional, handcrafted content that requires a considerable amount of time and manual labor. Utilizing these algorithms, PGC can generate endless varieties of in-game elements with minimal human input.

There are varying degrees of procedural generation, from purely random generation to heavily controlled systems with specific parameters. Some games use a combination of both to strike a balance between unpredictability and structure. In some cases, PGC co-exists with handcrafted content, supplementing the development process and providing an extra layer of diversity.

Notable Examples of Procedural Generation in Games

Minecraft

Minecraft is perhaps the most well-known example of a game that uses procedural generation. In Minecraft, PGC is employed to create a nearly infinite open-world terrain, with landscapes that include mountains, forests, caves, and bodies of water. Players can explore this vast world, mine resources, build structures, and defend against various creatures—all within an environment that is never the same.

No Man's Sky

No Man's Sky, a space exploration game, was created using procedural generation to develop an entire universe. The game boasts over 18 quintillion planets for players to explore, each varying in factors such as terrain, climate, and wildlife. The level of interaction and immersion in the game is greatly enhanced thanks to PGC, as players are encouraged to explore these unique and uncharted worlds.

Rogue-likes and Rogue-lites

Rogue-likes and Rogue-lites are game genres largely founded on PGC principles. These titles feature randomized levels, items, enemies, and permadeath (i.e., permanent death of the player's character) making every playthrough fresh and unpredictable. Titles like Dead Cells, The Binding of Isaac, and Spelunky are popular examples of games that rely heavily on procedural generation to create a diverse array of challenges for players with each playthrough.

Benefits of Procedurally Generated Content in Games

Cost and Time Efficiency

Developing large-scale, open-world games traditionally requires significant time and labor to design and implement the diverse array of landscapes, characters, and items needed. PGC can dramatically reduce the need for these resources, allowing developers to focus on other aspects of the game, such as mechanics or AI.

Infinite Replayability

Since procedural generation algorithms can create virtually limitless content, the replay value of games utilizing PGC is exponentially increased. Players are drawn to games that offer new experiences, and procedural generation ensures that no two playthroughs are identical.

Emergent Gameplay

PGC can foster emergent gameplay when the generated content interacts in unexpected, yet coherent ways. This can lead to unique events and interactions that surprise even the developers themselves, creating memorable experiences for players.

Future Challenges and Opportunities

While procedural generation has proven to be a valuable asset for developers, it also poses several challenges. Maintaining quality and consistency in the generated content is crucial, as poorly designed assets may lead to undesirable or frustrating player experiences.

Balancing the elements of randomness and control presents an ongoing challenge for developers. Striking the right balance ensures that the game feels dynamic without sacrificing coherence and player enjoyment.

As the technology and techniques behind procedural generation continue to evolve, there is vast potential for new applications in gaming. One opportunity is the advancement of generative AI algorithms that could facilitate the coherent design of entire game worlds, complete with stories, questlines, and characters. Additionally, adaptive algorithms may open up possibilities for evolving game worlds that respond to individual players' actions and choices, creating truly personalized gaming experiences.

Ultimately, the future of procedural generation in games lies in its ability to coexist with handcrafted design, allowing developers to create rich, dynamic, and immersive worlds that keep players engaged and captivated.

18.2 AI-driven Narrative and Character Development

Within the vast domain of artificial intelligence, one of the key areas of focus in recent years has been the potential for AI to create and innovate within the world of storytelling. This broad concept encompasses the development of convincing characters, dynamic narratives, and truly engaging worlds. AI-driven narrative and character development refers to the growing trend of using machine learning techniques and natural language processing tools to augment the creative work of human authors, screenwriters, and content creators.

The implications for the creative industries are profound, with AI-driven narrative and character development having the potential to revolutionize how stories and characters are developed through automation, assisting in the optimization of story structures, and providing tools for creators to more effectively realize their visions. In this section, we will explore the various facets of AI-driven narrative and character development, from the current state of the field to the challenges and opportunities that lie ahead.

Current State in AI-driven Narrative and Character Development

The current state of AI-driven narrative and character development is characterized by considerable progress and several exciting developments. Some of the most significant advancements in recent times include:

AI-assisted writing tools

With the development of AI-powered writing tools such as GPT-3 by OpenAI, the capabilities of AI in text generation have grown significantly. These models have demonstrated remarkable skills in generating fluent and contextually relevant text passages, which can be adapted in various content creation tasks, such as scriptwriting, generating dialogues, and even creating entire novels.

Automated story generators

Automated story generators are algorithms that utilize AI technologies like natural language processing, machine learning, and deep learning to create stories from scratch or using given constraints. Existing tools like Plotto, Annalisa, and Tropes suggest that AI can generate compelling and coherent story outlines to varying degrees, which can then be expanded upon and revised by human authors.

Character development tools

AI-driven character development tools can provide inspiration, generate backstory, or flesh out intricate character details. For example, AI Dungeon (an AI-powered text adventure game) is not only interactive but can deliver detailed character descriptions and backgrounds while being built upon the GPT-3 framework.

Challenges in AI-driven Narrative and Character Development

Despite the promising progress in AI-driven narrative and character development, the field is still faced with numerous challenges. Those challenges primarily stem from:

Creativity

While AI models have demonstrated the ability to generate highly-structured and grammatically accurate text, their capacity for truly original thought and creativity remains limited. They inherently rely on the patterns and creativity they learn from the data input, which may limit them to producing outputs that are derivative or too anchored in well-established tropes.

Context Understanding and Continuity

A key challenge facing AI-driven narrative and character development tools is their ability to maintain context and ensure continuity. AI models can sometimes fail to understand indirect references and maintain cohesion in character motivations over the course of the narrative, which can lead to jarring narrative inconsistencies.

Emotional Intelligence

Developing believable characters requires a deep understanding of human emotion, motivation, and psychology. AI models often struggle with accurately portraying complex human emotions, character growth, and relatable interpersonal relationships.

Opportunities in AI-driven Narrative and Character Development

Despite the challenges, AI-driven narrative and character development offers tremendous potential for content creators and the broader creative industries. These opportunities include:

Collaborative Storytelling

By combining the best of AI's text-generating abilities with human creativity, we can create fascinating stories with more depth, complexity, and variety. Collaborative storytelling with AI as a tool allows for a more efficient generation of a wide range of ideas and enhanced creativity.

Personalization and Customization

AI-generated narratives provide the opportunity for highly personalized stories that cater to individual preferences and interests. Combining AI-driven storytelling with personal data could enable tailored experiences, whether through customized narratives or personalized character arcs.

Dynamic Storytelling in Video Games and Interactive Media

The integration of AI-powered story generation into video games and interactive media could pave the way for truly dynamic and immersive experiences. This would offer narratives that respond and adapt to player choices, offering near-infinite storylines and outcomes, resulting in a never-before-seen level of interactivity.

In conclusion, the future of AI-driven narrative and character development offers a tantalizing glimpse of a world where creative professionals can push the boundaries of storytelling and craft experiences that captivate audiences like never before. By continuing to develop technologies that enhance creativity, foster collaboration, and facilitate dynamic and emotionally resonant storytelling, AI has the potential to become an indispensable ally to the creative process.

18.3. Adaptive game design using AI techniques

The gaming industry has always been at the forefront of technological advancements, pushing the boundaries of computer graphics, user engagement, and more recently, artificial intelligence. The future of games will likely focus on fostering more dynamic, personalized experiences for players. Adaptive game design, supported by AI techniques, can revolutionize the way we develop and experience games. This section will discuss various ways AI can be utilized in creating adaptive game design, as well as the advantages brought about by these advancements.

18.3.1. Procedural content generation

Procedural content generation (PCG) is an AI technique that helps developers create content, such as levels, characters, and items, on the fly. This approach can save time, increase replayability, and allow for infinite game worlds. PCG can be achieved through various algorithms, including:

- **Noise-based algorithms**: Noise functions, such as Perlin noise and Simplex noise, can create coherent and random-looking content. For example, these algorithms can be used to generate realistic terrain, clouds, or textures.
- **Fractal-based algorithms**: Fractals are complex patterns generated by repeated application of simple shapes. Fractal algorithms can be used to create natural-looking structures like mountains, coastlines, and trees.
- **Grammar-based algorithms**: Generative grammars, such as L-systems or shape grammars, can be used to create complex structures, like buildings, cities, or dungeon levels.

18.3.2. Dynamic difficulty adjustment

Dynamic difficulty adjustment (DDA) aims at adapting the game's challenge level to the player's skill, ensuring a satisfying experience for all players. AI techniques, such as reinforcement learning (RL) and Bayesian modelling, can help balance the game's difficulty, making it enjoyable for players with various skill levels. For instance, an RL-based AI could analyze in-game data such as player success rate and time spent, gradually adjusting the difficulty according to the player's skills.

18.3.3. AI-driven narratives

Traditional storytelling methods can limit player agency and lead to predictable outcomes. By incorporating AI techniques, narratives can dynamically adapt to players' actions, creating a more immersive and personalized experience. Examples of AI-driven narratives include:

- **Emergent narratives**: Rather than relying on predefined scripts or branching decision trees, emergent narratives arise from a complex interplay of game systems, player actions, and AI-controlled characters. This can lead to unique and unpredictable stories, where players have more agency in shaping the game's narrative.
- **AI-generated dialogues**: Natural language processing (NLP) techniques can analyze and generate human-like dialogues, allowing game characters to carry context-aware conversations with players. Through these interactions, players can uncover hidden storylines or influence the game's narrative.
- **Character-based AI**: Each AI-controlled character can have its own motivations, goals, and personality traits. This results in more meaningful, believable

interactions between the characters and the player, enriching the narrative.

18.3.4. Advancing player modeling

AI-driven player modeling can help developers understand various aspects of players, including their skills, preferences, playstyles, and engagement levels. Machine learning techniques such as clustering, classification, and regression can be used to derive insights from large datasets, enabling developers to improve and tailor game design for various player personas.

18.3.5. AI in game balancing and testing

Game balancing is a complex process, as developers need to ensure that various elements of a game are tuned to provide a fair and engaging experience. AI techniques can assist in identifying imbalances through automated playtesting or analyzing player data, allowing developers to fine-tune the game.

Automated playtesting using AI agents can quickly identify game-breaking issues, imbalances, and exploits. They can also help discover unexpected emergent behaviors arising from complex interactions between game systems, leading the developers to better design decisions.

18.3.6. Conclusion

Adaptive game design using AI techniques holds immense potential to enhance the gaming experience. Procedural content generation, dynamic difficulty adjustment, AI-driven narratives, player modeling, and AI-assisted game balancing are just a few ways in which AI can positively impact the future of game design. As developers continue to embrace AI, the gaming industry will see more engaging, personalized, and immersive experiences like never before.

Chapter 19: AI and the Creative Process

19.1 Introduction

As AI technology rapidly evolves and becomes more sophisticated, it is changing the landscape of how creative processes are approached and executed. From visual arts, music production, and writing to marketing, advertising, and product development, AI plays a significant role in pushing the boundaries of what can be achieved across various industries.

In this chapter, we will delve into how the creative process is influenced and enhanced by AI, discussing how generative AI models are enabling creative individuals to achieve new heights. We will also explore the challenges and ethical implications associated with AI-generated content, and ponder the possibilities that lie ahead as AI continues to shape the world of computational creativity.

19.2 The Role of AI in the Creative Process

AI is not merely a tool for streamlining or automating tasks; it is a transformative force with the potential to reshape the workflow and outcomes of creative projects. In this section, we will highlight the various ways that AI plays a role in the creative process.

19.2.1 Inspiration and Ideation

For many artists and other creative professionals, the ideation stage is an essential part of the creative process. AI can assist in this stage by analyzing massive amounts of data, identifying patterns, and suggesting innovative ideas. By examining vast datasets containing information on aesthetics, styles, and cultural trends, AI can inspire novel creative concepts that push boundaries and lead to the creation of original, groundbreaking content.

19.2.2 Collaboration and Co-creation

Generative AI has made it possible to produce art, music, and other creative content through collaboration between humans and machines. Through machine learning algorithms, AI systems can learn a user's creative preferences and styles, offering valuable suggestions and input that can enhance the final output. This synergy between human and AI allows for the exploration of new creative avenues and improved methods of execution, pushing the envelope of what is possible within a given medium.

19.2.3 Automation and Augmentation

AI's potential for automating and augmenting creative tasks can help free up time and energy for other aspects of the creative process. Mundane tasks – such as image resizing, color adjustments, or audio processing – can be delegated to AI systems, allowing artists and creators to focus on conceptualizing and refining their ideas. In other instances, AI can act as an assistant to help with tasks that demand a high level of precision and consistency, such as the intricate design of intricate patterns or repeating motifs in a composition.

19.3 AI-Generated Content: Opportunities and Challenges

The advent of AI-generated content has sparked a lively debate about its potential impact on the creative industries. This section will explore the opportunities and challenges presented by AI-generated content across various domains.

19.3.1 Opportunities

1. **Increased access and affordability**: AI-generated content can democratize access to high-quality creative output by enabling artists, smaller organizations, or those with fewer resources to produce professional-grade work at a fraction of the cost.
2. **Enhanced creativity**: The collaboration between humans and AI opens up unprecedented creative possibilities that can nurture novel ideas and opportunities for artistic growth.
3. **Personalization**: AI's ability to analyze and learn from individual user preferences can lead to highly personalized content experiences, tailoring recommendations, advertisements, entertainment, and more to cater to the specific tastes and interests of diverse audiences.

19.3.2 Challenges

1. **Intellectual property and copyright**: The question of copyright and ownership in AI-generated content is complex and not yet fully resolved, potentially leading to legal disputes and challenges in attributing rights to creators and their AI counterparts.
2. **Ethical considerations**: There are ethical concerns associated with AI-generated content, such as deepfakes, manipulation, and misinformation. Finding responsible applications of AI-generated content remains a key challenge for the creative industries.
3. **Cultural impact**: Some critics argue that the proliferation of AI-generated content could lead to the homogenization of art and culture, while others worry about the possibility of decreased opportunities for human creators as AI becomes more adept at producing high-quality work.

19.4 Conclusion & Future Outlook

Artificial intelligence is poised to have a profound and ongoing impact on the creative sphere. By offering exciting opportunities for innovation and collaboration, AI has the potential to revolutionize creative processes and shape the future of computational creativity. As we continue to develop more advanced AI models and navigate the challenges presented by AI-generated content, it will be essential to consider the ethical implications and foster responsible usage of this powerful technology. In doing so, the fusion of human creativity and artificial intelligence will likely continue to yield transformative results across a range of creative domains.

19.1. Augmenting Human Creativity with AI

As computational power continues to grow exponentially, the world of artificial intelligence (AI) is flourishing with new possibilities. When combined with our innate human creativity, AI unlocks unprecedented potential for innovation and change across industries. This synergy between human and machine will not only augment creative pursuits but also reshape them, yielding fruitful collaborations that drive unique solutions and novel creations.

In this section, we will delve into the various ways AI can augment creative processes and the potential benefits for enterprises:

1. Enhancing Creativity in Design and Ideation

AI-driven generative design tools are already transforming industries like manufacturing, automotive, and construction. These tools analyze user-defined goals and constraints, using algorithms to generate an array of design options that a human could not conceive on their own. This capability enables humans to explore novel solutions to challenges, ultimately leading to more robust and innovative designs.

Moreover, AI tools like natural language processing (NLP) and language generation can help cultivate creative avenues in writing, marketing, and communication. These algorithms can analyze vast amounts of data to understand linguistic patterns and generate new content or ideas, providing inspiration and assisting human creators.

2. Automation and Optimization of Creative Tasks

AI isn't just enhancing creativity—it's also amplifying it by automating repetitive and mundane tasks. Machine learning models can tackle simple creative assignments, like editing images or generating copy, freeing up time and effort for human creators to focus on more abstract and complex challenges. With AI handling tedious tasks, humans can work smarter, fostering efficiency and innovation.

Optimization is another significant aspect of AI-driven creativity. AI can quickly analyze results and provide feedback, allowing an iterative process of refinement. For example, AI algorithms can help optimize pricing for products or services, testing various models and automatically identifying the most effective one. This capability allows organizations to make rapid improvements and adapt to changing market conditions.

3. Expanding Creative Collaboration

Collaboration between humans and AI will revolutionize the creative landscape. A hybrid human-

AI creative team benefits from the strengths of both parties, enabling innovations that may be unattainable by a purely human team. For instance, AI can present a vast array of design variations that humans can then evaluate, refine, and adapt based on their expertise and vision.

Collaborative applications extend beyond design, as AI powered virtual assistants can enhance strategic efforts, brainstorming sessions, and decision-making processes, allowing for more informed creative choices. By embracing AI as a collaborative partner, enterprises can catalyze innovation and produce pioneering results.

4. Personalization and Customization

AI is revolutionizing personalization, enabling organizations to tailor experiences and offerings for individual consumers, clients, or stakeholders. Machine learning algorithms can analyze enormous datasets, identify patterns, and produce custom content or experiences. This feat influences fields such as marketing, sales, and customer experience—ultimately boosting both customer satisfaction and loyalty.

For example, retailers can leverage AI to create personalized marketing campaigns, recommendations, or even products based on customers' purchasing history and preferences, thereby boosting conversion rates and brand loyalty. AI can also help enterprises adapt their products, services, or messaging to suit different markets and demographics, ensuring optimal results.

5. Fostering New Perspectives and Innovations

AI's ability to analyze large amounts of data from diverse sources lends a unique perspective to creativity. For example, an AI trained on images or patterns from unrelated fields can generate original, out-of-the-box ideas that might otherwise have been missed. By questioning assumptions, AI can incite us to reconsider our entrenched views and inspire fresh innovative solutions to longstanding challenges.

In addition, AI can track and analyze emerging trends, shifts in consumer behavior, or new market opportunities, offering insights that inform creative direction. AI's bird's-eye view of the landscape is invaluable for strategic and creative decision-making, enabling organizations to stay ahead of the competition.

Conclusion

The fusion of AI and human creativity holds extraordinary potential for enterprises. By harnessing the power of AI to augment creative processes, we can unlock unforeseen possibilities, enhance productivity, and create groundbreaking innovations. Embracing AI as a creative ally will help humanity navigate an increasingly complex world and open doors to new artistic, scientific, and cognitive breakthroughs.

19.2. The Role of AI in the Creative Workflow

In the present-day corporate landscape, artificial intelligence (AI) is playing an increasingly significant role in the creative processes of many enterprises. From marketing and product development to research and analysis, AI's applications in creative workflows are changing the way individuals and organizations generate, consume, and distribute content. In this section, we'll delve deeper into the role of AI in creative workflows, exploring its various facets and potential impact on industry practices.

19.2.1. The Creative Workflow and its Components

A typical creative workflow can be broken down into various stages, each of which usually involves several discrete tasks. Although the specifics of these processes will inevitably differ depending on the industry or organization in question, a general workflow may include stages like:

1. Idea generation and brainstorming
2. Research and data gathering
3. Concept development and planning
4. Content creation (design, writing, or other forms of production)
5. Editing, refining, or revising
6. Reviewing and approval
7. Distribution or deployment

Each of these stages has the potential to be greatly influenced or even transformed altogether by AI technologies. Let's explore how AI tools can be employed to enhance and optimize them.

19.2.2. Idea Generation and Brainstorming

At the beginning of the creative process, individuals and teams seek to discover unique and valuable ideas that may later be transformed into a product, service, or piece of content. AI tools can help support this process by using generative algorithms that are designed to generate new ideas or content. These algorithms may draw from existing databases, analyze trends and patterns, or operate through a process of random trial and error.

For example, tools like Google's DeepMind, OpenAI's GPT-3, and other language models can facilitate idea generation by suggesting topics, presenting fresh perspectives on existing content, or proposing associations between disparate concepts. This can help creative professionals overcome mental blocks, access innovative possibilities, and more rapidly iterate on their ideas.

19.2.3. Research and Data Gathering

AI's data processing capabilities can significantly ease various stages of creative research. By searching, parsing, and distilling vast amounts of data, AI tools can quickly present relevant and useful information to creative teams. This can lead to more informed decisions, efficient adjustments, and superior ideation.

Natural language processing (NLP) technologies are particularly adept at extracting insights from textual sources, while computer vision algorithms can discern patterns and information from images, videos, or other visual content. Together, these capabilities can save creative professionals time and effort, allowing them to focus on other aspects of their work.

19.2.4. Concept Development and Planning

As creative teams hone their ideas, AI can play a supportive role in developing, visualizing, and coordinating these new concepts. AI-assisted design tools can rapidly generate numerous iterations of a design, or suggest potential developments to a concept, taking into account the team's specific preferences, guidelines, or objectives.

Project management tools harnessing AI can anticipate potential roadblocks and suggest optimal workflows, enabling creative teams to operate more smoothly and effectively. They may predict the personnel or resource requirements needed for a project or suggest the best allocation of tasks among team members.

19.2.5. Content Creation

The actual act of creating content—be it designing a logo, writing an article, or developing software—has also been impacted by AI technologies. Creative AI applications can generate content in various forms automatically, such as:

- Developing initial drafts of written content using GPT-3 and similar state-of-the-art language models
- Generating graphic designs or artwork through tools like DALL-E or RunwayML
- Assisting in composing music, as with Google's Magenta or OpenAI's Jukebox

These tools often serve as valuable collaborators for creative professionals; rather than replacing them, they aid in streamlining and refining the content creation process by suggesting ideas, handling repetitive tasks, or providing a starting point for further development.

19.2.6. Editing, Refining, and Revising

AI technologies can optimally assist in the revision process by identifying areas that require improvement or adjustment. AI-powered grammar and style checkers like Grammarly and ProWritingAid can enhance textual quality, while image recognition and computer vision algorithms can automatically detect errors or inconsistencies in visual content. These tools help creative professionals maintain high-quality outputs while minimizing mistakes.

19.2.7. Reviewing and Approval

AI applications can help streamline the review and approval process by automating some of the tedious and repetitive tasks involved. For example, AI-powered sentiment analysis tools can provide insights into how an audience might respond to a piece of content, while predictive analytics can forecast its potential impact or success.

In addition, AI tools can ensure that content complies with legal requirements, brand guidelines, or other relevant standards. By performing these tasks swiftly and efficiently, AI can reduce the time and resources spent on manual reviews.

19.2.8. Distribution and Deployment

Lastly, AI can optimize the distribution and deployment of creative content. Recommendation algorithms can determine the optimal audience or target market for a specific piece, while personalization technologies can tailor and adapt the content for different users or platforms. Furthermore, AI can gauge the performance and impact of distributed content, analyzing data to inform future creative endeavors.

19.2.9. Conclusion

The role of AI in creative workflows is vast and ever-evolving. As new algorithms, platforms, and tools are developed, AI's influence on creative processes will undoubtedly continue to grow. By embracing the potential of AI-driven innovation, organizations can greatly enhance their creative capabilities and reap significant benefits in this competitive, fast-paced world.

19.3. Human-AI collaboration in creative projects

As artificial intelligence continues to improve and influence various industries, creative projects are no exception. The collaboration between humans and AI is becoming increasingly important to enhance innovation, efficiency, and adaptability in various forms within creative industries. In this section, we will discuss the implications of human-AI collaboration in creative projects, explore noteworthy examples and collaborations, and provide insights on how this symbiosis could reshape the future of enterprise creativity.

19.3.1. The rise of generative AI in creative industries

Generative AI systems have been developed to create novel and aesthetically valuable content in various domains, including visual arts, music, literature, and design. These systems are typically based on deep learning techniques, such as generative adversarial networks (GANs), variational autoencoders (VAEs), and recurrent neural networks (RNNs). They are trained on large datasets of human-generated content, thereby learning to imitate and create new content by drawing inspiration from the existing data.

These generative AI models present new opportunities for human-AI collaboration in creative projects. This collaboration enables humans and AI systems to complement each other's strengths while overcoming their respective limitations. For instance, AI models can process and synthesize information from vast datasets, exploring new creative possibilities at an unprecedented scale. Meanwhile, humans can provide the necessary guidance, intuition, and cultural context to refine and direct the AI-generated content, ensuring the final output is genuinely valuable and aesthetically appealing.

19.3.2. Implications of human-AI collaboration in creative projects

Enhancing creativity and productivity

By collaboratively working with AI, creative professionals can push their creative boundaries and explore new artistic forms, styles, and concepts. AI systems can generate a substantial number of ideas, quickly providing inspiration and relieving humans from the burden of routine work, such as drafting and ideation. This allows creative professionals to focus on refining ideas, selecting the most promising ones, and bringing them to life more efficiently.

Expanding the scope of creative projects

With AI's ability to process large amounts of data, businesses can now experiment with new creative possibilities that were previously not feasible due to time or resource constraints. As a result, larger-scale projects can be undertaken, catering to a wider range of customer preferences and enabling the creation of highly personalized art, music, and other creative content.

Democratizing creativity

As AI technologies become more accessible and affordable, a broader range of individuals and businesses can harness their potential to realize their creative pursuits. This democratization of creativity may spur innovation and competition in the creative industries, enabling smaller enterprises and individuals to compete with established market players.

19.3.3. Notable examples of human-AI collaboration in creativity

Music and AI

The collaboration between musicians and AI has resulted in a variety of creative projects blending human expertise and computational power. Popular AI-based music generation tools, such as OpenAI's MuseNet, Amper Music, and Jukedeck, have enabled musicians to create original compositions by combining various styles, genres, and instruments.

Furthermore, artists like Taryn Southern and SKYGGE have released albums that feature AI-generated tracks, showcasing the potential of human-AI collaboration for chart-topping music.

Visual art and AI

The world of visual arts has also witnessed significant collaborations between artists and AI. Generative AI models, such as DALL-E by OpenAI and RunwayML, have been used to create novel images, illustrations, and even animations. For example, prominent contemporary artist Refik Anadol utilized AI-generated visuals to transform the façade of the Walt Disney Concert Hall in Los Angeles, creating a mesmerizing multimedia experience.

Writing and AI

In the literary world, authors and AI platforms have produced compelling narrative projects showcasing human-AI symbiosis. OpenAI's GPT-3 language model, for instance, has demonstrated its creative prowess by writing poetry, short stories, and even completing sections of novels in collaboration with human authors. Other examples include the AI-written novel "1 the Road" and the first-ever AI-human collaborated play, "Sunspring."

19.3.4. Future perspectives for human-AI collaboration in creative projects

As generative AI technology advances, human-AI collaboration in creative projects is poised to continue growing in significance. There are several promising directions and applications for these collaborations in the creative industries:

- Developing interactive, real-time AI tools for creative professionals to use in their workflow, allowing for seamless integration of AI-generated content within the creative process.
- Utilization of AI-generated content to aid prototyping and preliminary design in various industries, such as fashion, architecture, and product design.
- Leveraging AI for personalized content delivery, tailoring art, music, and other creative works to individual preferences and tastes.
- Using AI to analyze, predict, and recommend creative trends, enabling businesses to stay ahead of the curve in constantly evolving industries.

The era of human-AI collaboration in creative projects marks the beginning of a new chapter for the creative industries. As the symbiosis between AI-generated content and human creativity deepens, we are likely to witness a new wave of groundbreaking creative achievements that redefine the boundaries of art, music, and literature.

Chapter 20: Evaluating AI-Generated Creative Outputs

Evaluating creative outputs in any domain has always been a difficult and subjective endeavor. Assessing AI-generated creative outputs presents new challenges and opportunities for both individuals and businesses to evaluate their worth and impact. This chapter will provide an overview of several approaches and considerations for evaluating AI-generated creative outputs.

1. Technical Metrics

The first approach to evaluating AI-generated content is purely technical. By examining the algorithm's performance and the quality of its results compared to a ground truth or a human-generated reference, one can determine its effectiveness.

1.1 Accuracy and Fidelity

For AI-generated content, especially in areas like image, audio, and video synthesis, an evaluation of the accuracy and fidelity of the result is critical. The output should be compared against the desired reference or a human-generated equivalent. Metrics may include pixel-based comparisons, calculating loss functions, or measuring perceptual similarity through user studies.

1.2 Learning Metrics

Evaluating an AI model's ability to learn and adapt can provide insights into its performance. Metrics related to loss functions, convergence rates, and other learning-related statistics can offer valuable information about the underlying model and its suitability for a particular creative task.

1.3 Computational Efficiency

AI systems often involve significant computational resources. Evaluating the speed of the system, model complexity, and the ability to quickly generate high-quality results can provide insight into the overall efficiency of the AI model. This can help individuals and businesses determine the feasibility and cost-effectiveness of employing AI for a particular creative problem.

2. Creativity Metrics

In the context of computational creativity, a key aspect of evaluating AI-generated content is determining its novelty and quality within the creative domain.

2.1 Novelty and Surprise

An AI-generated output's novelty can be quantified by measuring its level of surprise and its difference compared to existing content. The generated output's divergence from known patterns or content in the domain, as well as its ability to offer a fresh perspective, can signify a level of creativity.

2.2 Quality and Aesthetics

The quality of AI-generated content is closely related to its perceived aesthetic value. Evaluating the quality of the output involves considering factors like the level of refinement, coherence, and complexity in the domain, as well as its relevance and appeal to the intended audience.

2.3 Originality and Uniqueness

Another metric to consider is the originality and uniqueness of the AI-generated content. The ability of the AI system to produce content that is distinct from existing content, or patterns in the domain, demonstrates its creative potential.

3. Human-Centric Evaluations

Ultimately, AI-generated creative outputs are often intended to be consumed or utilized by humans. Incorporating human-centered evaluation methods can help elucidate the success of an AI system at creating meaningful and engaging outputs.

3.1 User Studies and Surveys

One approach for incorporating human evaluation is through user studies and surveys, where judges or participants are asked to rate the AI-generated content in terms of creativity, novelty, quality, and other dimensions. These evaluations can help discern individual preferences and perceptions, which are often critical to the success of creative content.

3.2 Expert Reviews

Expert reviews can help account for domain-specific knowledge and expertise when evaluating AI-generated content. Industry experts or professionals can evaluate the AI-generated outputs based on their experience and understanding of the domain, providing a more informed perspective on the creative outputs.

3.3 Comparative Analysis

Comparing AI-generated content to human-generated content is another approach for human-centric evaluation. Participants can be asked to rank or rate AI-generated outputs alongside human-generated outputs, without knowing the source of each output. This blind comparison can reveal insights into the success of the AI model at producing outputs that are similar in quality and creativity to the human-generated alternatives.

4. Ethical and Societal Considerations

Finally, evaluating AI-generated creative outputs should include considerations of ethical and societal implications. The potential consequences of AI-generated content, such as issues of authorship, privacy, and the potential for misinformation or manipulation, should be taken into account when assessing the creative outputs and their potential applications.

Evaluating AI-generated creative outputs involves a multitude of factors and approaches, as the assessment of creativity is inherently subjective and multidimensional. By considering technical metrics, creativity metrics, human-centric evaluations, and ethical and societal considerations, enterprises and individuals can better appreciate the value, impact, and potential of AI-generated creative outputs in a wide range of domains.

20.1. Measuring creativity in AI-generated content

As we continue to develop more advanced generative AI and leverage it for a variety of enterprise needs, it becomes essential to understand how to measure the creativity inherent in the AI-generated content. This section will explore the various methods and criteria for gauging the creativity in AI-generated content, and discuss the future implications and potential applications of such measurements.

20.1.1. Defining creativity in the context of AI-generated content

When discussing creativity in relation to AI-generated content, it is crucial first to establish a clear definition. Creativity can generally be regarded as the ability to generate ideas, solutions, or products that are both novel and valuable. In the context of AI-generated content, creativity refers to the AI's capacity to develop unique and meaningful content that exhibits a certain level of inventiveness or originality.

20.1.2. Criteria and methods for measuring creativity

Various criteria and methods exist to measure AI-generated content's creativity. These methods often involve evaluating the generated content based on specific attributes, many of which can be traced back to established theories and models of human creativity.

20.1.2.1. Novelty

One essential aspect of creativity is the novelty of an idea or product. A key factor in measuring AI creativity is determining the extent to which the generated content is unique, distinct, or innovative. This can be achieved through various quantitative methods, such as:

- **Comparing against a dataset**: Assess the AI-generated content's novelty by comparing it against an existing dataset of human-generated content or a dataset of previous AI-generated content. The comparison could be based on similarity metrics, like cosine similarity or Jaccard similarity, revealing how much the generated content diverges from existing content.
- **Surprise or unpredictability**: Measure the extent to which the AI-generated content differs from what users expect.

20.1.2.2. Value

The value of the AI-generated content is essential when evaluating creativity. Ideally, the content should provide some meaningful contribution or usefulness for the intended audience. Methods to evaluate value include:

- **Relevance to the given task**: Assess whether the AI-generated content effectively addresses and fulfills the task or prompts it was given.

- **User feedback**: Gather user feedback on the AI-generated content, offering insights into how the content is perceived and how it has impacted the target audience.

20.1.2.3. Divergent thinking

An aspect of human creativity involves divergent thinking, where multiple ideas or solutions are generated for a given problem. In AI-generated content, this can be measured by:

- **Idea variation**: Assess the degree of variety present in ideas or solutions provided by the AI. For example, if given a problem or prompt and a requirement to generate several solutions, the AI should ideally create solutions that are significantly different from each other.
- **Generation of multiple solutions**: Count the number of plausible, alternative solutions provided by AI.

20.1.2.4. Flexibility

The flexibility of AI-generated content refers to its ability to embody diverse perspectives, themes, or styles. Flexibility can be measured by:

- **Thematic variation**: Establish whether the AI-generated content demonstrates a variety of themes or domains in response to a given prompt.
- **Adaptability to different contexts**: Test AI's ability to create content suitable for different settings or user types, such as formal, casual, professional, or creative.

20.1.2.5. Elaboration

Elaboration refers to the level of detail, intricacy, or complexity present in AI-generated content. This can be examined by:

- **Layering of ideas**: Assess the AI-generated content in terms of the number of layers or levels of ideas that are built upon one another, demonstrating complexity and depth.
- **Coherence**: Evaluate the coherence between different generated content components, revealing the degree to which the AI can provide structured and meaningful elaboration of ideas.

20.1.3. Future implications and applications for measuring creativity in AI-generated content

The ability to measure and evaluate the creativity of AI-generated content will have significant implications for enterprise applications, including:

- **Algorithm improvement**: Evaluating creativity can enable developers to refine and enhance AI algorithms, leading to more creative and valuable AI-generated content.
- **Customization**: Organizations can use creativity measurement to identify the most suitable AI-generated content for their specific needs, ensuring tailored and creative solutions.
- **Performance benchmarking**: Measuring creativity can enable businesses to establish performance benchmarks for AI-generated content

and aid in the selection of the most appropriate AI system based on creative performance.

- **AI in education and training**: As AI plays an increasingly larger role in education and training, measuring creativity will become vital to ensure that AI-generated content effectively fosters creative learning and problem-solving.

In conclusion, understanding how to measure creativity in AI-generated content is essential to harnessing its full potential for enterprises and computational creativity applications. By using a variety of methods and criteria to evaluate AI-generated content, businesses can derive unique insights, improve algorithms, and ensure their AI systems are adequately aligning with their creative goals.

20.2 Criteria for Assessing Computational Creativity

The development of generative AI models has opened new opportunities for computational creativity in various domains such as art, music, design, and writing. As AI systems become more sophisticated, businesses and users increasingly face the challenge of evaluating the creative outputs produced by these models. Assessing computational creativity involves distinguishing the factors that make a particular system creative and measuring the extent of this creativity.

In this section, we will explore criteria for assessing computational creativity, including novelty, value, quality, intentionality, and autonomy. This multi-faceted approach aims to form a holistic framework to evaluate generative AI output and guide enterprise decisions about adoption, development, and investment in AI-driven creative processes.

20.2.1 Novelty

Creativity is often synonymous with the production of novel ideas, artifacts, or processes. Thus, assessing novelty in computational creativity involves determining the extent to which a system's outputs are unique, surprising, and distinguishable from prior creations. Novelty can generally be measured in the following ways:

1. **Unpredictability**: The degree to which the output is unexpected or surprising when compared to existing creations or prior outputs.
2. **Diversity**: The range and variety of the output, considering both the range of styles and the differences between individual generated results.
3. **Originality**: The capacity of the output to present new and unique perspectives or combinations, as opposed to merely mimicking or refining existing creations.

20.2.2 Value

Beyond novelty, creative artifacts need to possess some sort of value or utility. To assess the value of outputs generated by a computational system, we can consider the:

1. **Relevance**: The degree to which the output is contextually appropriate or meaningful for its intended use, audience, or purpose.
2. **Aesthetic or Functional Value**: The aesthetic or functional qualities of the generated output, such as beauty, harmony or practicality.
3. **Problem-solving Ability**: The effectiveness of the output in addressing, solving or contributing to a specific problem or challenge.

20.2.3 Quality

Quality is a measure of the overall craftsmanship, refinement, and skill exhibited in a creative output. In assessing computational creativity, the quality of AI-generated output can be evaluated through factors like:

1. **Technical Proficiency**: The degree to which the generated output adheres to the principles, techniques, and norms of its respective discipline (e.g., composition in music, grammar in writing, etc.).
2. **Cohesiveness**: The overall unity, coherence, and fluency of the output, reflecting a clear structure and organization.
3. **Expressiveness**: The extent to which the output is able to convey emotions or ideas that resonate with audiences or users.

20.2.4 Intentionality

Intentionality examines the purpose or objectives driving a creative system or process. Evaluating the intentionality in AI-generated outputs would require an assessment of:

1. **System Goals**: The objectives or goals programmed into the generative AI system, which could include maximizing novelty, value, or specific characteristics.
2. **Task Appropriateness**: The degree to which the AI system is suitable for a given creative task, reflecting an understanding of the task's context, requirements, and constraints.
3. **Adaptability**: The capacity of the system to learn from feedback, and adapt or modify its output to align better with its creative objectives.

20.2.5 Autonomy

Examining a system's autonomy seeks to understand the extent to which AI-generated outputs are independent of human intervention or influence. A higher degree of autonomy is generally more desirable for computational creativity. Autonomy can be assessed by evaluating:

1. **Creative Control**: The degree to which the AI system independently makes choices and decisions throughout the creative process, rather than relying solely on pre-defined rules or explicit human input.
2. **Learning Capacity**: The ability of the AI system to learn, develop, and evolve its own creative processes over time, often involving analysis of previously generated outputs or external data sources.
3. **Collaboration**: The level of interaction and mutual innovation between the AI system and human users or other AI systems, reflecting a balance between independence and effective collaboration.

Evaluating computational creativity is inherently subjective and context-dependent. The criteria outlined in this section provide a comprehensive framework to guide decision-makers in assessing AI-generated outputs, but it is essential to recognize that these factors may be more or less relevant depending on the specific domain or application in question. Ultimately, understanding and assessing computational creativity is a critical step in harnessing the full potential of generative AI systems for enterprises and unlocking new opportunities in creative domains.

20.3. Addressing biases in AI-generated creative outputs

One of the key concerns surrounding the implementation of AI technology for various purposes, including generative AI, is the presence of biases. Such biases can have negative consequences for businesses, individuals, and society as a whole. Consequently, AI-driven models and creative outputs must be essentially free from these prejudices. In this section, we will discuss the sources of biases, examine their impact, and explore various techniques to help mitigate their influence in AI-generated creative outputs.

20.3.1. Sources of biases in AI

There are multiple points in the data pipeline where biases can emerge, such as during data collection, preprocessing, or model training. Often, biases stem from the following sources:

1. **Historical data**: Datasets required for training AI models can be biased due to historical patterns of prejudice or exclusionary practices.
2. **Data sampling**: Sampling imbalances in the dataset can lead to an insufficient representation of certain groups or viewpoints, leading to biases during training.
3. **Feature selection**: Certain features might unfairly favor one group or hold inherent biases, either due to their design or the application of the selected features.
4. **Labeling**: Humans labeling the data can introduce biases as they might carry their own personal judgments, experiences, and stereotypes.
5. **Algorithmic bias**: Certain algorithms might favor specific patterns, thus introducing bias during training or inference.

20.3.2. Impact of biases in creative outputs

Creative outputs generated by AI models are not immune to biases. They can often reflect the biases present in the data used for training. This can lead to several negative consequences:

1. **Reinforcing stereotypes**: Biased AI-generated content might perpetuate existing harmful stereotypes about certain groups, leading to further misunderstandings or prejudice.
2. **Exclusion**: Biased representations can result in the exclusion of specific groups or perspectives in AI-generated work, thereby disregarding their respective values and contributions.
3. **Misrepresentation**: Certain groups might be portrayed in an unfair or distorted manner in AI-generated outputs, which can cause offense and perpetuate falsehoods.
4. **Misinformation**: Biased AI models may draw conclusions or provide recommendations based on biased data, leading to the spread of misinformation and potentially harmful consequences.

20.3.3. Strategies for addressing biases in AI-generated creative outputs

To mitigate biases in AI-generated creative outputs, several approaches can be employed throughout the data pipeline, including data collection, preprocessing, and model training.

1. **Diverse data sources**: Utilizing a variety of data sources can help reduce the effects of biased data, as diversity can lead to more balanced datasets.
2. **Stratified sampling**: To ensure that all groups are adequately represented in the dataset, sampling methods can be employed to maintain proportionality between groups.
3. **Bias identification and measurement**: Before training, it is essential to conduct a thorough analysis of the dataset to uncover any biases present in the data. Various statistical methods can be applied to measure and identify biases.
4. **Data preprocessing**: Techniques such as re-sampling or re-weighting can be employed to address biases and establish a better balance in the dataset.
5. **Fair feature selection**: Careful selection of features to be used during the training process can help reduce biases. Features that perpetuate biases should be avoided or redesigned.
6. **Labeling guidelines**: Providing clear labeling guidelines to human annotators and employing third-party reviews can help maintain consistency and minimize the introduction of biases during labeling tasks.
7. **Transparent and explainable models**: Utilizing interpretable AI models can lead to a better understanding of the decision-making process and help to spot any biases present in the outputs.
8. **Bias-mitigating algorithms**: Employing algorithms that are specifically designed to mitigate biases can be beneficial. These algorithms can reduce both the effects of historical biases and biases emerging during the training process.
9. **Continuous monitoring and evaluation**: Regularly monitoring model outputs and evaluating feedback from users are necessary to ensure that

biases are not unintentionally introduced, perpetuated, or amplified.

10. **Collaboration**: Proactively engaging with stakeholders and encouraging collaboration can foster a diverse range of perspectives and increase awareness of potential biases.

By proactively addressing biases in AI-generated creative outputs, enterprises can improve the quality, efficiency, fairness, and accuracy of their AI systems, and better support their human workforce. The key takeaway is that taking responsibility for the ethical use of AI technology can lead to a more inclusive, productive, and beneficial environment for all parties involved.

Chapter 21: The Ethics of AI-Driven Creativity

As artificial intelligence (AI) becomes an increasingly capable partner in the pursuit of creative enterprise, the question of ethics comes to the forefront. AI-driven creativity, like all AI applications, poses unique ethical challenges. In this chapter, we will explore these challenges and consider ways to address them as we push the boundaries of computational creativity.

21.1 Ownership and Attribution of AI-Generated Content

When AI generates creative content, who should be given credit for the work? Is it the person or team who designed and trained the AI, or should it be the AI itself? This question has significant implications for intellectual property rights, royalties, and artistic recognition.

Traditionally, the ownership of creative works has been easily assignable to human authors or artists. However, the concept of ownership is vastly more complex when an AI generates content. The rise of generative AI necessitates considerations such as:

1. **Human-AI collaboration**: Does partial ownership of the creative output belong to the designer of the AI or the AI itself? How do we determine the extent of AI or human input in a collaborative work?

2. **Derivative works**: AI tools may build upon existing creative works from other artists. How do we ensure the rights of the original creators are protected?
3. **Training data**: AI models are often trained on large datasets from a variety of sources. How do we track the lineage and ensure proper attribution for the data used in creating an AI model?

21.2 Bias and Stereotyping in AI-generated Content

AI systems, including those involved in creative processes, often learn from large datasets that can include biases and stereotypes from the real world. These biases can be unintentionally reproduced, amplified, or even introduced by the AI.

To address these concerns, creative AI systems must be closely monitored and ethically trained to ensure that diverse, equitable, and inclusive perspectives are represented. Additionally, developers must ensure transparency in AI system design, allowing for the effective examination and correction of biases present in the system.

21.3 Privacy and Personal Data in AI-generated Content

The inclusion of personal or sensitive data within training datasets poses considerable privacy risks. In a world of facial recognition, voice synthesis, and personalised AI recommendations, it is more important than ever to protect individuals' privacy and control their personal data.

This is particularly important in the context of AI-generated content, whether it is in the form of art, writing, or other creative material. AI developers and users must navigate the ethical complexities of using personal information to create content while preserving the autonomy and privacy of individuals. The following considerations must be addressed:

1. **Anonymization**: Techniques such as data anonymization and differential privacy can ensure the protection of individual identities in training datasets.
2. **Consent**: Ensuring informed consent from individuals whose data will be used in AI training is crucial to preserving their privacy rights.
3. **Transparency**: Providing clarity on how personal data is used during AI training and generation can help engender trust in the AI's creative output.

21.4 Impact on Human Creativity and Job Security

The proliferation of AI-driven creativity has raised concerns about the potential impact on human employment in creative fields such as art, design, and writing. Will AI eventually outpace human creativity and lead to significant job displacement?

While AI-driven creative tools have increased in capability, they remain supplementary to human creativity, rather than replacing it. Humans possess abstract thinking, empathy, and subjective experiences that AI cannot replicate. Therefore, it is essential to promote a symbiotic relationship between human creators and AI, where AI assists and augments human creativity rather than overpowering it.

21.5 Ensuring Responsible and Ethical AI Development and Use

As we continue to explore the potential of AI-driven creativity, it is vital that we develop and adopt ethical guidelines and frameworks to ensure responsible innovation in the field. Developers, users, and regulators should collaborate to establish best practices that protect the interests of individuals, society, and the creative community as a whole.

Key elements of responsible and ethical AI-driven creativity include:

1. **Transparency**: Clear communication of the AI system's function, purpose, and limitations.
2. **Accountability**: Assignment of responsibility for AI-generated content and AI system behavior.
3. **Privacy**: Protection and advocacy for users' privacy rights.
4. **Inclusivity**: Promotion of diverse perspectives and the prevention of bias and discrimination.
5. **Education**: Encouraging public understanding of the ethical issues associated with AI-driven creativity.

By addressing these ethical concerns, we can help ensure a future where AI-driven creativity continues to enhance, support, and augment the human creative spirit, while safeguarding the values and diversity that contribute to the richness of human expression.

21.1 Ownership and Intellectual Property in AI-Generated Content

In today's world, AI-generated content is rapidly changing the landscape of creative industries. With the advent of more advanced AI algorithms and machine learning techniques, AI is now seen playing an influential role in fields as diverse as art, writing, music, and design. As we continue to push the boundaries of technology to produce even more complex and innovative AI-generated content, new questions arise surrounding the ownership and intellectual property (IP) associated with these creations. In this section of the book, we present the various implications, possibilities, and challenges to consider when addressing intellectual property and ownership aspects in AI-generated content.

Recognizing AI-Creations: The Current Intellectual Property Laws

Intellectual property laws are designed to protect the ownership rights of original creators or inventors of an idea, creation, or innovation. In general, IP laws are divided into four main categories: copyrights, trademarks, patents, and trade secrets, each of which serves a specific purpose.

Copyrights protect the originality of works expressed in a tangible medium (such as literature, music, and films), while trademarks are concerned with brand identity aspects like logos, symbols, or phrases used to distinguish goods and services. Patents, on the other hand, focus on safeguarding new inventions and innovations in technology. Lastly, trade secrets entail a unique set of confidential information valuable to a business, which is not publicly known.

The Challenges in AI-Generated Content and IP Laws

While our current intellectual property laws are designed to protect human-produced content, they fail to adequately address AI-generated content, mainly because AI was never taken into consideration during the development of these laws. This has led to a considerable degree of uncertainty, debate, and confusion about which laws should apply to AI-generated content.

Some challenges to consider include:

1. **Originality and creativity**: Our existing IP laws usually require a degree of human originality and creativity for protection. However, AI-generated content might not align with these criteria, as AI algorithms inherently lack the conscious intent and creative expression that define human creations.
2. **AI as author or inventor**: If an AI algorithm generates content independently, without human intervention, can it be considered the author or inventor? Our current laws only recognize human authors or inventors; therefore, granting legal rights to AI systems would require rethinking the foundations of intellectual property.

3. **Ownership interests**: If AI-generated content is granted IP protection, who would own the rights? Is it the AI system's creators, the ones who provide training data, entities implementing the AI, or the AI itself? Resolving such questions would require redefining ownership concepts whose scope is currently limited to humans.

Potential Solutions and Approaches to Address AI-Generated Content IP Issues

With AI-generated content posing new challenges to the intellectual property landscape, possible solutions and approaches must be considered to ensure clarity, fairness, and innovation for all parties involved.

Adapting IP Laws

Given the complex nature of AI-generated content, adapting existing IP laws or developing new ones to incorporate AI remains a challenging yet crucial step. Lawmakers need to address the issues of AI-generated content's originality, creativity, and authorship while preserving the incentives for invention, creation, and innovation that these laws encourage.

Human-AI Collaboration

As AI-generated content often results from a combination of human input and AI computation, sharing ownership rights between human creators and AI developers could be a possible solution. Under this approach, both the AI programmer and the individual utilizing the AI system would be considered joint authors (or inventors), thereby ensuring a degree of control and reward for both parties in the creative process.

Incentivizing Innovation through Alternative Rights Models

Alternative models to IP rights could encourage innovation while affording protection to AI-generated content. One such model is the adoption of open-source licensing schemes akin to those used in software development. This would grant access to innovations and creations without restrictions, fostering the sharing of ideas and promoting creative collaboration.

Embracing the Future of AI-Generated Content

The rapid advancements in AI-generated content and the subsequent challenges to the intellectual property landscape warrant a thorough reevaluation of existing IP laws and concepts. As legal developers and policymakers keenly examine these issues, stakeholders in the creative industries must be prepared for a transition to adapt to this new era of AI-mediated creativity.

Instilling clear guidelines, policies, and regulations for AI-generated content will not only ensure a fair and balanced ecosystem for IP protection; it will also pave the way for harnessing the potential of generative AI for the benefit of all stakeholders and promote the growth of human-AI synergies in the realm of computational creativity.

21.2. Ethical considerations in computational creativity

In the age of rapid advancements in generative AI and computational creativity, it is essential for enterprises to navigate a complex landscape of ethical considerations. By understanding and addressing these concerns, organizations can establish responsible practices that are essential for long-term success and trustworthiness.

This section will delve into the ethical challenges that arise in the realm of computational creativity, examining potential consequences and discussing strategies to guide businesses in their ethical pursuits. Some key areas include:

1. **Privacy**: As AI applications increasingly create content based on data provided by human users, privacy concerns become paramount. Organizations need to be certain that the data they collect from individuals – whether related to personal preferences, demographic information, or intellectual property – is safeguarded against misuse and unauthorized access. Clear consent mechanisms and robust data protection policies should be in place to minimize risks.
2. **Bias and Fairness**: Computational creativity algorithms typically depend on training data that is reflective of the real world. As a result, these datasets may contain inherent biases present within society.

Enterprises should be diligent in detecting and addressing such biases within their AI systems, ensuring that the outputs are fair and unbiased. This can be done through effective use of diverse datasets, algorithm tweaking to mitigate biases, and continuous monitoring.

3. **Authorship and Intellectual Property**: As generative AI begins to produce creative works on par with human collaborators, the question of authorship and intellectual property (IP) becomes increasingly complicated. Businesses must work closely with legal experts to define clear guidelines for IP ownership, licensing, and attribution in the context of computational creativity. Establishing fair partnerships and acknowledging the creative input of AI systems can help foster collaboration and respect among stakeholders.

4. **Transparency and Explainability**: Given the potential for AI-generated content to be highly influential, transparency about the underlying algorithms and decision-making processes becomes crucial. Organizations leveraging computational creativity should be prepared to disclose key information about their AI systems – from the training data used to the methodologies employed – to foster trust and mitigate potential risks associated with opaque AI practices.

5. **Human-AI collaboration**: As AI systems become increasingly capable of producing creative works, it will be essential to maintain collaborative, respectful relationships between human creators and AI-generated content. Organizations should provide opportunities for human and AI inputs to be combined effectively, considering how the creative process can evolve alongside generative AI capabilities while still valuing human intuition, emotions, and expertise.

6. **Societal Impact**: The deployment of computational creativity can have far-reaching consequences, leading to job displacement and questions surrounding human role and identity. By remaining aware of these potential impacts, organizations can make more responsible decisions throughout the development and deployment process of their AI systems. Strategies may include continuous monitoring of the societal influence of computational creativity, active engagement with stakeholders, and providing upskilling or reskilling opportunities for the workforce.
7. **Regulation and Standards**: Enterprises must keep a close eye on the evolving regulatory landscape surrounding AI applications, including potential guidelines for responsible computational creativity practices. By proactively developing and adhering to industry-wide best practices, organizations can demonstrate their commitment to ethical AI creativity and contribute towards trust-building in the digital age.

In conclusion, the ethical implications of computational creativity pose profound challenges for enterprises, urging them to balance innovation with human values and social consequences. A holistic, principled approach to the development and deployment of AI-driven creative solutions will be essential for businesses to navigate this complex and evolving landscape.

By cultivating ethical practices, organizations will not only safeguard their reputations and relationships with users but also contribute to a more responsible, forward-thinking, and ultimately more productive digital creative landscape.

21.3. Balancing AI innovation with ethical guidelines

As the world embraces the potential for transformational change brought about by generative AI, it is critical that enterprises and governments establish ethical guidelines to balance the potential benefits with possible risks. This chapter explores the need to create such guidelines and how to implement them effectively in organizations.

21.3.1. The importance of ethical guidelines

AI technologies have advanced at a rapid pace, and generative AI's ability to understand, learn, and create has led to numerous applications, from personalized medicine to art and literature. However, as with any groundbreaking technology, generative AI also brings potential risks, including concerns over the manipulation of information, bias in outcomes, and the loss of individual privacy.

Establishing ethical guidelines ensures that AI technologies are used responsibly and prevent the negative consequences that could arise from unregulated use. While some ethical concerns apply to AI more generally, generative AI poses unique challenges that must be taken into account.

21.3.2. Key ethical considerations for generative AI

Several ethical considerations are particularly relevant to generating AI:

- **Bias and fairness**: Generative AI models learn from data, and if that data contains biases, the model may produce biased outcomes. Ethical guidelines must ensure that AI systems are trained on diverse and representative data and consider fairness across various dimensions (e.g., race, gender, socioeconomic status).
- **Transparency**: A lack of understanding of how generative AI models work can lead to a lack of trust in their outputs. Organizations must strive for transparency in the development and application of AI, including sharing both high-level explanations of the technology and detailed information about how decisions are made.
- **Responsibility and accountability**: As AI systems become more complex and autonomous, it becomes challenging to determine who is responsible for their actions. Clear lines of accountability should be established for the development, deployment, and operation of AI systems.
- **Privacy**: Generative AI systems often require vast amounts of data to function effectively. Organizations must ensure that data is collected, stored, and used in a manner that respects individual privacy and complies with relevant data protection laws.
- **Safety and security**: Generative AI can potentially be misused, creating harmful content or enabling illicit activities. Ethical guidelines should include measures to mitigate risks associated with AI systems and ensure that they are secure from tampering or malicious use.

21.3.3. Implementing ethical guidelines

To ensure that ethical guidelines effectively direct the development and deployment of generative AI, a structured approach is required. The following steps outline a framework for implementing ethical guidelines within an organization:

1. **Establishment of principles**: Develop a set of ethical principles that will guide the organization's approach to AI technology. These principles should reflect the organizational values and provide a framework for addressing ethical concerns.
2. **Identification of relevant stakeholders**: Determine the various stakeholders involved in the generative AI ecosystem, including developers, data providers, users, and those affected by AI-generated outputs. Engage in ongoing dialogue with these stakeholders to build a shared understanding of the ethical issues at play.
3. **Creation of guidelines**: Based on the established principles and in consultation with stakeholders, create a set of guidelines tailored to the organization's specific context and generative AI technologies. These guidelines should address the key ethical considerations outlined earlier in this chapter.
4. **Training and education**: Ensure that employees, contractors, and partners involved in the development and deployment of generative AI understand the ethical guidelines and receive appropriate training on how to follow them.
5. **Monitoring and enforcement**: Establish processes to monitor the adherence to the ethical guidelines, and enforce consequences for non-compliance. This may include establishing an AI ethics committee or appointing dedicated personnel to oversee adherence to the guidelines.
6. **Revision and adaptation**: As AI technologies and their applications continue to evolve, revisit the ethical guidelines regularly to assess their continued relevance and make necessary updates.

21.3.4. Conclusion

As generative AI continues to transform industries and reshape the way we live and work, it is crucial for enterprises to balance its innovative potential with appropriate ethical guidelines. By establishing and implementing a robust set of ethical guidelines, organizations can unlock the full potential of generative AI while minimizing potential risks and fostering an environment of trust and transparency around this transformative technology. As AI and generative AI become ever more integrated into our lives, a commitment to ethical practices will set the stage for responsible growth and continued innovation.

Response writing tips

Utilizing Generative AI to enhance the process of creating content for a variety of applications, businesses can harness the power of new technology to reduce time and effort spent on content production. Generative AI can facilitate the creation of everything from marketing materials and support documentation to website content and social media posts.

When implementing Generative AI, the length of the generated response is a crucial factor. Recently we have seen advances in the development of long-form Generative AI models such as OpenAI's GPT-3, which can generate responses as long as necessary.

In this chapter, we will discuss the importance of long-form responses for enterprises and how Generative AI can be harnessed to meet those needs. We will delve into practical applications of Generative AI and explore case studies across various sectors to understand how these technologies can create new opportunities for growth and innovation.

4.1 Why Long-form Responses are Important for Enterprises

Long-form content has several advantages over short-form content when it comes to enterprise applications. A few of these benefits include:

1. **Comprehensive Information Delivery:** Businesses need to share a wealth of content ranging from product descriptions to help material to ensure

their customers and stakeholders have access to complete, accurate information. Long-form responses can provide detailed insights and comprehensive explanations to satisfy their requirements.

2. **Improved SEO:** Long-form content often ranks higher in search engine results pages (SERPs). When Generative AI-generated content can scale the length and depth of the response, it helps boost visibility and credibility for the enterprise in search results, leading to potential new leads and increased customer engagement.

3. **Increased Audience Engagement and Retention:** When AI-generated content can provide substantial value to the reader, it tends to engage them for longer durations. This increased engagement, in turn, contributes to improved customer retention rates and increased likelihood of conversions.

4. **Fuel for Content Marketing:** With the ever-growing importance of content marketing, businesses need a constant stream of fresh, high-quality content to feed their marketing strategies. Long-form AI-generated content can accelerate content production while maintaining the level of detail and depth consumers expect from modern businesses.

4.2 Exploring Generative AI Possibilities in Different Industries

4.2.1 Healthcare Industry

Generative AI can be used to automatically create long-form educational materials, patient communications, and research summaries. For example, pharmaceutical companies can use Generative AI to develop comprehensive articles detailing new research findings, enabling easier interpretation and adoption of new medications by medical professionals.

4.2.2 Financial Services Industry

Banking and financial services organizations can employ Generative AI to create in-depth reports on market trends, risk analysis, and other critical factors. These detailed AI-generated reports can provide clear insights into complex financial data, helping stakeholders make informed decisions.

4.2.3 Retail Industry

AI-generated content can provide detailed product descriptions, customer reviews, and how-to articles to enhance user experiences on e-commerce platforms. Furthermore, retailers can utilize Generative AI to create personalized long-form content, such as emails or blog posts, tailored to each customer's preferences, driving increased customer loyalty and sales.

4.2.4 Education Industry

Generative AI can be used to curate personalized learning materials and long-form articles that meet the specific needs of students. These AI-generated study materials can provide a deeper understanding of the topic, helping students improve their comprehension and retention of the material.

4.3 Challenges and Future Outlook

Despite the exciting potential of Generative AI, businesses must consider the challenges that accompany its implementation. One such challenge is ensuring the quality and accuracy of the generated content, as low-quality or misleading information can harm a business's reputation. Another concern is the ethical implications of using the generated content, as content creators and businesses must consider issues such as attribution, copyright infringement, and plagiarism.

Several developments are expected to influence the future of Generative AI, potentially enhancing its capabilities further. These advancements could push the boundaries of what AI-generated responses can achieve in terms of length, coherence, and relevance. As cutting-edge models like GPT-3 continue to be refined, the future of generative AI for enterprises and computational creativity will likely prove to be transformative.

In conclusion, long-form Generative AI can provide numerous benefits to businesses, helping them meet the increasing demand for high-quality, engaging content across a range of applications. Automation in content generation not only accelerates content production but also fosters innovation and unlocks new opportunities for growth. By understanding how Generative AI can be harnessed to create detailed long-form content, enterprises can stay ahead of the curve and meet the needs of today's rapidly-evolving digital landscape.

Chapter 22: The Future of Computational Creativity

1. Introduction

As we move closer to a future where AI continues to develop at an unprecedented rate, the implications of artificial intelligence on various industries are apparent. One field where AI has tremendous potential is computational creativity. The ability of intelligent systems to generate ideas, solutions, and even art has inspired researchers and innovators across a spectrum of fields. In this chapter, we will explore the potential directions for the future of computational creativity and dive into the benefits and challenges it presents.

2. Widening scope of applications

In recent years, we've observed a plethora of examples where computational creativity has left its mark. From AI-generated artwork selling for tens of thousands of dollars to algorithms composing original music, computational creativity has come a long way. In the future, these applications are expected to expand into numerous domains, including various artistic disciplines, marketing, scientific research, and more.

2.1. Art and entertainment

Generative art has already made significant strides, and as AI models become more advanced, we can expect even more innovative and aesthetically pleasing artwork to emerge. This will likely ignite a broader conversation about the meaning of art and the value we place on human-created versus AI-generated pieces. Consequently, this could redefine the role of artists in society and reveal new perspectives on human-AI collaboration.

Furthermore, we may witness computational creativity influencing the entertainment industry. Scriptwriting, character modeling, and film direction could benefit from AI-driven creativity, helping create more immersive and engaging stories.

2.2. Scientific research

In fields such as drug discovery, materials science, and synthetic biology, computational creativity can revolutionize the way researchers discover and develop novel solutions. Intelligent systems may provide insights and propose fresh approaches that humans may not have otherwise considered.

2.3. Education

The role of AI in education is already beginning to expand. In the future, computational creativity could be used to customize learning curricula, facilitate creative problem solving, and foster an appreciation for the sciences and the arts in students.

3. Opportunities for collaboration

The integration of computational creativity into various sectors doesn't signify the replacement of human creativity, but rather, it can serve as an enhancement. AI and human creators can collaborate effectively to produce original and pioneering work.

3.1. Augmented creativity

In the future, computational creativity could function as a valuable tool for supplementing human thought and inspiration. AI systems might be employed to generate rough ideas or execute initial experiments, thereby freeing up time and resources for human practitioners to iterate, refine, and develop these concepts.

3.2. Hybrid art

Rather than viewing computational creativity as a purely separate field, we can begin to view it as a new medium for humans to work with. Artists and scientists, for instance, can use the output of generative AI models as raw material for further exploration and manipulation, establishing a new style of hybrid creative output that genuinely fuses human ingenuity and AI-driven insight.

3.3. Education of AI models

There will be increasing opportunities for humans to educate AI in creative fields, be it through fine-tuning existing models or curating data. This transfer of human knowledge and intuition onto computational systems will become an essential skill in the age of computational creativity.

4. Ethical and societal considerations

As we move toward a future where computational creativity plays a more prominent role, several ethical and societal implications must be considered.

4.1. Ownership and copyright

The advent of AI-generated work raises questions about ownership, copyright, and value attribution. Legal and regulatory frameworks must evolve and establish clear guidelines for dealing with these issues.

4.2. Originality

As AI becomes more prevalent in creative fields, defining "originality" and determining the merit of creative output may become increasingly complicated. Society may need to reevaluate its perspectives on creativity and incorporate AI's contribution into these definitions.

4.3. Human expression

The integration of computational creativity into various artistic domains might prompt a reexamination of the role of human expression in the creative process. Discussions surrounding the place of AI-generated art and the significance of human emotion in artistic creation will likely intensify as we move forward.

5. Conclusion

The future of computational creativity bears the promise of diverse opportunities and incredible advancements. As we navigate this fascinating terrain, ongoing collaboration between humans and AI, as well as careful consideration of the ethical and societal implications, will be crucial in ensuring that the potential of computational creativity is harnessed for the greater good.

22.1. Predictions for AI's impact on creative industries

The pervasive adoption of artificial intelligence (AI) technologies has the potential to transform the way humans interact with the digital world, impacting numerous industries that rely on human creativity. In this section, we will discuss how AI is poised to revolutionize various creative industries, such as design, music, film, writing, and gaming. We will explore some of the key predictions regarding the dawning age of AI-driven computational creativity and discuss the challenges and opportunities it presents for the future.

22.1.1. Design and Visual Arts

AI has already begun to penetrate various aspects of the design and visual arts industry. From generating logos and brand identities to creating compelling advertisements and virtual reality experiences, AI-powered design tools are making their way into the hands of designers around the world. Some of the predictions related to AI's impact on this industry include:

1. **Automated design generation**: AI-powered algorithms will continue to improve their ability to generate unique and visually appealing designs based on user inputs or automatically, with minimal human intervention.
2. **AI-assisted design evaluation**: AI algorithms will be employed to analyze and critique design proposals, providing real-time feedback on aspects such as aesthetics, style, and composition to help designers iterate quickly and improve their work.
3. **Improved design personalization**: AI will enable designers to create highly customized experiences that cater to individual user preferences, demographics, and context. This will result in highly personalized designs on a scale never before possible.
4. **Crowdsourced design**: As AI tools become more prevalent, collaborative platforms that allow users worldwide to submit designs and ideas will prosper. AI systems will help to organize, evaluate, and synthesize these contributions into cohesive, aesthetic, and highly creative designs.

22.1.2. Music and Audio Production

From composing music to synthesizing and processing sounds, AI has the potential to significantly alter the landscape of the music industry. Here are some predictions for how AI might impact this creative industry:

1. **AI-driven composition**: AI algorithms will continue to mature to compose music across a wide range of genres, styles, and moods. AI-generated

music will become increasingly difficult to distinguish from human-created compositions.
2. **Audio synthesis and processing**: AI systems will offer novel and creative ways to synthesize sounds, process audio signals, and generate effects. This will open up new avenues for experimentation and creativity in music and sound production.
3. **Collaborative music creation**: AI-powered platforms will enable musicians to collaborate over distances, crossing geographical and stylistic boundaries to create new and innovative music.
4. **Music recommendation and curation**: Machine learning algorithms will drive more personalized and nuanced music recommendations and curation, helping users find the perfect song or artist for any mood, moment or event.

22.1.3. Film, Television, and Video Production

AI is expected to reshape the landscape of film, television, and video production in several ways. Here are some key predictions for this creative industry:

1. **Scriptwriting and storytelling**: AI systems will emerge as powerful tools in writing scripts and dialogues, helping writers explore new storytelling techniques and cater to diverse viewers' tastes.
2. **AI-powered special effects**: AI will play a crucial role in generating realistic visual effects and animations, automating tedious tasks and reducing production costs without compromising quality. This will empower creators to experiment with new visual styles and techniques, regardless of their budget constraints.
3. **Automated video editing**: AI will assist editors in pacing, selecting shots, and making creative

decisions, speeding up the post-production process and reducing human error.
4. **Data-driven decision-making**: AI analytics will help production companies make data-driven decisions about project investments, talent recruitment, promotional strategies, and audience targeting.

22.1.4. Writing and Journalism

As AI-powered natural language processing (NLP) technologies continue to evolve, its potential impact on the writing and journalism industry is becoming increasingly evident. Some key predictions for this creative field include:

1. **Automated content generation**: AI algorithms will progressively get better at generating written content, from simple news articles to complex narratives, adapting to the style and tone of different publications.
2. **AI-assisted writing tools**: AI will facilitate writers' work by providing real-time suggestions on grammar, tone, style, and structure, helping them refine their prose and reach their target audience more effectively.
3. **News filtering and summarization**: AI systems will enable personalized news feeds that curate articles, filter out irrelevant content, and provide concise summaries tailored to each reader's interests.
4. **Fact-checking and verification**: AI-powered tools will assist journalists in verifying facts, detecting fake news or misinformation, and assessing the credibility of sources, ensuring that the information disseminated is accurate and reliable.

22.1.5. Gaming and Interactive Entertainment

AI has already made significant advances in the gaming industry, notably in developing game agents and enhancing player experiences. Here are some predictions about the future impact of AI in this creative realm:

1. **Procedural content generation**: AI algorithms will facilitate the generation of game assets, terrains, and narratives in real-time, providing players with unique and dynamic experiences that adapt to their play styles.
2. **Smart NPCs (Non-Player Characters)**: AI will be increasingly used to create intelligent and engaging NPCs that exhibit more human-like behaviors, contributing to more immersive and believable game worlds.
3. **AI-driven game design**: AI-powered design tools will enable game developers to create games more efficiently, streamline production pipelines, and enhance player experiences with innovative gameplay mechanics.
4. **eSports and competitive gaming**: AI systems will play a crucial role in shaping the future of competitive gaming and eSports, from enhancing coaching tools to improving match analytics and fostering fair-play mechanisms.

22.1.6. Conclusion

In summary, the impact of AI on creative industries is profound and far-reaching. From design to music, film to writing, and gaming to interactive entertainment, AI-powered tools and technologies stand poised to revolutionize the way we create, consume, and engage with creative content. As AI continues to advance, its potential to democratize creativity and promote inclusivity, collaboration, and innovation is boundless. However, the same technologies also bring new challenges and ethical considerations to the table, which must be thoughtfully addressed as we traverse the uncharted territory of AI-driven computational creativity.

22.2. Emerging Trends and Advancements in Computational Creativity

Computational creativity is a rapidly evolving field that seeks to build intelligent systems capable of producing creative outputs, such as art, music, and literature. In recent years, there have been several key advancements and emerging trends in the field, driven by the increased availability of data, improvements in computational power, and the development of novel algorithms and techniques. In this section, we will explore some of these trends and advancements shaping the future of computational creativity.

22.2.1. Generative Adversarial Networks (GANs)

Generative Adversarial Networks (GANs) have been a significant breakthrough in the field of computational creativity. Introduced by Ian Goodfellow and his colleagues in 2014, GANs consist of two neural networks – a Generator and a Discriminator – that compete against each other during the learning process. The Generator creates fake samples, while the Discriminator evaluates the quality of these samples, attempting to distinguish them from real samples. This adversarial approach allows GANs to generate high-quality, diverse, and creative outputs in a wide variety of domains, including image synthesis, style transfer, and even 3D object generation.

22.2.2. Transformer Models and Language Generation

Transformer models, such as GPT-3 (Generative Pre-trained Transformer 3) by OpenAI, have revolutionized the field of natural language processing (NLP) in recent years. These models employ a self-attention mechanism to analyze and generate human-like text, demonstrating impressive capabilities in tasks such as translation, summarization, and content generation. As a result, transformer models have attracted significant interest as a tool for facilitating computational creativity in the domain of literature, poetry, and storytelling, enabling the generation of creative textual content that is both coherent and contextually relevant.

22.2.3. Multimodal Models

While early computational creativity research often focused on single-domain applications, there is a growing trend towards developing models capable of generating creative outputs across multiple modalities. Multimodal models aim to understand the relationships between different forms of data, such as text, images, and sound, and leverage these relationships to generate more complex and nuanced outputs.

For example, DALL-E, another model developed by OpenAI, combines aspects of both GPT-3 and GANs to generate high-quality images based on textual input. This ability to generate creative content across multiple domains opens up new possibilities for applications in areas such as multimedia storytelling, digital art, and music composition.

22.2.4. Reinforcement Learning

Reinforcement learning (RL) is a subfield of artificial intelligence in which an agent learns optimal behavior through trial and error, by interacting with its environment and receiving feedback in the form of rewards or penalties. This approach has been increasingly applied to computational creativity problems, allowing systems to explore novel solutions and optimize their creative output based on user-defined rewards.

For example, in the domain of music generation, RL has been used to develop models that can create unique melodies or harmonies by exploring and learning from a range of different musical styles. This approach allows the creative process to be guided by the model's own exploration of the creative space, rather than relying solely on pre-existing patterns or templates.

22.2.5. Collaborative AI-Enhanced Creativity

Another emerging trend in computational creativity is the development of systems that offer creative assistance to human users, rather than replacing them entirely. These AI-enhanced tools aim to augment human creativity by offering suggestions, insights or partial solutions that users can build upon or modify as required.

For example, AI-enabled design tools can help architects explore a broader range of potential design solutions by generating alternative layouts or suggesting new material combinations. Similarly, AI-driven text editors can assist writers in generating story ideas, refining character arcs, or even suggesting entire passages of text as needed.

22.2.6. Ethical Considerations and Bias Mitigation

As computational creativity systems become more sophisticated and widespread, ethical considerations around their application and use also become increasingly important. Issues such as fairness, accountability, and transparency are critical, as is the need to prevent the perpetuation of biases present in the training data used by these systems.

To address these concerns, researchers are developing techniques to detect and mitigate biases in creative outputs and increase the transparency of the decision-making process underpinning these systems. This includes approaches such as auditing algorithms, implementing fairness constraints, and encouraging diversity in AI-generated content.

In conclusion, the future of computational creativity is poised to be shaped by advances in GANs, transformer models, multimodal models, reinforcement learning, and collaborative creativity. These trends, coupled with growing awareness of ethical considerations and bias mitigation, will continue to catalyze innovation in the field and unlock new possibilities for creative applications of AI in the enterprise context.

22.3 Preparing for a World with AI-Driven Creative Solutions

As AI-driven creative solutions continue to advance, it becomes increasingly essential for enterprises to adapt and prepare for the changes that these technologies will bring. In this section, we will discuss some primary aspects that companies need to consider while preparing for the world with AI-driven creative solutions. These aspects include understanding the potential roles of AI in creativity, addressing the ethical considerations, redefining the creative workforce, fostering a generation of AI-savvy leaders, embracing interdisciplinary collaboration, and optimizing investment strategies in AI technologies.

Understanding The Potential Roles of AI In Creativity

To effectively leverage AI-driven creative solutions, it is crucial first to understand the potential roles of AI in creativity. The evolving AI technologies could transform creative processes in various industries, including but not limited to, art and design, marketing and advertising, content generation, product development, and scientific research. Organizations need to research and identify which tasks and processes could benefit from AI's capabilities, from offering data-driven insights to improving decision-making or enhancing creative output.

Addressing Ethical Considerations

With the integration of AI-driven creative solutions comes the responsibility to address ethical considerations, including ownership, intellectual property, transparency, biases, and privacy. Companies must understand and outline the responsibilities and rights related to AI-generated creative outputs. As legal frameworks continue to develop in this emerging field, organizations need to collaborate with regulatory bodies and stakeholders to ensure ethical usage of AI-powered creativity.

Redefining the Creative Workforce

The implementation of AI-driven creative solutions will undoubtedly have an impact on the workforce landscape. Organizations must shift their perspective to prepare for a new generation of creative professionals whose skills and talents are augmented by AI technologies. In this new world, human creativity will still be highly valued, but employees will need to develop complementary skills to navigate and utilize AI tools effectively. Training and education programs that equip professionals with the necessary knowledge and expertise to adapt to this AI-infused environment will be essential in the preparation process.

Fostering a Generation of AI-Savvy Leaders

As AI plays a more significant role in shaping creative industries, organizations must prioritize cultivating leaders who understand these advanced technologies' nuances and capabilities. Investing in talent development programs that focus on AI awareness, understanding, and implementation will help companies bridge the knowledge gap between traditional creative leadership and AI-driven creative solutions. Future leaders must be equipped with both the knowledge and skills to guide the strategic implementation of AI-based creative initiatives.

Embracing Interdisciplinary Collaboration

The future with AI-driven creative solutions calls for interdisciplinary collaboration, as multiple fields will be responsible for harnessing AI's potential. This interdisciplinary collaboration can manifest in different forms, such as teaming art educators with technologists, collaborating between data analysts and marketers, or connecting scientists with creative experts. Encouraging the cross-pollination of ideas and expertise will enrich the value that AI-driven creative solutions can bring to the organization.

Optimizing Investment Strategies in AI Technologies

To effectively prepare for a world with AI-driven creative solutions, enterprises must optimize their investment strategies in AI technologies. This includes allocating resources to AI research and development, enabling AI experimentation within different departments, and investing in AI training and education programs. Companies must also explore partnerships with other organizations or institutions to leverage the collective expertise in AI development and application. By prioritizing and optimizing investments in AI technologies, enterprises can stay ahead of the curve and remain competitive in a rapidly evolving landscape.

In conclusion, the emergence of AI-driven creative solutions presents new opportunities and challenges for enterprises. By understanding the potential roles of AI in creativity, addressing ethical considerations, redefining the creative workforce, fostering a generation of AI-savvy leaders, embracing interdisciplinary collaboration, and optimizing investment strategies in AI technologies, organizations can better position themselves to navigate and leverage the transformative impact of AI on the creative landscape. By preparing for this AI-driven future, businesses can capitalize on the immense potential that these creative solutions offer, ultimately driving innovation, efficiency, and growth.

Chapter 23: Conclusion: Embracing the Future of Generative AI

As we step into the future, the transformative potential of generative AI for both enterprises and computational creativity becomes increasingly evident. We are on the cusp of a new era in which ground-breaking applications of AI will reshape industries, augment human expertise, and spark creativity within the realm of the arts. In this concluding chapter, we take a moment to envision the world of possibilities that lie ahead, while also remaining cognizant of the challenges we need to tackle for ethical, responsible, and beneficial integration of AI into our lives.

Reimagining Industries and Workspaces

The implementation of generative AI in various industries will lead to more efficient and streamlined processes. For instance, in the healthcare sector, the ability of AI models to analyze vast amounts of data and generate crucial insights can prove invaluable. They can help in the early detection of diseases, the discovery of new drug compounds, and the formulation of personalized treatment plans. Patients can expect better healthcare outcomes due to these advancements, while hospitals and other care providers may reap the benefits of improved resource allocation and optimized patient care pathways.

In the design and production domains, generative AI can facilitate the creation of innovative products with minimal human effort, while optimizing for cost and sustainability. For instance, generative design tools can enable architects to create environmentally-friendly building structures that can adapt to various climatic conditions. Similarly, manufacturing sectors could employ generative AI to develop complex production workflows that reduce waste, maximize yield, and minimize costs.

Creative industries, such as film, music, and marketing, stand to be revolutionized by the potential applications of generative AI. From developing engaging marketing campaigns to composing evocative soundtracks, these tools can be used to both augment human creativity and produce original content without relying on existing templates. The impact of such advancements will reverberate through the entire creative spectrum, posing intriguing questions on the essence of creativity and ownership of AI-generated artworks.

Professional and Collaborative Dynamics in the era of Generative AI

The integration of generative AI technologies in the workplace will necessitate a reevaluation of the skills required for thriving within ever-evolving professional environments. The demand for interdisciplinary skill sets will increase, with professionals needing a combination of domain knowledge, data science expertise, and creative thinking abilities. As AI becomes more prevalent, businesses will actively seek experts adept in AI ethics, governance, and policy-making - ensuring that the development and implementation of these technologies are guided by a considerate, responsible approach.

The relationship between humans and generative AI within the workplace is likely to be more collaborative than adversarial. Instead of seeing AI solely as a threat, it can be viewed as an opportunity to maximize workplace efficiency and empower employees to focus on more crucial, strategic tasks. Generative AI can serve as a reliable partner in the co-creation process, offering insights and ideas hitherto unexplored, which can serve as excellent catalysts for human creativity. By working in harmony with AI systems, professionals can leverage the strengths of both parties, creating a more effective and inventive workspace.

Navigating Ethical Challenges and Ensuring Responsible AI Development

While the potential of generative AI is vast, careful attention must be paid to the ethical considerations that accompany it. Issues such as job displacement, potential misuse, and bias in AI-generated outcomes need to be addressed proactively. Policy-makers, organizations, and AI researchers must work together to develop legal frameworks, governance structures, and ethical guidelines that will steer the advancement of AI technologies in the right direction.

Efforts geared towards making AI systems more interpretable, explainable, and transparent must continue unabated. Enabling humans to understand the rationale behind AI decisions is crucial for building trust in AI systems and fostering their responsible integration into society.

Bias in AI-generated outcomes, be it unintentional or due to inherent limitations, must be scrutinized, acknowledged, and rectified. Stakeholders must ensure that AI technologies do not perpetuate harmful stereotypes or exacerbate existing inequalities.

Embracing the Future Together

As we move forward with the development and implementation of generative AI, it is essential that all stakeholders - from policymakers and researchers to businesses and the public - join forces in embracing its potential responsibly. Establishing a future where generative AI serves as an enabler of better lives, enriched workplace experiences, and enhanced creativity necessitates cooperation and a shared commitment to ethical guidelines and values.

Together, we can help create a world where generative AI contributes to a brighter future, championing human ingenuity, fostering collaboration, and realizing the myriad possibilities that lie within the vast, uncharted expanse of computational creativity.

23.1 Key Takeaways and Lessons Learned

As we have explored the world of Generative AI for Enterprises and Computational Creativity, many valuable insights and lessons have been gained. This section of the book summarizes those findings as key takeaways, serving as potential guiding principles for organizations and individuals looking to harness the power of generative AI in the future.

Key Takeaway 1: Generative AI is a driving force for innovation

Generative AI enables enterprises to explore uncharted territories by providing a powerful mechanism to generate novel and creative solutions. It can assist in designing new products, improving existing ones, and even fostering breakthroughs in various fields such as healthcare, finance, and art. It is crucial for organizations to fully understand the potential of generative AI to stay at the cutting edge and maintain a competitive edge in their respective industries.

Key Takeaway 2: Data quality and quantity are critical

The foundation of any successful generative AI model lies in the quality and quantity of data it is trained on.

Data should be diverse, representative, and unbiased to ensure that the AI produces the desired output, free from unwanted biases. Investing time and resources in collecting, annotating, and curating data sets will be essential for the successful implementation of generative AI applications.

Key Takeaway 3: Collaboration is key in the age of AI

With the ever-growing complexity and advancements in the field of AI, it becomes increasingly important for enterprises to collaborate effectively with other organizations, research institutions, and academia. Fostering a culture of open innovation and knowledge sharing will help drive the development and adoption of generative AI for enterprises.

Key Takeaway 4: Ethical considerations should not be overlooked

As AI continues to play a more substantial role in our lives, ethical concerns surrounding generative AI should be considered and addressed. This includes issues of fairness, privacy, accountability, and transparency. Organizations should establish guidelines and best practices that govern their use of AI to ensure that the technology is used responsibly and does not cause unintentional harm.

Key Takeaway 5: Embrace the human-in-the-loop approach

A successful generative AI system should not be seen as a replacement of humans, but rather as a tool that enhances human creativity and capabilities. Leveraging the strengths of both AI and human expertise can lead to synergistic outcomes, where AI helps automate tasks and generate novel ideas, while humans bring their critical thinking, reasoning, and domain knowledge to refine and validate AI-generated results.

Key Takeaway 6: Experimentation and adaptation are crucial

As generative AI techniques continue to evolve rapidly, organizations must be prepared to adapt and experiment with the technology. It is crucial for organizations to maintain a learning mindset and be open to incorporating new techniques, updating models, and refining applications based on feedback and results.

Key Takeaway 7: Invest in skill development and education

As generative AI becomes increasingly important for enterprises, there will be a growing need for a skilled workforce that understands the technology and can effectively utilize it for various applications.

Organizations must focus on reskilling and upskilling their workforce and invest in continuous learning programs to stay ahead of the curve. This includes supporting a culture of learning, providing access to resources and training materials, and partnering with educational institutions to build talent pipelines.

In conclusion, generative AI holds immense potential to revolutionize the way enterprises operate and bring about groundbreaking innovations. By keeping these key takeaways in mind and adapting to the rapidly evolving AI landscape, organizations can harness the power of generative AI to unleash their full creative potential and steer their respective industries into a more productive and innovative future.

Chapter 23.2 - The Transformative Power of Generative AI and Computational Creativity

As we continue to explore the applications and implications of artificial intelligence in the enterprise landscape, generative AI and computational creativity are increasingly becoming an essential focus. In this section, we'll delve into the transformative power of these technologies, the benefits they can bring to various industries, and the challenges they may face along the way.

What is Generative AI and Computational Creativity?

Generative AI refers to the development of artificial intelligence systems that can autonomously create content, designs, and solutions without direct human input. These AI systems are capable of learning from vast amounts of data, identifying patterns, and generating novel, optimized, and creative outputs.

Computational creativity, on the other hand, is a field of AI research that explores the ability of computers to emulate or simulate human-like creative processes. It involves designing algorithms that can generate content, such as text, images, music, and designs, that are not only original but also pass a certain quality threshold deemed as "creative" by humans.

How Can Generative AI and Computational Creativity Transform Enterprises?

1. **Product and Service Innovation**: Utilizing generative AI and computational creativity can lead to groundbreaking product and service innovations, giving companies a competitive advantage in the market. By allowing AI systems to analyze vast amounts of data, identify trends, and generate new ideas, businesses can tap into a world of creative possibilities that were previously unimaginable. For example, some fashion companies have already started experimenting with AI-generated designs for new clothing lines, while some car manufacturers are using generative designs to create lightweight, fuel-efficient vehicle components.
2. **Cost Reduction and Efficiency**: Implementing generative AI and computational creativity can lead to significant cost reduction and improved efficiency in various organizational operations. By automating tasks that previously required human intervention, such as content generation, design, or problem-solving, businesses can save time, money, and resources, allowing them to focus on other strategic priorities.

3. **Enhanced Customer Experience**: Generative AI and computational creativity can help businesses deliver personalized and engaging experiences to their customers. AI algorithms can analyze customer preferences, behaviors, and emotions to generate tailored content, products, or services, ultimately creating more meaningful and memorable interactions. For instance, AI-driven customer engagement platforms can curate personalized marketing content that has a higher chance of resonating with individual customers.

4. **Augmented Human Creativity**: Generative AI should not be seen as a threat to human creativity but rather as a powerful tool that compliments the creative process. By combining the capabilities of AI algorithms with human expertise, businesses can create innovative solutions that are both data-driven and guided by empathy, intuition, and experience. This collaboration can lead to the discovery of novel ideas and solutions, which are more effective, valuable, and appealing to customers.

Challenges to Overcome

Realizing the full potential of generative AI and computational creativity in the enterprise environment is not without challenges. Some of the key hurdles that need to be addressed include:

1. **Ethical Considerations**: As AI gains the ability to generate content autonomously, ethical concerns related to plagiarism, copyright infringement, and the overall ownership of creative outputs must be addressed. Clear guidelines and regulations will be required to ensure fair and responsible usage of generative AI.

2. **AI Governance**: Effective management and governance of AI systems are crucial in mitigating potential risks and biases. Organizations must establish governance models that promote transparency, accountability, and trust, ensuring that AI algorithms align with business objectives and ethical principles.
3. **Talent and Expertise**: The full potential of generative AI and computational creativity can only be realized when organizations possess the right talent and expertise. This includes specialists in AI development, data science, and product or service design, as well as cross-functional teams that can effectively collaborate and innovate.

Despite these challenges, the transformative power of generative AI and computational creativity is undeniable. As enterprises continue to embrace these technologies, they will unlock new opportunities for innovation, growth, and improved customer experiences. With a forward-thinking and responsible approach to AI adoption, businesses can benefit immensely from the inevitable advancements in generative AI and computational creativity.

23.3 Envisioning a Better Future with AI

In this chapter, we'll explore the potential benefits of leveraging Generative AI in various enterprise sectors and the potential for it to drive incredible advancements in computational creativity. We will delve into several key areas, such as AI-driven decision-making, creative AI applications, and fostering a symbiotic relationship between artificial intelligence and humans. By taking a closer look at these developments, we can begin to paint a comprehensive picture of a better future enabled by Generative AI.

23.3.1 AI-Driven Decision-Making

Decision-making is a core aspect of enterprise management. Leaders continually face an overwhelming number of choices that shape the future of their organizations. Generative AI has the potential to confront these issues with remarkable precision, analyzing vast quantities of data from an array of sources to help inform decision-making at every level. By training these systems on historical data, organizations can train AI to consider countless scenarios, identify patterns, and evaluate the potential impacts of various choices.

23.3.1.1 Data As The New Oil

In an era where data has become immensely valuable, organizations can reap the benefits of their access to vast sets of information. By utilizing Generative AI models to streamline the decision-making process based on this data, enterprises can gain a significant advantage over their competition. AI-driven insights offer organizations the opportunity to conduct deeper market analysis, forecast sales with greater accuracy, manage inventory more efficiently, and optimize resource allocation across every aspect of the business.

23.3.1.2 Operational Efficiency

Generative AI can contribute significantly to optimizing operations, spanning from supply chain management to human resources. By accurately identifying the demand for various goods and resources, AI can optimize stock levels and anticipate demand shifts. Furthermore, AI can identify opportunities for process improvements, leading to reduced costs and enhanced output. Advanced analytics and deep learning models can analyze employee performance, suggesting better-fit roles or identifying where staff training should be enhanced.

23.3.1.3 Improved Strategic Focus

AI-driven decision-making allows top-level management to focus on more strategic, future-oriented goals. By automating the analysis and decision-making related to routine tasks and operations, human input can be directed towards expansion, innovation, and building a sustainable competitive advantage.

23.3.2 Creative AI Applications

Generative AI can redefine the landscape of computational creativity, fuelling advancements in design, media, and entertainment.

23.3.2.1 Art And Design

AI-driven automated design systems can prove invaluable in various domains, from web design to video game development. When applied to graphic design, AI algorithms can generate visual elements that satisfy specific criteria, drastically reducing the time and effort required to complete a design process. Generative AI has also fostered a new wave of digital art, with artists using tools such as DeepArt to create transformative works of art that challenge the boundaries of human imagination.

23.3.2.2 Journalism And Content Creation

The ability to generate written content presents profound implications for journalism and content creation as a whole. AI algorithms can be employed to generate news articles, blog posts, and even more creative forms of writing, such as poetry and short stories. While humans will still have a crucial role in refining and editing this content, Generative AI can enable unprecedented levels of productivity.

23.3.2.3 Entertainment Industry

In the film and music industries, Generative AI can revolutionize the creative process. Algorithms can help generate movie scripts, suggest plotlines, and create compelling character profiles. Emerging technologies such as GPT-3 demonstrate impressive capabilities in generating coherent dialogue, potentially transforming traditional scriptwriting processes. Additionally, music composition and production can be invigorated by AI-generated soundtracks that fit specific moods or themes.

23.3.3 Human-AI Symbiosis

As Generative AI proves its potential in fostering new levels of creativity and innovation, the relationship between humans and AI must be nurtured and developed.

23.3.3.1 Collaboration

Artificial intelligence and human creativity should be viewed as complementary forces, each bringing unique perspectives and skills to enterprise environments. Fostering collaboration between AI and human employees can lead to enhanced productivity, innovative problem-solving approaches, and improved quality of output.

23.3.3.2 Ethical Considerations

The integration of AI into any enterprise requires thoughtful reflection on potential ethical implications. Organizations must be mindful of the potential consequences of such technologies while developing and implementing AI systems, taking measures to ensure privacy, fairness, and transparency to maintain trust and credibility.

23.3.3.3 Education And Reskilling

As AI becomes an integral part of modern enterprises, it is crucial to invest in education and reskilling programs for the existing workforce. Preparing human employees for the future of work and nurturing their ability to collaborate alongside AI-driven systems is vital in optimizing the symbiotic relationship between AI and humans.

In conclusion, with careful planning and thoughtful implementation, Generative AI has the potential to revolutionize enterprises and computational creativity in unprecedented ways. By embracing AI-driven decision-making, exploring creative AI applications, and nurturing a symbiotic relationship with humans, enterprises can reshape the future of work and create a better, more innovative future.

Content Disclaimer:

AI-Assisted Content Disclaimer:
The content of this book has been generated with the assistance of artificial intelligence (AI) language models like CHatGPT and Llama. While efforts have been made to ensure the accuracy and relevance of the information provided, the author and publisher make no warranties or guarantees regarding the completeness, reliability, or suitability of the content for any specific purpose. The AI-generated content may contain errors, inaccuracies, or outdated information, and readers should exercise caution and independently verify any information before relying on it. The author and publisher shall not be held responsible for any consequences arising from the use of or reliance on the AI-generated content in this book.

General Disclaimer:
We use content-generating tools for creating this book and source a large amount of the material from text-generation tools. We make financial material and data available through our Services. In order to do so we rely on a variety of sources to gather this information. We believe these to be reliable, credible, and accurate sources. However, there may be times when the information is incorrect.
WE MAKE NO CLAIMS OR REPRESENTATIONS AS TO THE ACCURACY, COMPLETENESS, OR TRUTH OF ANY MATERIAL CONTAINED ON OUR book. NOR WILL WE BE LIABLE FOR ANY ERRORS INACCURACIES OR OMISSIONS, AND SPECIFICALLY DISCLAIMS ANY IMPLIED WARRANTIES OR MERCHANTABILITY OR FITNESS FOR ANY PARTICULAR PURPOSE AND SHALL IN NO EVENT BE LIABLE FOR ANY LOSS OF PROFIT OR ANY

OTHER COMMERCIAL OR PROPERTY DAMAGE, INCLUDING BUT NOT LIMITED TO SPECIAL, INCIDENTAL, CONSEQUENTIAL, OR OTHER DAMAGES; OR FOR DELAYS IN THE CONTENT OR TRANSMISSION OF THE DATA ON OUR book, OR THAT THE BOOK WILL ALWAYS BE AVAILABLE.

In addition to the above, it is important to note that language models like ChatGPT are based on deep learning techniques and have been trained on vast amounts of text data to generate human-like text. This text data includes a variety of sources such as books, articles, websites, and much more. This training process allows the model to learn patterns and relationships within the text and generate outputs that are coherent and contextually appropriate.

Language models like ChatGPT can be used in a variety of applications, including but not limited to, customer service, content creation, and language translation. In customer service, for example, language models can be used to answer customer inquiries quickly and accurately, freeing up human agents to handle more complex tasks. In content creation, language models can be used to generate articles, summaries, and captions, saving time and effort for content creators. In language translation, language models can assist in translating text from one language to another with high accuracy, helping to break down language barriers.

It's important to keep in mind, however, that while language models have made great strides in generating human-like text, they are not perfect. There are still limitations to the model's understanding of the context and meaning of the text, and it may generate outputs that are incorrect or offensive. As such, it's important to use language models with caution and always verify the accuracy of the outputs generated by the model.

Financial Disclaimer

This book is dedicated to helping you understand the world of online investing, removing any fears you may have about getting started and helping you choose good investments. Our goal is to help you take control of your financial well-being by delivering a solid financial education and responsible investing strategies. However, the information contained on this book and in our services is for general information and educational purposes only. It is not intended as a substitute for legal, commercial and/or financial advice from a licensed professional. The business of online investing is a complicated matter that requires serious financial due diligence for each investment in order to be successful. You are strongly advised to seek the services of qualified, competent professionals prior to engaging in any investment that may impact you finances. This information is provided by this book, including how it was made, collectively referred to as the "Services."

Be Careful With Your Money. Only use strategies that you both understand the potential risks of and are comfortable taking. It is your responsibility to invest wisely and to safeguard your personal and financial information.

We believe we have a great community of investors looking to achieve and help each other achieve financial success through investing. Accordingly we encourage people to comment on our blog and possibly in the future our forum. Many people will contribute in this matter, however, there will be times when people provide misleading, deceptive or incorrect information, unintentionally or otherwise.

You should NEVER rely upon any information or opinions you read on this book, or any book that we may link to. The information you read here and in our services should be used as a launching point for your OWN RESEARCH into various companies and investing strategies so that you can make an informed decision about where and how to invest your money.

WE DO NOT GUARANTEE THE VERACITY, RELIABILITY OR COMPLETENESS OF ANY INFORMATION PROVIDED IN THE COMMENTS, FORUM OR OTHER PUBLIC AREAS OF THE book OR IN ANY HYPERLINK APPEARING ON OUR book.

Our Services are provided to help you to understand how to make good investment and personal financial decisions for yourself. You are solely responsible for the investment decisions you make. We will not be responsible for any errors or omissions on the book including in articles or postings, for hyperlinks embedded in messages, or for any results obtained from the use of such information. Nor, will we be liable for any loss or damage, including consequential damages, if any, caused by a reader's reliance on any information obtained through the use of our Services. Please do not use our book If you do not accept self-responsibility for your actions.

The U.S. Securities and Exchange Commission, (SEC), has published additional information on Cyberfraud to help you recognize and combat it effectively. You can also get additional help about online investment schemes and how to avoid them at the following books:http://www.sec.gov and http://www.finra.org, and http://www.nasaa.org these are each organizations set-up to help protect online investors.

If you choose ignore our advice and do not do independent research of the various industries, companies, and stocks, you intend to invest in and rely solely on information, "tips," or opinions found on our book – you agree that you have made a conscious, personal decision of your own free will and will not try to hold us responsible for the results thereof under any circumstance. The Services offered herein is not for the purpose of acting as your personal investment advisor. We do not know all the relevant facts about you and/or your individual needs, and we do not represent or claim that any of our Services are suitable for your needs. You should seek a registered investment advisor if you are looking for personalized advice.

Links to Other Sites. You will also be able to link to other books from time to time, through our Site. We do not have any control over the content or actions of the books we link to and will not be liable for anything that occurs in connection with the use of such books. The inclusion of any links, unless otherwise expressly stated, should not be seen as an endorsement or recommendation of that book or the views expressed therein. You, and only you, are responsible for doing your own due diligence on any book prior to doing any business with them.

Liability Disclaimers and Limitations: Under no circumstances, including but not limited to negligence, will we, nor our partners if any, or any of our affiliates, be held responsible or liable, directly or indirectly, for any loss or damage, whatsoever arising out of, or in connection with, the use of our Services, including without limitation, direct, indirect, consequential, unexpected, special, exemplary or other damages that may result, including but not limited to economic loss, injury, illness or death or any other type of loss or damage, or unexpected or adverse reactions to suggestions contained herein or otherwise caused or alleged to have been caused to you in connection with your use of any advice, goods or services you receive on the Site, regardless of the source, or any other book that you may have visited via links from our book, even if advised of the possibility of such damages.

Applicable law may not allow the limitation or exclusion of liability or incidental or consequential damages (including but not limited to lost data), so the above limitation or exclusion may not apply to you. However, in no event shall the total liability to you by us for all damages, losses, and causes of action (whether in contract, tort, or otherwise) exceed the amount paid by you to us, if any, for the use of our Services, if any. And by using our Site you expressly agree not to try to hold us liable for any consequences that result based on your use of our Services or the information provided therein, at any time, or for any reason, regardless of the circumstances.

Specific Results Disclaimer. We are dedicated to helping you take control of your financial well-being through education and investment. We provide strategies, opinions, resources and other Services that are specifically designed to cut through the noise and hype to help you make better personal finance and investment decisions. However, there is no way to guarantee any strategy or technique to be 100% effective, as results will vary by individual, and the effort and commitment they make toward achieving their goal. And, unfortunately we don't know you. Therefore, in using and/or purchasing our services you expressly agree that the results you receive from the use of those Services are solely up to you. In addition, you also expressly agree that all risks of use and any consequences of such use shall be borne exclusively by you. And that you will not to try to hold us liable at any time, or for any reason, regardless of the circumstances.

As stipulated by law, we can not and do not make any guarantees about your ability to achieve any particular results by using any Service purchased through our book. Nothing on this page, our book, or any of our services is a promise or guarantee of results, including that you will make any particular amount of money or, any money at all, you also understand, that all investments come with some risk and you may actually lose money while investing. Accordingly, any results stated on our book, in the form of testimonials, case studies or otherwise are illustrative of concepts only and should not be considered average results, or promises for actual or future performance.

Copyright and Other Disclaimers:

This book, "Day Trading with Robinhood: Trade Like a Pro," is an independently published work and is not affiliated with, endorsed by, or sponsored by Robinhood Markets, Inc. or any of its subsidiaries or affiliates. The author and publisher of this book have no association or connection with the Robinhood app, and any opinions, views, or strategies expressed within this book are solely those of the author and do not represent the opinions or viewpoints of Robinhood Markets, Inc. or its affiliates. The information provided in this book is for educational and informational purposes only and should not be considered as financial, investment, or professional advice. Readers are encouraged to consult with a licensed financial professional before making any investment decisions.

General Disclaimer: The information, strategies, and techniques presented in this book are for educational and informational purposes only. They do not constitute financial, investment, tax, or legal advice. The author and publisher are not responsible for any financial losses or other damages that may result from applying the information contained in this book. Before making any investment or trading decisions, readers should consult with a licensed financial professional.

Risk Disclaimer: Investing and trading in stocks, options, ETFs, and other financial instruments carry inherent risks and may not be suitable for all investors. The value of investments can go up or down, and investors may lose their principal. Past performance is not indicative of future results. The author and publisher of this book do not guarantee any specific outcomes or results from using the strategies and techniques discussed herein.

Testimonials and Examples: Any testimonials, case studies, or examples presented in this book are provided for illustrative purposes only and do not guarantee that readers will achieve similar results. Individual success in trading depends on various factors, including personal financial situation, risk tolerance, and the ability to consistently apply the strategies and techniques discussed.

Copyright Notice: All rights reserved. No part of this publication may be reproduced, distributed, or transmitted in any form or by any means, including photocopying, recording, or other electronic or mechanical methods, without the prior written permission of the publisher, except in the case of brief quotations embodied in critical reviews and certain other noncommercial uses permitted by copyright law.

Trademarks: All product names, logos, and brands mentioned in this book are property of their respective owners. Use of these names, logos, and brands does not imply endorsement by or affiliation with their respective owners.

Printed in Great Britain
by Amazon